MOUNTAIN

MOUNTAIN

A LIFE ON THE ROCKS

STEVE
BACKSHALL

First published in Great Britain in 2015
by Orion Books

1 3 5 7 9 10 8 6 4 2

A CIP catalogue record for this book
is available from the British Library.

HB ISBN 978 1 4091 4403 8
TPB ISBN 978 1 4091 4404 5

Typeset by Input Data Services Ltd, Bridgwater, Somerset

Printed and bound by CPI Group (UK) Ltd, Croydon CR0 4YY

Orion Books
The Orion Publishing Group Ltd
Carmelite House
50 Victoria Embankment
London, EC4Y 0DZ
An Hachette UK Company
www.orionbooks.co.uk

The Orion Publishing Group's policy is to use papers that
are natural, renewable and recyclable products and made
from wood grown in sustainable forests. The logging and
manufacturing processes are expected to conform to the
environmental regulations of the country of origin.

To Helen
As soon as I saw you,
I knew an adventure was going to happen.

CONTENTS

LIST OF ILLUSTRATIONS

SECTION TWO

18. Mt Kuli, Borneo (Cede Prudente)
19. Climbing Kuli with Tim (Johnny Rogers)
20. Johnny climbing the ridge on Kuli (Tim Fogg)
21. With Tim and Johnny on the summit of Kuli (Johnny Rogers)
22. Camp Two on Cho Oyu, Mahalangur Himal (Dave Cole)
23. With Tarx on Cho Oyu (Rohan Kilham)
24. With Sammi and Dave at Camp Three on Cho Oyu (Dave Cole)
25. Tibet in the shadow of Cho Oyu (Dave Cole)
26. The team in front of Upuigma, Venezuela (John Arran)
27. Waking up on top of Upuigma (John Arran)
28. Climbing vertical ropes (Steve Backshall)
29. Climbing Upuigma (Keith Patridge)
30. Sunrise on Upuigma (Keith Partridge)
31. On the portaledge on Upuigma (John Arran)
32. In the summit forest of Upuigma (Keith Partridge)
33. John shortly after reaching the top (Keith Partridge)
34. The mystery Upuigma frog (John Arran)

SECTION THREE

35. Ivan sat on the ledge (John Arran)
36. Upuigma (John Arran)
37. Descending Kaieteur Falls, Guyana (John Arran)
38. Laya village, Bhutan (Steve Backshall)
39. Laya villagers (Steve Backshall)
40. Lizzie crossing the Weasel river on Baffin Island, Canada (Steve Backshall)
41. Mt Asgard on Baffin Island (Steve Backshall)
42. Twilight on Asgard (Steve Backshall)
43. Dinner on Asgard (Steve Backshall)
44. After midnight on Asgard (Steve Backshall)
45. Heading towards Asgard base camp (Steve Backshall)
46. Auyuittuq National Park (Steve Backshall)

INTRODUCTION

'Only those who will risk going too far can possibly find out how far they can go.' *T. S. Eliot*

Ching! The sickening metallic clatter of ice axe piercing thin ice and impacting on rock beneath. Chips of ice shatter and explode, peppering my face, spiralling off into the void beneath me. Teetering on crampon tips, a stifled gasp as bodyweight threatens to swing me off into space. Sweat beads as toes shuffle to redistribute weight, before sucking in a deep breath to still my racing heart. Millimetre by millimetre, so as not to throw myself off balance again, I raise my head, craning my neck to look up. Above is a vertical rock corner, its blank faces offering no holds for ice-axe tips. Many hundreds of metres more and beyond my gaze is the summit of Ben Nevis, where in the summer grandparents in khaki shorts and sandals will open a thermos of soup and eat their cheese-and-tomato sandwiches. Little do they know that the north face at their feet offers some of the stiffest winter mountaineering challenges known, and that its faces and gullies can be as deadly as Everest. My fingertips blaze with fierce, agonising pain. Caused when intense cold shuts down circulation to your extremities, and then the blood flows back in again, it's known here as 'the hot aches', and to Americans as 'the screaming barfies'. There's nowhere in the world you get it worse than in Scottish winter climbing. In the Greater Ranges you'll usually be mountaineering well below freezing, which may sound more intimidating, but is actually quite easy to prepare for. Conditions are usually dry, warm high-tech gloves keep digits safe from harm. Here in a Scottish January, though, the climbing is too technical for thick insulated mitts, and the temperature fluctuates from a little above to a little below freezing . . . but sopping soggy wet. Your gloves soak through, then freeze. There is little you can do to stop the deep chill into your fingertips. Illustrious mountaineer Andy Cave describes it as 'like small shards of broken glass being hammered into the fingertips'. I'd have to concur.

It's moments like this that make me question this passion of mine. Why do this to myself? Terrified for many hours on end, in genuine danger of death or disablement, at the very least bitterly cold, at worst verging on hypothermia. No chance of waxing lyrical about the magnificent highlands view, as thick clouds have been punishing us with rain, sleet or snow since before dawn. We could be halfway up the Blackpool Tower for all we've seen of the vista. My climbing partner and I have been pushing on, heads bowed, barely speaking a word all day so can't even claim the joy of companionship or camaraderie. Why? Why am I doing this to myself? I look up once more. There in the crack that lines the rocky corner is a sod of frozen grassy soil. I tentatively tap at it with my ice axe, then offer a downward swing into it. Thunk! It seems good. I shift gently, preparing to commit all my weight to the new hold. As I make to move my first axe, with a wrenching sensation the clod of soil comes loose, my axe flies backwards and I punch myself in the face with it. My whole body swings sideways like an opening barn door, pivoting with my body weight held on the point of my first axe. My life hangs there, on a thumb's width of steel hooked around a nubbin *of rock. If it dislodges I will fall at least five metres on to jagged rocks.*

It holds. Scrabbling my feet around in snow on the thin grassy ledge, I gingerly get myself back up to standing, breathing heavily. Soil-soaked blood from my eyebrow dribbles into my eyes. Heart hammering out of my chest, I press my face to the cold rock, like some chilly Dorothy whimpering 'There's no place like home.' I close my eyes, and wish I could be transported anywhere else but here.

Two hours later, we cut our way through the cornice at the top of the north face. It's the last obstacle to the summit, a breaking wave of solid windblown snow hanging over us. I hack into the hardened, dust-peppered snow with my axe, giving myself a narrow chute to pull myself through, plunging my arms in up to the elbows, climbing like a Victorian toddler hauling themselves up a sooty chimney. The snow drops down my neck, into my boots and clogs up my sleeves. That doesn't matter now. I push my axe, then my head through the crust above, and haul myself panting out on to my belly. Minutes later my partner the White Rabbit pops out of his hole, a tunnelling convict emerging to freedom . . . and another world. As we stand there on our nation's highest point, a gust tears the black clouds apart and dusky golden sunlight breaks through, creating a light of otherworldly alien quality. The peaks below suddenly become glowering ancient mountain trolls and white-haired ogres shining impossibly neon in that weird gold light; swirls of smoky crystal dust spin and sparkle around the precipice. It is too, too real, a moment of utter perfection earned from fear and frozen fingertips. In the back of my mind is a nagging insistence. We need to keep moving, or we'll freeze. We're also well behind schedule, which means we'll be down-climbing in the dark. But just a minute more; this is ours and ours alone. No other human being in the whole world will ever witness this perfect moment.

All the most ecstatic moments of my life have been either with wild animals or in the mountains. Sometimes both. They have a power over me no drug could ever compete with. The connection to nature and animals at least I can rationalise, and explain in words. It's between three and five million years since we humans shared an ancestor with the chimpanzee. If you were to hold hands with your mum, she with your gran, and her with her own mother, and so on in one unbroken line back through the generations, it would only take 300 miles or half a million generations before the members holding hands would look like modern chimps. There is no modern zoological classification that doesn't lump us in with the other Great Apes. For the entirety of our comparatively short evolution as the species *Homo sapiens*, we have lived in the outdoors, and animals have been essential to us. To our cave-dwelling ancestors, those animals were potential friends, like wolves and horses that could be tamed, or threats like sabre-toothed cats, snakes and big hairy spiders. Or more prosaically they could be something tasty to roast over our primeval bonfires. For our ancestors, knowledge of and curiosity in the wild world around them would have been essential to their survival. A fascination with animals has been a trait favoured by natural selection throughout the six-million-year evolution of the human race. Within the last half-century we have started to live sedentary lives, indoors, and wild animals have become for most people only an occasional diversion. Fifty years is not even a half-hiccup in evolutionary time. Certainly not long enough to kill psychological elements so fundamental to us and our success as a species. The primal past lives on in the dark corners of our brain, in the mists Jung called the 'collective unconscious'. When we spend time in the wilderness, and with animals, we commune with our ancestors stood holding hands back into the distant past. It satisfies us in ways we cannot possibly compute.

The same can be said of being in the outdoors in general, and of being physically active. Both of these things activate our endocrine systems, releasing endorphins such as dopamine, the 'happy hormone' that gives you a sense of well-being. Fight it if you like, but there doesn't need to be any philosophy involved; being outside and physically active makes us exultant in a quantifiable way. It's chemistry, pure and simple.

A desire to climb is perhaps more deeply ingrained in our make up than we might realise, and may also have been favoured by natural selection. As we became bipedal, our hands were freed up to use tools, perhaps the beginning of modern culture. While there was no need for everyone in a tribe to maintain the skills necessary to remain master of the vertical realm, there would be real advantage to, say, one person in a hundred being a natural climber. Climbing would enable one specialist member of the group to clamber up to a vantage point, enabling them to scout for game, route or foes. It would be a good way to escape the attentions of predators or head-hunting rivals. And there is food up high; birds' nests full of eggs and chicks, coconuts, bee hives full of honey hanging from rock-faces (until recently our only natural source of sugar, prized beyond gemstones), fruit and nuts dangling from boughs. Having one or two people in a tribe who had a 'head for heights' and were agile in ascent would have been valuable for the survival of the group. On St Kilda, the local people scampered around barefoot on precipitous seacliffs to gather birds' eggs and the birds themselves, their big toes growing unusually large to enable them to grip like fingers. And recent research shows that 1 in 13 modern humans still possess a 'mid-tarsal break', allowing the same midfoot flexibility as found in chimps – an adaptation for gripping and climbing. In New Guinea I saw the same adaptation, in local peoples who would scamper up trees to get a good view above the jungle, an unusual gap between big toe and the next allowing them to grasp trees.

But why the mountains? I have done extended expeditions in every conceivable environment, spent years in tropical rainforests, the Arctic, swamps, deserts, oceans, temperate forests and savannah.

I adore every one of these for its own reasons, but none compare to standing on the summit of a peak, surveying the world below as the sun creeps up over the distant horizon. In those moments I know exactly how people who have been struck by religious ecstasy feel. So what is it about the mountains that makes me feel so utterly, sometimes unbearably alive?

In some ways, you could argue that it is down to another suite of chemicals. Like dopamine, adrenalin is a powerful drug. It courses through the veins, giving a hit as addictive as crack cocaine. But adrenalin junkies don't last long in mountaineering. As the saying goes: 'There are old climbers, and there are bold climbers, but there are no old bold climbers.' In fact, if you speak to any of the idols of the climbing arts, it will soon become apparent that their love of climbing did not arise from a desire to play with death. Far from having a death wish, they relish life too much to risk losing it. No, for them it is about control. It is about honing their skills and experience to such a level that they can be safe in situations that to the rest of the world would mean certain death. To an extent, I have experienced this in my day job filming 'Deadly' animals. To get to a stage where you can catch a full-grown crocodile, handle the world's most venomous snakes, or dive in bluewater alongside a Great White shark takes confidence garnered from a lifetime of experience. Forty years of learning the hard way, building up from catching grass snakes in the compost heap, are what allow me to catch a king cobra without getting killed. I have in some small way set myself apart from my fellow man, and can glory in my own skill, my own specialness. I can convince myself that I am master of my own destiny (even if I am sometimes kidding myself!).

In a sanitised world where we are protected and told what we can and can't do on a daily basis, this is a profound rebellion. The climber too makes a statement that, for that moment in time when they are hanging over the abyss by their fingernails, they and they alone are responsible for their life. It is a battle for freedom in a world of red-tape and rules that seems bent on making us conform. It is the existential, ecstatic scream of a lunatic: 'I am free!'

There is much more to it than this dime-store pocket-book psychology, more joy than could ever be contained in these few pages. But it has taken a long time for me to reach these conclusions. In that time, I have summited an 8,000-metre peak, and many harder small ones in all the greater mountain ranges. I've made first ascents, and had major triumphs . . . but many more abject failures. Not to mention six years and twelve operations recovering from a fall that should have killed me. A lot of rock has passed beneath my fingers in that time. As with all love affairs, it had to begin somewhere, and first dates aren't always auspicious . . .

The first thing I need to get out of the way is that I am not much of a climber. And I am not saying this merely to be humble. Some years back, I was huffing and puffing my way up a particular rock route in the Lake District when a ruddy-cheeked man of about seventy arrived below, and told me cheerfully that he had soloed the same climb wearing roller skates and boxing gloves. It turned out that this was not a joke. He genuinely had.

Climbers of his era set their Cumbrian jaws against climbs I would struggle with today. And they did it wearing hobnailed boots, with a loop of hemp rope tied round their waists – more for peace of mind than anything else; if they'd actually fallen they'd probably have pulled their climbing partner off with them. Their protection consisted of knots of rope and shipwright rivets, nuts, bolts and old engine parts crammed into cracks. By contrast, today's climbing tyros are professional athletes equipped with sponsors' gear engineered from titanium and high-tech polymers. In physique they are sylphlike and sinuous. Their strength-to-body-weight ratios are superhuman; they can do pull-ups off a single finger with a dumbbell in the other hand, and climb overhanging rockfaces hanging on to holds invisible to the naked eye. They are more akin to gymnasts or ballerinas of the vertical world than any other kind of sportsman.

No one would use any of these words to describe me. I have the proportions of a light heavyweight boxer. I'm strong, fit and determined, but also heavy. This body was passed down from a hefty rugby-playing father, and honed through a lifetime of judo and other contact sports (plus a love of burgers and beer). My muscle bulk is excess weight, and one of many reasons why I will never be at the cutting edge of any kind of climbing. I am average at best. Many of my finest achievements in the hills have been down to climbing alongside partners with far superior abilities, who have made big things possible for me. For this I owe many of the world's finest climbers a great deal; a plodder like me has no right to have shared my rope with so many legends.

If you want to read of the superhuman few who sprint up the north face of the Eiger in an afternoon, or who have summited all the 8,000-metre peaks without oxygen, then this book is not for you. Their tales abound in climbing literature and are not hard to find; the appendix at the back will point you in the right direction. *This* book, is about my love affair with mountains. It's about big adventures, about exploration, outlandish achievements, about not being good enough, failure, being scared, and also moments when I've been so overwhelmed with joy that tears stream down my cheeks and can't be stopped. I hope at the end of it, you too might wish to head to the hills, even if it is to stroll in Snowdonia for a few hours, stopping off somewhere for a nice cream tea.

As long as I can remember, I've loved clambering up stuff. Often purely so I could jump off once I got to the top. My first serious brush with death was aged about eight doing a high dive off a pier at the beach. The pier was two storeys high, the water about half a metre deep. My mum cannot talk about it even now; she watched me do an elegant swan dive, then stop dead, like Wile E. Coyote diving into a pool that Bugs Bunny had sucked all the water out of. I still don't know how I walked away from that. I was also particularly into what is now known as 'Deep water soloing', but back then was called 'Rock climbing with water below you for when you fall off'. It's a miracle I made adulthood. This may seem sheer madness, but in actual fact climbing comes naturally to us humans. Babies, when they have something placed into their hands, will grasp it in the same way as any other primate. In monkeys, this allows them to cling to their mother as she swings through the treetops, and soon to do the same themselves. Human babies too, can suspend their own body weight from their hands with ease, and we're all familiar with the grins on toddlers' faces as they swing over the jungle gym, their petrified parents waiting nearby, mobiles poised with the ambulance on speed dial.

My ever-adventurous mum and dad were not the cautious kind. There was never any mollycoddling of my sister and I. Instead we were encouraged from birth to learn about the world through our mistakes. The fact that we grew up on a smallholding surrounded by woodlands and the seemingly infinite Surrey heaths beyond, made it possible for them to turf us out of the house every morning, and not expect us home till hunger or darkness drove us back. Even now I still feel a definite sense of guilt for every minute that I am inside; unbearable if the sun is shining. They took us camping to Snowdonia or the Brecon Beacons several times a year, and my most enduring memories were of miserable days wandering up easy peaks like Moel Siabod or the Carneddau. I remember trudging upwards, peering out through the tiny slit in the hood of my anorak at huge black slugs and lumps of sheep wool in the grass, drawstrings pulled as tight as possible to keep out the rain. And then when the rains finally cleared, sitting round our feeble little Hexalite stove trying to boil up enough water for a cuppa while the midges did their darnedest to make every second a misery. Perhaps the strongest memory was from when my sister Jo was four and I was six. We were camping out in a valley dominated by what seemed to be towering summits. As night fell, a torrential storm rolled in. To begin with, it was comforting to sit inside our little haven as the rain battered the canvas about us, but as the night went on, the nearby river began to rise until it flooded our tent. Jo and I were sleeping on inflatable lilos, and were floating around the tent, still blissfully asleep while Mum and Dad battled in the soaking darkness to keep both us and our home from being swept away. Eventually the tent collapsed (which had been bought for pennies from the Free-ads in the back of the *Camberley Times*), and we were carried out to curl up in Dad's rusting old beige Austin Princess. Jo and I were still tiny enough that the back seat seemed like a king-size bed, but it must have been a fitful and uncomfortable night for Mum and Dad. Next day they drove all the way home, across the Severn Bridge with a hurricane wind trying to blow them off into the Atlantic, the whole bridge swaying side to side. They stitched up the battered old tent, got back in the car, and drove all the way back again to carry on with their holiday. They didn't give up easy.

In 1984 I was one of approximately fifteen million people – 30 per cent of the UK population – who watched Hamish MacInnes, Joe Brown and his team climb the Old Man of Hoy, a famous spindly sea stack off Orkney in Scotland. I was staying at my grandparents' two-up two-down in Birmingham, and was so enthralled that they allowed me the rare treat of watching through dinner with my tea tray on my knees. It seemed like some Hollywood stunt performed by superhuman spidermen, and it never occurred to me that I would go on to climb routes equally as difficult in my adult years.

My first ever rock climb was memorable for all the wrong reasons. It was on a school field trip to Tremadog in Wales, aged about thirteen. We scrabbled about half-heartedly on some grimy rock in grey drizzle, wearing big red helmets and oversized harnesses, at a time when looking good to girls was the most important thing in life. In fact, that trip was most memorable because I was sent home in disgrace after being found in a girl's bed. Sadly, this was not because I was some teenage lothario – far from it. Four or five of us boys had been having a midnight feast in the girls' dorm room when we heard teachers coming upstairs. To avoid being rumbled, we'd all scrambled for the nearest hiding place. When the lights were turned on, two boys were found in the cupboard, another under the bunks, one behind the door . . . and me, cowering under Katy Hunter's duvet. It should have been immediately apparent that we were fully clothed, giggling, good kids, and we should have been sent to bed with a ticking off. Unfortunately the centre was run by a particularly pious Christian order. They delivered a fire and brimstone lecture about the dangers of STDs and teenage pregnancy, which reduced the girls to floods of tears, before sending us all home in disgrace. So it's hardly surprising that the climbing failed to make an impression.

I did a bit of bouldering at university, but was too obsessed with rugby and martial arts to consider joining the ranks of skinny climbers. The first proper rock climb I can remember doing was after I had left uni and gone to Japan to study martial arts. Japan is the home of both judo and karate, which I have studied off and on for most of my life. The way I saw it, after a year's serious training in Japan, I could set up my own dojo here in Britain. In order to pay the bills, I worked as a model (yes – in those days in Japan being a foreigner was enough!), and as an extra on Japanese telly, doing adverts for Nintendo and plum wine. I reconciled myself to the humiliation with the fact that Brad Pitt, Sean Connery and George Clooney were all doing the same thing, selling out for a hefty whack of Japanese yen. My day job, though, was teaching English. Soon after starting, I was assigned a student called Hideyuki; mostly because he was so utterly hopeless at English that none of the other teachers wanted him. I didn't mind; I was much more interested in studying Japanese anyway, so he ended up teaching me more than I did him. The added bonus was that Hideyuki was a rock climber, and offered to take me into the hills. We spent several weekends out near the ancient capital of Kyoto doing my first vertical rock routes, and though I was far from talented, I was instantly hooked. It was a case of perception switch. Until then, a rockface had been merely a dead end, something whose only potential was danger. All of a sudden, it became a challenge, a vertical gym where I could beat my fears and the natural limitations of my species. It was a foregone conclusion that, on my return to the UK, I would have to learn more.

Last month I sat down for a pitching meeting with an executive producer from the BBC Natural History Unit. As with all such meetings, I'd primed myself for him being dismissive and cynical about me and my abilities – to write me off as a kid's presenter while simultaneously pinching all my ideas. I'd run through every scenario in my head, and was ready for anything he could throw at me, and any criticism that might rubbish the concept I was there to sell. So his opening gambit threw me totally off guard.

'I think you should get some therapy,' he said.

I laughed, thinking it was a joke. But he was totally serious.

'When are you going to think enough is enough?' he said. 'When will you stop trying so hard, and just be comfortable with what you've achieved?'

I hadn't prepared any answer to that. I made some mumbled wisecrack about having come along to pitch my idea for a television series, not to have my head shrunk.

'No, I'm serious,' he continued. 'You need to see a therapist. If you don't figure out what it is that's driving you, you'll never be happy. It is simply impossible to do everything, to achieve everything, and while you keep on trying, you are going to drive yourself insane.'

Luckily, the exec moved on seamlessly to my big idea, so I didn't need to address the question. Which was just as well, because I had no answer.

Obviously I haven't been to see a therapist, I'm way too much of a control freak to do that. Instead, I decided to write it all down. I had a month on a boat headed to the Antarctic in high seas, during which there wouldn't be much else to do, so I decided to splurge it all out on my laptop, and see where it got me.

This book is the result of that brief and uncharacteristic spell of introspection. What I discovered on those long days on the Southern Ocean, is that I have always been driven by the fear of failure, and by what frightens me. If I see or hear of something that scares me, then I need to beat that fear. Within days it has changed from the thing that frightens me most, to the thing I most have to do. That's why the mountain that draws me on most is K2, the most dangerous and challenging on Earth; and why the single climb I most coveted was the endless blank granite face of Mount Asgard on Baffin Island. That's why I decided to go back to school and work towards my biology degree, despite being hopeless at science and having the maths skills of an eight-year-old. That's why I decided to run across the Sahara, despite being a lousy runner. And of course, it's why I decided to learn to dance in public on the nation's biggest TV show, when I would feel embarrassed dancing in the crowd at a mate's wedding.

But what is this utter mania to achieve? No sooner have I finished writing one book than I sign up to write another. Even before the blisters and rucksack rub have healed from one expedition, I am planning the next. Ranulph Fiennes once said that 'nothing is more responsible for the good old days than a bad memory'. Instead of dwelling on 'long-latent memories of gangrene and crotch rot' and 'horrid times and subsequent self-promises never to do it again', Fiennes keeps on going because the negatives are 'eclipsed by rose-coloured recollections of journeys past'. I can see where he is coming from. As I write these words, I am in training for my second go at an ultra-endurance race, excited and driven by the challenge, and by memories of the camaraderie and sense of achievement after my first attempt. Yet everyone I know reminds me that I *hated* this race last time, declaring it a soul-destroying trawl without an ounce of fun, and vowed I would never think of doing it again.

My friend Ed Stafford, who became the first person to walk the length of the Amazon, has an incisive view of this never-ending search for fresh challenges: 'Having a moderate amount of adventure in your life is healthy'. Ed says; 'However, if adventure becomes your life, you have lost something. You have become addicted to a thrill, a rush, and have lost sight of responsibility and meaning. You have become a serial escape artist and need to stop, and work out what you are escaping from.' It's clear from Ed's writings that he believes many explorers have a character defect that prevents them making normal connections with people. They are in many ways emotionally retarded, and as a result can do extraordinary things without any apparent psychological issues ... but their relationships with family and friends are detached and dysfunctional. The evident cost of this cold independence has forced me to reassess my own motivations, and that's proved one of those occasions where introspection is not particularly comfortable.

In balance I don't think I fit the profile. I'm not removed or isolated from the people that care about me – far from it. And I am not driven to escape life; I love life more than anyone I've ever met. My motivations are much more akin to those of George Mallory, who derived from his adventures 'just sheer joy'. I'm just a big labradoodle puppy with his head stuck out the car window of life, tongue lolling, ears flapping, with empty mind and open heart. I have felt the ecstasy of exploration, of discovering places for the first time, and I would agree with Mallory; 'joy is, after all, the end of life. That is what life means and what life is for'. And the mountains infect me with a euphoria that is something of a pantheistic, quasi-religious experience. Sometimes when you're climbing, and you've been pushed to the limit, and felt as if your life was in danger for extended periods of time, you come back and the world seems different. Colours seem brighter, tastes more pronounced, senses heightened. Adventure has allowed me to be a traveller in an undiscovered destination of hyperreal over-saturated colours, and to discover joys beyond words. If I sometimes seem like an unbearable zealot, it's because I want other people to share this joy. Essentially, I'm a Jehovah's Witness, doorstepping the unwary, with the promises of a new panacea. The elixir of adventure!

BEGINNINGS

'This, therefore, is a faded dream of the time when I went down into the dust and noise of the Eastern market-place, and with my brain and muscles, with sweat and constant thinking, made others see my visions coming true. All men dream, but not equally. Those who dream by night, in the dusty recesses of their minds, wake in the day to find that all was vanity; but the dreamers of the day are dangerous men, for they may act their dream with open eyes, and make it possible.'   *T. E. Lawrence*

Looking down the north face of the Eiger is like gazing down into the nine circles of suffering in the pit of Dante's inferno. It's a sickening, dizzying drop, that seems to pull you outwards, luring you to throw yourself into the abyss. It is no longer the challenge that led Hitler to covet an ascent for his Ayrian race, much as later leaders coveted space and the Moon. But it is still undeniably a fierce objective, and as dangerous as any climb can be. Unless caught in the midst of a freeze, the rock runs with slimy water and a constant cascade of gravel, and occasional hefty rockfall. Brutal föhn winds can still change the character of the Eigerwand, wall of death, in a matter of hours. It's a place where even the hardiest mountaineer can lose nerve, yet its hulking finger beckons irresistibly to anyone who has ever wielded an ice axe. It draws in young men like a silk-kimonoed courtesan beckoning from an opiate haze. No good can come of the encounter, yet it summons all the same.

I first became a mountaineer and a serious climber because of a girl. Our meeting was pretty ludicrous when I think about it now. In my early twenties, while doing my first proper job, working as an author for the Rough Guides series, I had an occasional sideline as a model on QVC, the shopping channel. I cannot quite believe I'm admitting this. When they were trying to flog worthless fitness equipment to lonely goggle-eyed people sitting at home (who would buy the equipment, look at it once, then shove it under the bed), I would be in the background in a tiny vest and shorts, flexing my biceps. It was humiliating, and my friends used to crucify me about it, but it paid more for a weekend's easy work than my full-time employers the Rough Guides paid for six months, so I took it on the chin. On my first QVC gig, I was to appear alongside a female counterpart. We'll call her Sam. A former professional athlete, she was six years older than me and seemed to be incredibly exotic. She was also a climber.

Our first date was climbing at Harrison's Rocks in Tunbridge Wells. I'd never fixed the top rope before, but didn't own up to this, instead watching her doing it nonchalantly, while trying to take mental photographs of what she was doing. I then set off to do it myself, desperately hoping I'd get it right and not drop her on her head. Worse was to come: a few weeks later, finding that we were both going to be in North Wales at the same time, we arranged to meet up for a climb. It was the Milestone Buttress of Tryfan. This is very much the preserve of beginners, who come here to learn the dark arts of traditional climbing. 'Trad', as it is known in climbing circles, is the first level of climbing where you can actually hurt yourself, or even die. Up till then I'd only done 'Sport', where you're cosseted by using prefixed bolts in the rock. When climbing trad, you carry 'gear' with you, 'protection' mechanisms that are designed to be jammed into cracks and crevices. If you've done your job right, when you fall, they'll catch you. If you do it wrong, they simply lift out of the crack and dangle on the rope like a bunch of Christmas lights – and are about as much use.

Luckily, as we arrived at the route, there was another couple preparing to go on ahead of us. The guy looked like he knew what he was doing, and had hung all his gear through his harness gear loops neatly, with cams and nuts on one side, and 'quickdraws' on the other. I was so intent on taking it all in that it was a moment before I realised Sam had asked me something.

'You're OK with this?' she repeated. 'I mean, you have led trad before?'

'Hell yeah,' I replied. 'This crag looks pretty gnarly, might have to do a few dynos.' (I had recently watched *Cliffhanger*, and at least knew how to talk a good game.)

She looked at me sceptically, but there was no way I was going to back out now. Instead, I slipped on my climbing shoes and shot up the first slab. Luckily, this bit was easy, so I didn't bother with any protection, and instead got up and out of her view before I found a crack and took out the first piece of gear. I started trying to slot it into the crack, like a toddler attempting to cram a square peg into a round hole. I tried out almost everything on my rack (all the gear together) before finding one that sort of fitted. I rammed it in by punching it with my fist, and clipped a quickdraw through it. Then I clipped my rope through the carabiner. Breathing a heavy sigh of relief, I climbed up to a good belay point. What now? Luckily, the girl from the pair who'd climbed ahead was still there. They'd set up a simple belay, by throwing two slings over some big rocks, which she had clipped into to secure herself, before tending her partner's rope through her own harness. I waited till she moved on, then copied exactly what she'd done. 'OK, come on up!' I shouted. Sam was up to me in a few minutes, and then started to climb through. This is what pairs of climbers do in order to be more efficient. When she was up to her belay, she fixed it up. 'Safe!' she called down, then 'Off Belay'. I gathered up my stuff and started to climb. 'Climb when ready!' she called out. Oops. Another lesson learned. I looked at each piece of gear she'd placed carefully, trying to suck in the technique. Luckily the route was easy, or I'd have exhausted myself. When I got to her belay point, again I copied exactly what Sam had done when coming up to me, before climbing through again. Her belay was a complicated spider's web, with three different pieces of gear, all equalised out perfectly, a work of art, and capable of holding a swinging truck.

My pitch should have been about twenty metres, but at the end of that was a site that would have needed a complex belay, so I kept on climbing. I climbed right through the next pitch, and shortly before I ran out of rope, found myself at the top of the whole route on easy ground. The first pair were there already. 'That was pretty ballsy,' the girl said, 'taking both pitches in one go like that.'

'I'm always telling you,' the guy said, 'no point hanging around, best to get out of danger as quickly as possible. No need to put in another belay if you can just extend the pitch.'

She huffed. They had clearly argued over this before. The pair of them had packed up and were stomping off along the well-worn path down Tryfan before Sam topped out alongside me.

'You know that was supposed to be two pitches at the end there?' she asked with an air of accusation.

'Well, I always think it's best to get out of danger quickly,'

I answered. 'It was easy ground, no point putting in another belay if you can just extend the pitch.'

On the way home, I stopped off at a shop in Betws-y-Coed and bought a 'Rock climbing for Beginners' book and a bit of gear. The leisure centre near my parents' house had an old crumbly brick wall alongside the basketball court, and I went up there every day for a fortnight, pressing my gear into gaps in the masonry, determined to crack this climbing lark.

Imprudent and reckless though it had been, my eyes had been opened. I'd been to Snowdonia many times since childhood, and had always thought it to be the preserve of elderly ramblers and cub scouts. Suddenly, I had a newfound skill that turned even humble Snowdonia into a place of ferocious challenge, where I could set myself apart from the crowds within a few vertical feet of the ground. I had seen the respect on the faces of walkers as I strode past with a rope over my shoulder, and had seen the valleys below with the condescension of the conquering hero. I was a climber.

The following year, I learned another lesson on Milestone Buttress. I was taking several non-climber friends up the same route for their first climb. At a broad grassy ledge, I stopped, took my backpack off, and to my pals' amazement took a disposable barbecue, steaks and a bottle of red wine out of my pack. They were suitably impressed as I started to cook up an outdoor BBQ for them all. Slightly less so when the huge mountain rescue helicopter pulled in and hovered metres from the cliff face, to find out if we were in difficulty. I had to put out the barbecue with the bottle of wine, which slightly dampened the impressive gesture.

I never did own up to Sam that I'd never taken lead before that day. Or that I had held her life in my hands without even the slightest notion of what that meant. In the years that followed I had many climbing partners and learned what it meant to share a rope with someone; the profound trust required to put your life in someone else's hands quite literally. I was introduced to ice climbing, to mountaineering and ski mountaineering, to sport climbing hot rock in beautiful places all over the globe. By now I was employed by National Geographic as their 'Adventurer in Residence', which gave me the opportunity to combine my growing passion with my job. My first mountaineering expedition was to Switzerland, with the goal of climbing the icon all climbers aspire to: the Eiger.

The Eiger lies in the Bernese Oberland, a stunning region of German-speaking Switzerland, and is one of the Oberland giants, along with the Mönch and the Jungfrau. The three mountains (the names translate into English as the Ogre, the Monk and the Virgin) form an intimidating line towering over the immense Concordia glacier. I personally had something approaching an obsession with the Eiger, mostly because until very recently it was the only mountain other than Everest I had heard of, but also because of an illicit childhood viewing of Clint Eastwood's *Eiger Sanction*. A monster that killed all who attempted her, a mountain that even beat Eastwood.

Back when I started climbing, it was the only mountain I was interested in, which in mountaineering circles places me alongside the tourists who buy their way up Mont Blanc carrying Nikons the size of washing machines. That said, I defy anyone with an adventurous bone in their body to stand beneath the Eiger's legendary north face and not want to be on it.

Before making the ascent, I spent a day scoping out the outdoor shops in Grindelwald, choosing my equipment with more care than ever before. Firstly it was all seriously expensive, and I still wasn't earning enough to lavish the cash on exactly what I wanted. Secondly, it seemed that every purchase, from my Gore-Tex jacket to my ice axes, could prove the difference between me living and dying.

We spent the night in one of the network of alpine huts dotted about the mountains to accommodate trekkers and mountaineers. The combination of over a hundred people sleeping side by side in one of these immense dormitories, at altitude, most of them getting up at around 3 a.m. to begin their attempt on whatever summit, is absolutely guaranteed to prevent sleep. We were lucky enough to be bunked with about twenty Italians who chattered all night long, stinking, snoring, farting and burping. They also rewarded my painstaking attempts to get dressed silently and in the dark, by getting up earlier the following morning, turning on all the lights and proceeding to chatter themselves silly while everyone else in the room lay seething, with their pillows wrapped around their heads.

Weather conditions were not in our favour: a metre of snow every night, with gale-force winds that kept us huddled in the hut playing endless games of cards. When we finally made it out of the hut on the third morning, the only peak that was safe to climb was the Mönch, at 4,100 metres. Unfortunately, everyone else in the hut was faced with the same choice, which meant that everyone decided to climb the Mönch, and all of us were squeezed on to a single ridge in places no more than a foot wide, with precipitous drops on either side. This was OK while we were ascending the peak, but after summiting, we had to battle our way down past the people who were still on their way up, which meant having to wait for several hours on an exposed icy ridge, buffeted by piercing winds. It was also the first time in my life that I got to experience moving across a glacier.

Glaciers are one of the most exciting, curiously beautiful and frightening environments on Earth. They are constant challenges in mountaineering; ever-changing and moving rivers of ice that can be everything from the easiest and simplest route to travel, to the most lethal places which should be avoided at all costs. (Excuse the short geography lesson, but I'll be using these following terms lots through the rest of the book!) Classically, a glacier is formed by snow gathering high up in the mountains. These snowfields are known as the 'accumulation zone' – kind of like the headwaters of a river system. As layer upon layer of fresh snow lands, it compresses the layers below to ice. Once it reaches a depth of about thirty metres, the huge weight causes the compressed snow and ice to start flowing ever so slowly downhill, dragged by gravity. It hugs the landscape, carving and smoothing the rock as it goes. Eventually it reaches a point where more of the ice is being removed than accumulating; this is called the 'ablation zone'. Between the accumulation and ablation zones is the 'firn' line or zone, where the snow is somewhat compacted but has not yet turned into glacial ice. Along the way, glaciers pick up rocks and debris – some scraped out of the surrounding environment, some from rockfalls that tumble on to the ice and get frozen in. Eventually, as the glacier runs out of steam, it dumps these rocks in ridges known as moraines. Old moraines, made up of boulders dumped millennia ago which have become consolidated and bound together, are usually covered in lichen and moss. For mountaineers, these make terrific thoroughfares because it's possible to travel along them quickly and safely. Moraines that are still in flux, on the other hand, are a living nightmare of toppling rocks, shifting gravel and crevasses, and are to be avoided if at all possible.

Hanging glaciers in the mountains can be not much bigger than a football pitch, but in the Arctic and Antarctic, glaciers can get to be the size of nations. The Lambert Glacier in Antarctica is generally considered to be the biggest; it's currently 60 miles wide and 250 miles long, which is about the size of Denmark! And while most glaciers are no more than 30 metres deep, so crevasses can only be around 20 metres, the Lambert is about 2,500 metres deep!

So far, so simple. Glaciers are a river of ice flowing down a mountain. But like any river system the water flows over the landscape in a variety of ways. When the ground is flat and broad you get nice tame lakes; when you come to steep ground, you get waterfalls (or in glaciers, icefalls). Like a river, glaciers can be calm underneath but choppy on the surface. In water, this would present as waves. On a glacier, you get crevasses. Crevasses are gullies, cracks and crevices, and though they can be strangely hypnotic, with shades of blue and green you don't see anywhere else in nature, they are also formidable. Every season, in every notable range, people will die in crevasses on glaciers. They vie with avalanches for the most dangerous feature of life in the big hills. And while experienced mountaineers can work out the most risky locations and times in terms of avalanche risk, the best you can do is take a calculated gamble on where crevasses might be. As someone who has been a white-water kayaker since I was twelve, I find it helps to look at the glacier as if it was a river, and try to figure out where the rapids will be. The 'zones of tension' where ice drops, is compressed, made convex, avoids obstacles or splays out are classic places to encounter big crevasses.

The time of year and recent weather are among the most vital factors to take into account when exploring a glacier. In Alaska, we spent two weeks living on a glacier in the middle of summer. It never snowed, and the bare surface of the ice was completely exposed. We spent many days abseiling into moulins – huge swirling caverns formed in the ice by surface meltwater as it drains into the guts of the glacier. Normally you avoid these features at all costs, but without any snow covering, the glacier was a benign and predictable place to be. While caution was still required in dynamic areas such as icefalls and the snout, where it was calving into the sea, for the rest we wandered around on the ice without roping up, as nonchalant as if we'd been in a summer meadow. The only unexpected challenge was that after a week I woke up to find that my nose was almost touching my tent ceiling. It turned out that the ice around my tent had been imperceptibly melting in the sun, but my tent had been shading its own footprint. When we took down and moved our tents, we left behind half-metre-high pedestals of ice in the exact shape of our tents.

The flip side of this is being on a glacier during the Arctic winter; then the snow cover is so deep that any crevasses are buried many metres below the surface. In this situation you again can easily forget you're even on a glacier. Glaciers are at their most dangerous in spring, early and late summer, and autumn, when snowfall can cover the crevasses with snow bridges that hide the rift beneath, but might not take a person's weight. Then the whole place becomes a pitfall-trap-laced hell, where any hapless footstep can mean doom.

Everyone who makes a habit of venturing on to glaciers will end up falling into a crevasse at some stage. How well you are prepared for that eventuality will determine whether the outcome is a bit of a giggle, or death.

Heading up to climb a technical route on the Mont Blanc du Tacul early one summer, we crossed over a glacier covered by a uniform foot of snow. Every hundred metres or so, there'd be a 'crump' noise, a trapdoor of snow would open up, and your feet would fall away into the blackness beneath. It was impossible to predict the depth, but certainly sufficient that you wouldn't want to tumble in and find out. Correctly roped up, and with large packs on, we'd merely fall in up to our waists, before crawling out on our stomachs, usually chuckling at the fun of it all. Had we been less prepared, had we been less careful about monitoring the tautness of our ropes, it would have been anything but funny. To move across terrain like this solo, you would need to be on skis to spread the weight. Jon Krakeur relates how when travelling solo he'd bought two long curtain poles and strapped them to his pack, so that when he tumbled in, they'd bridge the gap and stop him falling in!

The key with moving on glaciers is also the most important tip for anyone embarking on expeditions or adventures of any kind. If there is only one piece of advice you take with you from this book, make this it: Never try anything out for the first time in anger. Whether it's a piece of kit or a skill, try it out on a dry run, never leave it until you're out there in the field, doing it for real.

At the milder end of the scale, I once did a non-stop 24-hour adventure race, and took along a brand of sausage rolls I'd never eaten before. They had onions in them that repeated on me, and eventually made me so sick I couldn't eat anything. On my first major jungle expedition I took a nice new pair of zip-off trousers with me, only to discover that the zips rubbed against the back of my knee. By the end of day one I had a bleeding welt, which I couldn't dress – worse still, I had another month in the field with only those trousers to wear. On another occasion, after months of training to paddle 125 miles non-stop in twenty-four hours for the Devizes to Westminster kayak race, I had a last-minute panic on the day of the race that I might get blisters. So, for the first time, I put climber's tape on my fingers as a preventative measure. After two hours, the glue from the tape rubbed off on to the paddle shaft, then started to grip my hands ... giving me blisters. We had to stop, and wipe it all off with white spirit, and my hands fell apart.

Everything is exacerbated in the field, when you're tired and stressed, and when you have no alternatives. While it might be unpleasant having an untested energy gel mess with your digestion, at least it won't kill you. Not knowing your crevasse rescue techniques, or fumbling in a panic because you haven't practised what steps to take in an emergency, could well end in disaster. I did my first glacier course many years ago, but nowadays, whenever I'm on a long trip in the mountains, especially if I'm working with a new partner, I take some time to run through rescue drills on easy ground.

With Mönch summited, the next day we decided to have a crack at the Jungfrau – a somewhat harder proposition, requiring a three-hour slog across the glacier to reach the foot of the climb. It hadn't been climbed in over a week, and we had to break trail through thigh-deep snow. There is, though, something unique about setting out into the mountains over fresh snowfall. The virgin surface of the snowpack betrays any who have passed before you. If the snow is unmarked, you instantly feel like a trailblazer. Everything about the big mountains confounds normality. Here, weather and landscapes make big impressions and have big implications, exposing you to phenomena that non-mountaineers will never experience. As an electric storm approaches, your ice axes start to audibly hum and buzz with static, and the hairs stand erect on your arms and neck. As you walk a ridgeline with the sun above you and seething hazy clouds below, a perfect circular rainbow glows on the white. As you continue to walk, your own dark silhouette suddenly appears in the centre of the rainbow. This 'Brocken spectre' visible only to you is one of the bonkers auras and apparent hallucinations to confront your thin-air-addled brain. Often perfect halos form around the sun or moon, reflected light through minute windblown ice crystals. I've seen 'sundog parhelions' and 'sunvex Parry arcs' where sequences of rainbows in geometric patterns cover the entire mountain sky, with upside-down rainbows known as 'circumzenithal arcs'. Up there you're in a world of wonders you never even knew existed until you find yourself gazing with the eyes of a child on phenomena too magical to put into words.

The same Italians who had made sure we didn't sleep wink in the dorms at night had been watching our burly guide, and timed it so they left the hut right on our heels. As he broke trail, they followed in his huge footsteps. Every time we rested, they would stand around yawning and looking at the sky nonchalantly, or checking out their kit, until we started off again.

By the time we got started on the actual climb, the weather suddenly broke, and we were rewarded with extraordinary blue skies framing delicate snow cornices, with plumes of snow trailing upwards in the strong westerly wind. There was still deep snow on the ridges, and we witnessed several sizeable avalanches as we struggled upwards.

As if the Italians hadn't endeared themselves sufficiently over the previous few days, as the summit came within touching distance they finally decided it was time for them to take their turn at breaking trail – scooting on ahead of us to be the first in the fresh powder on top. God we hated them!

We reached the summit of the Jungfrau by midday, having been climbing for about five hours. We were all the first on the summit for a good few days, and it was sensational to sit towering above some of the highest peaks in Europe. But the first rule of mountaineering is that the summit is only halfway there, a maxim which was to prove very true as we began our descent of the Jungfrau. The direct sun was rapidly turning the thick powder snow to slush, which clung to our crampons and covered them in a sheath of ice that we'd have to smash off with our axes every other step. If you forgot to knock off the ice, it would form into a slippery wedge that completely negated the use of our crampons, and we would slip down the near vertical slopes on our backsides, desperately digging our axes into the ice to stop ourselves plummeting off into space. Tramping back across the glacier at the foot of the Jungfrau finished me off. When we finally made it to the

Jungfraujoch station, I collapsed in the snow and waited for sleep to take me.

The ascent from the Eiger our side is two kilometres of knife-edge ridge, with the slopes on either side plummeting away to nothingness. The ridge is too sharp to walk on, so you have to use it as a rail, walking on your crampons on the edge of the cliff face. Unfortunately, with so much snow covering the ridge, this was not possible, so we had no option but to bin the Eiger and come down. Deciding that discretion was the better part of valour, we left the high mountains behind, and headed off in search of warm rock at sea level. But what I had seen had deeply affected me. In fact, I'll go further than that: it had changed me for ever.

Your experiences in the mountains are so beyond those of the normal world. Up amongst the craggy, ice-carved pinnacles, life itself seems to hang in the balance with every movement. You witness things of an exquisite, too-real beauty that photos cannot convey. Suddenly everything has changed and will never be the same again. You want to grab 'normal' people by the lapels and shake them, saying, 'You haven't seen what I have seen, come with me into the mountains, I can show you marvellous things, a new world!' When I returned down to 'ground' level after that first mountaineering experience, I was reeling with the same kind of Nature shock as I'd felt coming back from my first extended jungle expedition.

It was my very own *Hurt Locker* moment, wandering around the supermarket looking at the hundred brands of breakfast cereal in a daze, wondering how the real world would ever be enough again. As Maria Coffey put it: 'The return home can be a rude awakening for the climber. For weeks or months he has had a simple, uncluttered life. He has been out fighting dragons, moving through landscapes of mythical proportions, dealing with fundamental issues of courage and survival. Suddenly he is back in the slow river of domestic life, a never-ending flow of chores, demands, and small mundane concerns.' I staggered around the streets of Grindelwald and looked at the tourists as if they were an alien species. I was the only one who knew the truth, who knew of the wondrous world that lay up there, beyond their wildest dreams.

SUFFERING SINAI

SUFFERING SINAI

'It is not the critic who counts; not the man who points out how the strong man stumbles or where the doer of deeds could have done them better. The credit belongs to the man who is actually in the arena, whose face is marred by dust and sweat and blood ... who at the best knows in the end the triumph of high achievement, and who at the worst, if he fails, at least fails while daring greatly, so that his place shall never be with those cold and timid souls who neither know victory nor defeat.'   *Theodore Roosevelt*

Rubber soles molten on the throbbing heat of the rockface, I shuffle backwards over a cavernous drop. Far beneath me, a pit trap of jagged boulders is a faint and menacing mirage. My pack is the weight of a small fridge-freezer, and cuts remorselessly at my shoulders as I abseil off into thin air, 140 metres of brittle crackling rope my passage to the canyon floor. All around me granite walls soar into pencil-sharp peaks; beneath their vastness I am a tiny, sweaty spider, dangling on a thread down a gargantuan, long-dry waterfall . . .

The last few years of the millennium, and first few years of the 2000s, were highly significant for me for many reasons. I was working as 'Adventurer in Residence' for the National Geographic's television channel, making self-shot and self-edited adventure, wildlife and conservation films. I would make my base in one of the many National Geographic offices around the world – Sydney, Delhi, Washington DC, London or Tel Aviv – and work for months at a time, living in hotels or on the sofas of fellow Nat Geo colleagues, researching and editing my films. It was an incredibly exciting time; every expedition I suggested was instantly funded and filmed, and I was knocking off scores of the finest adventures, wildlife spectacles and exotic destinations of my fantasies. It was also the time when I learned my craft as a filmmaker. I had two series that were made with conventional crews, which gave me the opportunity to learn camerawork, sound and direction from seasoned pros. Every chance I had to take a camera and learn how to use it, I'd grab with both hands. The Nat Geo executives showed me enormous trust, allowing me to produce, research and edit my own programmes. These skills I would then use in completely self-filmed expeditions. On these, I would be the archetypal one-man band; just me, two cameras and the wilds. One of these cameras I would hand-hold, turning it towards myself to talk into the screen. The other I would set up on a tripod so that it could show how I was filming myself, thus letting the audience in on how it was being done, preventing them asking who the cameraman was. (This also gave me a certain amount of leeway; no one expects the camerawork to be professional quality if they can see the challenges you're up against to get the shots!) To make the most of this post-modern device, I'd leave the camera running longer than necessary and edit into the programme those messy moments when I was turning the camera on and off, or when I was going back to pick up the camera, having left it in situ for a walking shot.

Sometimes this worked brilliantly, sometimes ... not so much. On my debut expedition film, I was walking across the Negev Desert and came to a remote source of water. A tiny puddle full of bugs and green slime, but water nonetheless. I put the camera on a tripod on one side of the puddle, and squatted down on the other to talk about how sources of water like this become an oasis in the desert, a life-giving panacea to every animal in the environment. At that moment a gust of wind blew up the valley, caught the huge fluffy mic on top of the camera, and sent it toppling into the puddle. I jumped up to grab it as quickly as I could, but there was nothing to be done. It was dead. I had killed my camera. In the desert. By drowning it. Luckily, I had the second camera to fall back on, so it wasn't a disaster. My next expedition in the desert was also to feature an epic fail thanks to meagre water supplies, but this time the consquences would be far more serious.

Wadi Abu Khushab, 'the Canyon of the Whispering Ghost', is buried deep in the desert mountain ranges of southern Sinai. Squeezed between Israel and Egypt, Sinai is an almost entirely desert nation, with 60,000 square kilometres of burnt rock and splintered cliff faces; a wilderness as dry as a mouthful of warm sand. The mountains are geological newborns, formed by the uplifting of the Sinai peninsula four to five million years ago, and so they have not yet been worn by time and retain dramatically jagged forms. The canyon of Abu Khushab follows one of the minor fault lines that riddle this area, and since the mountains were lifted, floods have carved dynamic forms in the volcanic granite and metamorphic rocks. It was the perfect destination for my next big step in film-making: a full documentary about a journey that would look sensational on camera.

The expedition was the idea of Tsur Shezaf, an Israeli foreign correspondent, and the same man I'd walked across the Negev with.

Tsur is a remarkable man: opinionated, occasionally infuriating, but wise; an entertaining raconteur with an extraordinary range of experiences, and someone I was proud to call a friend. Our walk across the Negev together had been my first proper trip into a desert environment, and I'd fallen in love with it – in no small part due to his passion for the place and his knowledge of how to survive there. Initially, everything about the desert had frightened me. It seemed an alien environment where an Englishman simply did not belong, and I battled against it, making myself thoroughly uncomfortable in the process. But gradually, under Tsur's tutelage, I learned how to feel utterly at home there. We'd rest in the early afternoon when the scorch was most incessant and whenever we found shade, but push on hard during the cooler parts of the day. Every evening we'd make a simple bread out of flour and water, bake it in the fire and eat it with a sesame paste called halva (one of the finest endurance foods on Earth – I still favour sesame snaps over modern energy gels and bars), and in the morning we'd burn tamarisk twigs in the fire, then walk in the embers to harden our feet. I fell deeply in love with the environment, and particularly the wild majesty of desert mountains.

Someone who dodges bullets for a living may not seem the ideal travel agent, but Tsur sold the Sinai canyon as one of the most beautiful places he had ever seen; and he's seen a few (though mostly after they've been invaded or carpet-bombed). Tsur told me there had only been a handful of expeditions there since the 1970s, when it was discovered by Israeli pilots flying overhead on illicit reconnaissance missions. It felt like a forgotten alien world.

Our party was six strong, the other members hand-picked by Tsur. Ofer, Dicla, Lotem and Gomer were hard as nails; after finishing their stint of national service in the Israeli army, they were working as desert guides in the Negev. We boarded two jeeps that dropped us off near a ramshackle Bedouin camp not far from St

Catherine's monastery on the eastern Sinai peninsula, with the Red Sea to one side and the mountains to the other. The camp was little more than a series of black flapping blankets forming a tent, where we sat on cushions and shared tea. There's a very precise protocol for how tea should be served and who drinks first, and in days gone by there would have been serious repercussions for getting it wrong. Nowadays, and for tourists like me, they are far more forgiving – although not when it comes to sugar. Over half the cup is full of gloopy sweetness, and you can barely get the single glug of hot liquid down without gagging.

To reach the mouth of the canyon, we would have to climb to a mile above sea level over the course of several days. It was summer, and the temperature topped forty degrees for about eight hours a day. As no one had been into the canyon in recent memory, we had no intel on what the opportunities would be for fresh water, so we each carried a minimum of fifteen litres, which meant we were hauling over forty kilos on our backs in total. That's about four crates of lager (with which we could have had far more fun).

Watching the jeeps drive off into the distance as we stood sweltering next to packs as immovable as bungalows was a tense moment. We were now three days' walk from the nearest settlement and had no means of contacting the outside world. And there would be no period of gentle adjustment to get used to our packs or the heat; instead we immediately began scrabbling up the punishing mountainside of mammoth boulders and loose scree, sweat leaking out of our skin.

That night we made camp in a narrow valley, so much heat radiating off the rocks around us that it was too hot to even cover ourselves with a sheet. Night in the desert is so quiet it seems to roar in your ears; so silent it's deafening. With the nearest town hundreds of kilometres away, there is no light pollution, and desert skies are infinitely clear of clouds, so the stars above are as perfect as you'll ever see. Lying down in a rocky bed under the whimsical star-light seemed a romantic proposition at first, but after a few hours it felt like . . . well, like sleeping on rocks.

As we progressed further into the wilderness, we looked up on to the mountainsides and saw Nubian ibex picking their way over the steep rubble. They're extremely rare, with only a few thousand in the wild, but are in all other senses an archetypal caprid or 'goat antelope'. They're impossibly nimble, leaping about on vertical cliffs as if they are playing hopscotch, and the males have huge horns which they use for tumultuous rutting battles. They're generally considered to be a subspecies of the alpine ibex, despite the fact that their worlds are so different; the alpine variety tiptoeing over lush green mountain meadows that are covered by snow half the year, while their Nubian relations inhabit the driest, hottest moun-tains on Earth. Ibex are ludicrously at home in the world's most vertiginous places, impervious to the fears and fragility that assail humans in this environment. It was therefore a curiously forebo-ding moment when we came across an ibex carcass lying at the base of a dry waterfall, its rheumy eyes looking up at us as if in surprise. It was partially mummified, the flesh turned into tanned leather by the searing sunlight, and there was barely a bug on it, as if the canyon was too challenging even for flies.

The dry waterfall was about fifteen metres high, with a vertical face and a dry pool at the bottom. By 6 a.m. the sun was already peering into every crevice, and by eight it was unbearable. I led the way up the vertical face, which had decent footholds and was relatively straightforward, and then the others followed one by one. All went well until it was Dicla's turn. She started asking a lot of questions about the climb, which is always a sign that someone's nervous, but with a bit of coaxing she set off. About halfway, she stopped and started to wobble. Her feet were gyrating in the stress and fatigue reaction climbers refer to as 'disco leg'. This did not look good. Seeing my chance to play superhero, I descended and began to climb behind her, using my body as a brace so she couldn't fall. By this method I managed to get her up the face and out – shamelessly flexing behind her all the way. It makes me cringe now, looking back. But perhaps my posing bravado was illustrative of something deeper. Something that might explain why we do things like climbing in the first place.

Dicla's dayjob was working in a desert university under the renowned Israeli biologist Amotz Zahavi, originator of the handicap principle. This is to me one of the most fascinating ideas in biology, and relates directly to sexual selection. The idea is that animals exhibit many features in order to attract a mate. Most commonly it is the male who puts on a variety of displays to prove to the female that he is strong, fit, has good genes that can be passed on to her offspring and, where applicable, will be a powerful father who can protect her and her progeny. Most of these signals have to be fairly obvious, hence the huge back muscles and sagittal crest of a mountain gorilla or the thick mane of a lion. Some appear so over the top as to present a hazard to the owner. The exorbitant feathers of a male bird of paradise, for example. Sure, they make the bird easier to see in the rainforest darkness, but they also make them more obvious to predators. And think of the ludicrous trailing tails of quetzals, astrapia or widowbirds, a major impediment when it comes to evading a wild cat or circling hawk. The most obvious example is the peacock's tail. Of course it's beautiful, and peahens find them irresistible, but what about the handicap to their chances of survival? Zahavi argued that this is exactly the point. A peacock has this tail to point out to females that he can survive to maturity *despite* his handicap. 'Imagine how fit I must be,' he seems to be saying, 'to have made it to adulthood dragging this behind me.' It points to the fact that he must be exceptional at gathering food, at avoiding disease, and at escaping predators. It is a signal, a note to the unknowing and unconscious judgement of females, that this suitor is a force to be reckoned with.

In his seminal work *The Third Chimpanzee*, Jared Diamond points out that such signals are commonplace among human beings, too, particularly young males, with their hyperactive libidos and hormones. 'The female who selects such a male is like the medieval damsel testing her knight suitors by watching them slay dragons. When she sees a one-armed knight who can still slay dragons, she knows she has finally found a knight with great genes. And that knight, by flaunting his handicap is actually flaunting his superiority.'

Is it possible that a flash young buck driving a fast car to within inches of crashing is actually advertising to mates that he is so fit he can survive despite his stupidity? Is getting blind drunk an example of handicap principle? Jared Diamond suggests that it is. 'Ten thousand years ago, we "displayed" by challenging a lion, or a tribal enemy. Today we do it in other ways, such as by fast driving or by consuming dangerous drugs.' Do we climb mountains and run ironman triathlons to prove, on some subconscious level, that our genetics and our physical prowess is potent enough to win out, regardless of the insane risks we expose ourselves to? Diamond's answer to this is somewhat depressing:

'The messages of our old and new displays nevertheless remain the same; I'm strong and superior. It's a message to our rivals, our peers, our prospective mates – and to ourselves. The smoker's kiss may taste awful, and the drinker may be impotent in bed, but he or she still hopes to impress their peers or attract mates by the implicit message of the superiority. Alas the message may be valid for birds, but for us it's a false one. Like so many animal instincts in us, this one has become maladaptive in modern human society. If you can still walk after drinking a bottle of whisky, it may prove you have high levels of alcohol dehydrogenase in your liver, but it implies no superiority in other respects.'

In other words, the desire to risk our lives is a throwback to a time when such signals may have been the best way, but those signals don't work any more. So if Diamond is right, many young men have died or been injured while risking their lives in an effort to attract the opposite sex by resorting to these outdated methods. And I was about to join the ranks of the fallen.

The path led ceaselessly upwards, following a gully that ran between the peaks. In places the vertical walls were only a few metres apart, elsewhere they would open out into broad open valleys, the slopes a Mars-scape mess of dark flint and red sandstone. By the time we reached our highest point, I was totally out of water and starting to question Tsur's judgement in bringing us here. Finally, though, we started to descend, and then as the shadows lengthened we came to our first sign of water: a solid rock basin in a tight wadi, shaded from the sun almost all day long. The pool was no bigger than a double duvet, but looked inviting, so I flopped head first into it.

Now this being the desert, this pool wasn't over-endowed with water. I felt my head clatter off the rock bottom, and remember thinking, Oh God, I hope no one saw me do that. Then came the groans of my fellow travellers. I had set the camera up on a tripod before my little stunt, and it had caught everything. Later, when I was editing the sequence, I replayed it over and again, watching myself nearly becoming a paraplegic countless times. Ignoring the pain, I tried to make a joke of it, until I looked down. There was claret gushing everywhere, it looked like I'd taken a shower in tomato juice. When I stumbled forward, trying to get out of the pool, it became obvious my balance had gone and I couldn't get my footing. From the speed with which everyone mobilised, I knew that something serious had happened. Within seconds they had me laid out and the wound pressured; when they finally got up the courage to take a look, their reactions told me everything. My head had split like a ripe watermelon, the gash was down to my thick skull, and three inches long.

I tried to laugh and joke while they tended to me, inwardly wishing everyone would go away and leave me to my shame. I saw Lotem brewing up hot water to irrigate the wound. She was looking down and shaking her head, with a look on her face that said, 'Boys – they're all morons.' Ofer shaved my forehead in a perfect semicircle, giving an insight into how I'll look when I'm sixty. He then stitched me up, and asked around for a suitable dressing. The only thing that the girls could find that would fit the bill was a panty pad. It was so humiliating, I'd be walking around the desert trying to look rugged . . . with an Always Ultra strapped on my head.

It was going to take equally as long to get to civilisation whichever direction we chose, so we decided to press on. Furious that my moronic macho antics had put the trip in jeopardy, I slogged on ahead, determined not to prove a burden. That day's hike was one of the hardest of my life. The gradient was intense, on scree that carried us two metres backwards for every step forward. Once out of the gully and on the mountainside, there was no escape from the sun. We guzzled down water by the gallon, and it flowed straight out of our skin, evaporating instantly and leaving a salty frosting over everything. My tongue swelled up like a furry 'Welcome' mat, and what was left of my brain swelled and thumped in my head.

We were making our way to a high saddle, at about 1,500 metres above sea level, which would then lead us down to the valley that harboured the canyon. Nearing the saddle, we ran out of water again. After drinking almost constantly to keep moving, this was rather sobering. We were relying on there being water ahead to refill our bottles, but it would be no exaggeration to say that if we reached the pools and they were dry, we would be in big trouble. Walking in those conditions with no water makes every step increasingly sluggish, the mouth gets more and more sticky-parched, and you can feel your body shutting down. Before long it's auto-pilot time, all you can do is trudge with eyes half-closed, totally fixated on getting to the pools. Fortunately, after a fluid-less hour, we rounded a corner and found a shallow rock basin with a smidgen of green sludge in the bottom. We stuck our faces in and guzzled it like champagne.

It was late when the walls of the gorge began to narrow and we found ourselves at the top of the first dry fall. At the bottom was a long, dark green pool. We set up the ropes and I rappelled down, swam across the pool and set up a zip line to bring down the sacks. Desperate for rest and food after sixteen hours' trekking, we cooked up some rice and tuna, then bedded down for the night.

First light brought me out of a sick, exhausted torpor, utterly bewildered, and with no idea where I was. Despite the dazzling beauty of the surroundings, it was quite a nasty surprise to slowly come to. This wasn't a tequila hangover but a nasty head wound, and instead of being in hospital on intravenous antibiotics, I was lying under vertical or overhanging granite that towered hundreds of metres above us. The only way was on, down the canyon's thirty dry falls to where the jeep would meet us in several days' time.

As the sun began to rise, the colours grew from deep red through shades of orange on the fangs of the granite spires above us, the sun's rays peeking over the steep sides of the canyon to dance on the pools that sulked below many of the falls. Each of these falls would present its own particular set of challenges that would have to be overcome in order to get ourselves and the bags to the bottom. On the higher falls we'd send the bags down on a zip line, or carry them as we abseiled; on lesser falls the bags got chucked over on a rope. The shallower pools we could wade across, but others were so deep we had to swim across, dragging our packs in a small inflatable kiddy's canoe we had brought along for the purpose.

After another sixteen-hour day, we reached the highest fall, at over seventy metres. There was no way we were tackling that one in the dark, so we pitched camp right at the top of it, taking a mental note of which direction to take if we needed to pee in the night; it would have been a hell of a flush had we wandered the wrong way. The girls changed my dressing in the dark and, aside from ripping off what little remained of my hair, came to the conclusion that infection had set in. It was another restless and uncomfortable night's sleep.

The next morning I felt like my eyes were stuffed full of sleep. As the day drew on it became evident that my face had swollen up like a balloon from infection. My shame was now complete. I would be presenting to camera on this, my grandest adventure, with my whole head inflated, eyes reduced to puffy slits, and a feminine hygiene towel stuck to my forehead. The one compensation for my humiliation was the views. This was the most dramatic part of the canyon, with spiky spires jagged teeth above, and each fall over fifty metres high. Boulders the size of houses had been swept down the gullies during flash floods of unimaginable power, and now lay wedged between the narrow canyon walls, often forming ceilings above us that we would have to stoop beneath, or windows we'd have to abseil down through.

The Sinai mountains are unlike any other mountain range I've spent time in. There is evidence of human occupation going back two hundred thousand years; the reddish sandstone housed the main mines for the major edifices of the Ancient Egyptians, and all the patriarchs of the Jewish and Christian faiths were said to have spent time here. The place is teeming with history and religious artefacts, but it is the wilderness that makes the biggest impression. The towering, unclimbed, black and red fang-like peaks seemed to permanently frown down on the canyon, aware of their own majesty and mocking us with their might. The highest peak in the peninsula is 2,600 metres, and as the crow flies not far from the secret canyon we were now concealed in. Sinai is not a big place, and we were probably never that far from the coast, but entrenched in the canyon, with no means of contacting the outside world, we might as well have been a thousand miles from civilisation. With symptoms of heatstroke adding to the thudding in my head, I needed out, and soon.

It was about an hour after sunset, with the last light near gone, when we dropped down one last short fall and saw a figure dressed head to toe in Bedouin white sitting on the wadi floor waiting for us. It had taken him an hour to hike up the canyon, then he'd spent six hours waiting for our arrival and was on the point of leaving when we turned up. We did the last hour in pitch darkness, and many hours later we wandered stinking and filthy into about the best hotel Sinai had to offer, me still with a blood-stained panty pad stuck on my head. I had my head completely shaved to even out the fashion faux pas of the Franciscan monk hairdo, and we got to a local hospital the next day, where they pumped me full of antibiotics to subdue the infection. I had got off lightly, but in many dark days in the edit suite, as I watched the footage of me nearly paralysing myself over and again, I had cause to reassess my leap-before-you-look approach to life. If I was going to make a living for myself in the world's most extreme places, I was going to need to grow up. From here on in I would be a more cautious me, risk-assessing my actions, always thinking 'what if' before acting.

Looking back, that dumb dice with death is probably the thing that has kept me alive. There are areas of adventure in which you can be a bit of a renegade and still make it to a ripe old age. Sport climbing, for example, where the leader clips their rope through in-situ bolts that you could dangle a truck from; you have the exhilaration of pushing the boundaries to the limit, and you're pretty much guaranteed to fall every single time you climb – but in relative safety. When it comes to mountaineering and big expeditions, this is not the case. You have to rationalise your actions, putting them into the context of what the consequences would be should even something minor go wrong. A twisted ankle in the big hills is a potentially life-threatening injury. Drop a glove or a climbing shoe high up on a Himalayan mountain route and you will lose toes or fingers to frostbite. There is no room for bravado or being a hero; your survival depends on taking a parsimonious approach to risk. As my life has progressed, I have discovered more and more respect for the wise old souls, and less and less for the young tyros bounding about like jack rabbits. Either they will curb their enthusiasm, as I learned to, or their lives will be short.

THE SCHOOL FOR HIGH ACHIEVERS

'He who would learn to fly one day must first learn to stand and walk and run and climb and dance; one cannot fly into flying.' *Friedrich Nietzsche*

A blizzard of wind-whipped ice flakes needle at my eyeballs, chill penetrates through every tiny gap in ill-tethered clothing, fingertips burn hot with cold. The tent ropes whip about like flailing unmanned firehoses as we shout to each other above the ferocious gales. Faces red-raw, we fight to tie down the huge tent which the gale has transformed into a giant parachute that seems intent on carrying us off with it. The storm has been our constant torment for two days, and we've had to fight to stay on our feet. With visibility near zero, we've been forced to keep within an arm's length of the teammate in front, as otherwise we would soon be separated – with dire consequences. Our whole world has shrunk to a claustrophobic white cave. You either wear snow goggles, which clog in minutes, rendering you blind, or rely on keeping your eyes narrowed to tight slits so your eyelashes keep the snow out. It's the archetypal white noise, a weird blend of sensory overload and deprivation, wind roaring in our muffled ears.

We have become shuffling, grim half-beings, thinking of nothing more than each single step.

After such bleakness, the next moments possess a high-definition clarity I have never experienced before or since. All of a sudden, gusts of rainbow-glinting snow and raging clouds rip apart, the winds drop and release their airborne white cargo. Within seconds we go from barely being able to see our own feet, to standing beneath one of the most magnificent views on the planet. Horn-shaped Shivling, often said to be the most beautiful mountain on Earth, and three-peaked Bhagirathi, smile down on us. Thousands of metres of vertical rock-face in polished grey granite peppered with diamond-dust ice crystals shine like celestial thrones. Stunning at any time, but after our days in a frozen tumble drier the effect is ethereal, hyperreal, as if you could reach out and stroke your fingertips down its facets. Even the weather-beaten Tibetan porters stop and gaze in wonder. The miracle lasts only minutes before whirlpools of cloud eclipse the view. It will be three days before we see it again.

My stint as 'Adventurer in Residence' with National Geographic was one of the happiest and most challenging periods of my life, giving me the chance to learn my trade both as a broadcaster and as a professional expedition leader. However no job with a title that preposterous could last, and after five years it came to an end. For a while it seemed that my onscreen time would end with it, and I was bound for a career behind the camera in production. But a friend put me in touch with the BBC's Natural History Unit, where I took on a director/presenter role on their long-running kids' wildlife series *The Really Wild Show*.

As I didn't have much money, and no place to stay in Bristol, I pitched my tent in a caravan site on the edge of town and cycled into the office every day to research my grand plans. The *Wild Show* producer showed me a remarkable amount of trust, allowing me to completely own my portion of the show, coming up with my destinations, stories and schedules. I'd tease the calendar out as much as possible, getting as many days away on my adventures as I could. This was a trade-off for the fact that I provided ridiculous value for money. Not having an agent at the time, I had negotiated my own contract. Badly. I had pretty much told them in my first interviews that I'd do the job for free, and then set about making sure that was almost what happened. I was earning in a week what the other presenters earned in a day, but was also doing the directing, research, shooting second camera and stills. I had to pay all the bills on my own credit card and claim it back at the end, as well as dealing with irate contributors, and if anything went wrong then it was my neck on the line. While the other presenters were accompanied by a full crew, I just travelled with my trusted cameraman Mark Vinall.

Mark had many advantages. He was a superb underwater cameraman, as well as doing topside. Mark was a commercial diver who had spent many years of his life diving professionally on oilrigs. He told me about 'saturation diving', which meant going down in a compressed dive chamber the size of a portaloo and living on the seabed for a month at a time, occasionally diving out into the dark murk to carry out work on the rig. Mark had finally quit after seeing one of the chambers brought up to the surface, still pressurised to the equivalent of two hundred metres of pressure. He described how a tiny fissure formed in the rivets of the chamber, and 'both occupants were evacuated out through a gap of about two centimetres'. They had to rinse the liquid remains of his colleagues off the deck of the oil platform with a hose. Far from deciding to take up something safer, Mark had taken to exploratory cave diving, leading expeditions into dark flooded cave systems all over the world. He told of being stranded without air miles below ground in unexplored flooded caverns, and nearly blowing up an entire mine shaft and burying himself beneath hundreds of tonnes of rock. In his older years he had matured and calmed, but retained a vast legacy of experience in how things should not be done!

This meant that Mark could take care of all the diving risk assessments and practicalities, which was a big load off my plate. His calm and confidence with all things SCUBA was also massively beneficial. We would spend hundreds of hours underwater together, and I always looked to him for guidance and help when submerged. For the most part I wore a full-face mask with a hard-wired line back into the camera, which meant I could talk and the sound would be recorded. This allowed us to work as a two-person unit. Nowadays, a similar operation would require a hefty risk assessment that would take months, and I wouldn't be allowed out without a dive supervisor to stay on deck in comms with the underwater crew at all times, someone dedicated to help me with the full-face mask and sound recording, and a dive buddy! The fact that we cut so many corners allowed us to do things that had not been attempted on such a low-budget programme before. The experience confirmed my certainty that in television, as in expeditions, it is all about your crew. One exceptional experienced person can achieve the same as a score of average ones. You cannot put a price on having people on your team that you KNOW, without question, will not only have their own job covered but will also have your back.

Mark ran sound as well as pictures, and would work every hour of the day every day if I asked him to. In all the time we were away together we bickered constantly but never properly fought. He asked for one morning off in perhaps six months away, and never, ever missed a single wildlife shot. If something cool happened behind me, I didn't need to ask, I knew Mark would have got it. We were the perfect workaholic, socially-dysfunctional pairing.

It was the ultimate trimmed-down crew, formidably intense, with eighteen-hour days being the rule, but the set-up worked remarkably well for us, giving my inner control freak full reign. We also developed a relationship where we knew exactly what the other was about to do. For example, while we were filming mountain gorillas in Uganda, I was doing a piece to camera when a tiny baby gorilla started wandering towards me. As my attention transferred to the baby, Mark's camera focus and tilt perfectly followed my gaze, only to return to me as the gorilla took me by the hand. On another occasion I was talking to camera on the front of a boat off the coast of Australia when a humpback whale breached fully out of the water to the side of us. Somehow Mark whipped around, zoomed and focused in a millisecond, before whipping back to me the second the spray had dissipated. We filmed whale sharks and tiger sharks, raced a cheetah, dived in flashing silvery baitballs with penguins zipping about our ears, and danced a beautiful aquatic waltz with a quintet of female sea lions. It felt as if we were achieving the impossible on a daily basis, and that people around the Natural History Unit were starting to take notice. That year we'd done an extended trip through Central America and the Galapagos, filming our entire contribution for the year's series in one six-week trip.

This left quite a large portion of the year open for big adventures, and the one environment the job was not taking me to was the mountains. In my time off I'd go into the Scottish Highlands with pals, bagging Munros (mountains over 3,000 feet) and cramming my fingers into cold rock. I was pushing myself harder and harder with every trip, but it was becoming increasingly obvious that my ambition was starting to bypass my ability. If I was going to achieve anything noteworthy in the big mountains, it was not going to be through technical rock-climbing, at which I would never be anything other than fecklessly average. It would have to be in the big mountains, where my strength would be a benefit not a hindrance. But you can't simply wander off into the high Himalaya without the right training. Not if you want to keep all your fingers and toes.

When many think of the Himalayas, they think of Nepal and Tibet, but northern India offers some of the most fabulous Himalayan scenery and culture to be found anywhere in the world: from the high-altitude deserts and Tibetan wonderland of Ladakh, to the dazzling pointy peaks of Manali, Kashmir and the Garhwal. But even for the most self-sufficient mountaineer, climbing the peaks is an expensive business that requires months of planning. There is, though, a loophole that offers the opportunity to ascend awe-inspiring summits, live under canvas at altitude for a month, go ice-climbing in glacial crevasses, monkey up challenging rock routes and learn every skill necessary to plan your own Himalayan expedition . . . and all for less money than a weekend's climbing in the Alps. Originally set up to train military recruits in high-altitude warfare, India's four mountaineering institutes are situated in some of the most stunning parts of the Himalayas.

Of course, with a price tag of only five hundred US Dollars for five weeks, including everything from food to equipment and training, there has to be a catch. The training is run by the Indian military, and they don't care who you are or how important you might be back home, you'll still be treated like the lowliest private in the army. The course maxim is 'to introduce recruits to the realities of Himalayan mountaineering by exposing them to hardship, hunger, physical exertion and extremes of temperature'.

I first heard of the courses while working on a clean-up operation on another high peak in the Ladakh area of the Indian Himalayas. We had spent several days above 5,000 metres on a popular trekking peak, cleaning up the mess left by the previous year's expeditions. Literally tonnes of human waste get left behind. Most of it was what you'd expect: excrement and paper, fuel cans, rum bottles, tattered tent pieces, etc. What came as a surprise was the amount of shoes we found. There were hundreds, from crappy flip-flops to plastic mountaineering boots. What on earth could possess someone to ditch their shoes on a mountain? Are there an abnormal amount of frostbite injuries sustained on Stok Kangri that cause people to lose their feet? Or do climbers decide once they're up here amid the thick snow and boulders that shoes are an unnecessary impediment? In fact it's inexplicable to me that there's any junk left behind whatsoever. Stok Kangri is a straightforward climb and the walk in is not severe, but it's enough of an effort that you must love the mountains to make the trek. So why would you then go and ruin it with all your old crisp packets and sweetie wrappers?

Due to political unrest on the border of Jammu and Kashmir and Pakistan, climbing permits to summit mountains in the region had been rescinded, so we were prevented from summiting the peak. The expedition was far from wasted though, as I got to spend time with the Indian Mountaineering Foundation (another, far less evil, IMF). The members of that expedition made a lasting impression on me, and have truly introduced me to a class of old school, true Indian gentlemen. The respect I have for them is boundless.

The first was a Mr Sudhir Sahi. He was an incredibly unassuming man, who carried an entire library's worth of information about the mountains in his head, and could tell you the height in feet or metres of every pass or notable peak around the globe, as well as the dates and participants of every expedition to climb it. Unlike many people with an amazing amount of information to impart, he never left you with a sense of having been lectured. He was so self-deprecating, he seemed to be almost apologising for all the wonderful facts he was imparting. I could have listened to him for hours.

In stark contrast, the leader of the expedition, Mr Sonam Wangyal, seemed to ooze strength and authority. If I were to draw the face of an old-school mountain man, it would be his. Like many Indian military men, he wore a black, fluffy, goat-wool beret; his skin was weathered, his deep-set Tibetan eyes looked out through large, square-framed, no-nonsense glasses, and his granite-firm jaw betrayed the determination that had led him to summit Everest and Nanda Devi, and countless other peaks. He'd been on around sixty major expeditions, had climbed with Chris Bonnington, Doug Scott and others, and had been training high-altitude military personnel since long before I was born. He was the epitome of the classical, quiet hero, and I am sure on an expedition his men would follow him anywhere. The 'quiet' bit turned out to be a bit of a misnomer though; as soon as we got into the mountains he underwent a complete transformation, turning into an irrepressibly loud and enthusiastic presence. As we struggled, heaving and panting, up the mountains, he danced up singing Ladakhi songs – probably filthy, judging by the reactions of the porters.

And then there was Colonel Nath, the director of the IMF. He was another quiet and unassuming character, and another true gentleman. Despite being a very big deal in the Indian military, and in global mountaineering, he gave the impression that we and any problems we might have were the most important items on his agenda. There were times I was so grateful I could have hugged him – but I'm sure that's not done in his world.

They're a breed that has no time for the ignorance and selfishness of modernity; there's no sense of ego or self-importance, for all that they have achieved and seen things of which we can only read about. I've stumbled on a few of their kind wherever I've been in the mountains, and it has impressed me tremendously. Something about the mountains does this to people. Many young mountaineers and climbers can be arrogant and egocentric, looking to climb the most impressive grades possible, make their mark on the hills, to conquer them and in doing so make their name. But spend long enough in this environment and I guess you become humbled by the mountains, by their power, their terrible fury and their ever-changing beauty. Next to these places, man seems small and insignificant.

These gentlemen of the high places saw in me a kindred spirit in need of guidance, and hammered home to me the importance of training and experience. When I explained that the desire was there but I was held back by a serious lack of cash, they suggested that I head to one of the Indian mountaineering institutes and take advantage of the courses they offered.

I had to wait until the following spring before I could get enough time off work to book six weeks in northern India. From Delhi, I took the third-class train up to Hardiwar, home every twelve years to the famous Kumbh Mela, the largest gathering of human beings on planet Earth. On one single April day, ten million people gathered here to bathe in the sacred River Ganges; over the course of the one-month-long Kumbh Mela, one hundred million took part. It's difficult to imagine what it must be like to be part of that gathering; it's not a big town, and pretty crowded at the best of times.

From the station in Hardiwar, I took a cab to the outskirts of town, then spent two days hitchhiking to Uttar Kashi in the Garhwal Himalaya. The campus itself is gorgeous, with manicured gardens full of native Himalayan plants, alive with sound of songbirds, surrounded by pine forests, and beyond them the dazzling snow-smothered spiky peaks of the Garwhal. Walking into the Institute was seriously intimidating. Everywhere I looked were seriously fit military men in uniform; even the gardeners wore green uniforms with regulation haircuts and 'tashes. Seen from the driveway, the tower of the artificial rock-climbing wall – the first in

India – dominates the compound, and then the buildings and great hall of the Nehru Institute of Mountaineering come into view. The hallways were adorned with artefacts from bygone days of Himalayan exploration: preposterous hefty wooden axes, woollen clothing and the leather hobnail boots worn by the first men ever to attempt 8,000-metre summits. There were grainy black-and-white photos of men whose names are familiar to any student of mountaineering: Shipton, Hillary, Norgay, Messner . . . and Sonam Wangyal, who I'd met on Stok Kangri. He hadn't told me he'd been Everest's youngest summiteer at the age of twenty-three!

It felt like my first day at university. With the caveat that I was now old enough to be one of the professors, and the other recruits . . . were not. In my late twenties, I was a decade older than most, and not far off double their size. Also, everyone else I saw there in the corridors was Indian; dark-skinned, black hair and eyes, whippet thin, built for this kind of enterprise. I could not have been more incongruous if I'd been a Masai warrior wandering the streets of Tokyo. I was sharing a tiny, but spick-and-span dorm room with ten recruits, who all conversed in Hindi, and spoke very little English.

There are two main courses at NIM: Basic, which introduces initiates to every aspect of Himalayan mountaineering and, once you've completed that, Advanced, which attempts a considerable peak and qualifies initiates to put together a high-altitude expedition. Recruits for the Basic course needed to be fit and hardy, but required no experience at all. Despite my letters of recommendation from Mr Wangyal, this was where I'd been placed. There were over a hundred of us in the Great Hall for our induction, most of which was in Hindi. I went to my too-tiny bed on the first night thinking I'd made a terrible mistake. This conviction grew stronger when, what seemed like ten minutes later, the drill sergeants came banging on our doors, yelling that we had to be up and ready to go NOW! We barely had time to pull on our trainers before we were running through the campus to a concrete drill square, where we were put into regimented lines, and taken through a drill of stretches and exercises so antiquated that it was like being in a 1930s military recruitment movie. Once that was done we trooped out, double file, into the hills beyond. The sun was barely up, yet we were presented with full-size oil barrels and told to run them to the top of the nearest peak. My second day at altitude, I was far from acclimatised and my lungs felt as if they were on fire. But you couldn't let the pace slacken, not even for a minute. Other recruits, desperate to make a good impression, were running uphill through the trees, barely seeming to break sweat.

In previous months, for one of my television programmes, I had taken part in the Israeli army's paratrooper selection course, running sixty miles overnight in full battle dress and carrying a heavy pack. I'd trained hard for it, and was still in excellent shape. But that didn't seem to count for anything here. I could barely draw breath, sweat was pouring off me, and I was being overtaken every few seconds by another Indian whippet, all the while wondering what on earth I'd let myself in for. Hours of hard running and carrying later, we finally traipsed into the mess for breakfast. I looked at my watch. It was not yet 8 a.m.

After a bowl of what looked like gruel, we were taken to a large tarmac exercise area. My heart sank at the prospect of more drills, but it turned out we were there to get our kit. Huge piles of equipment were distributed to my fellow students: harlequin colourful home-sewn waterproof climbing suits, rucksacks, foam sleeping mats, ice axes that looked to have been formed from melted down scrap metal. Yet again, I stood out like a sore thumb. I'd brought all my own flashy high-tech equipment, so every time they called out, 'Steve Backshall – sleeping bag', I'd have to shout 'Personal' to let them know that I had my own. After about seven or eight items, the other recruits were smirking to each other, even calling out in unison, 'Personal!', when my name was called. Some of the recruits only had flip-flops and tattered cast-off clothing, and there was me with my Gore-Tex, Teflon, carbon fibre and fancy brand names. I've never felt so privileged, so much at risk of being Mr 'All the Gear and No Idea'.

Once we were all kitted out, the hundred or so youngsters looked like a team in their oversized yellow-and-black uniforms. Albeit a team of bumblebees. I was beginning to wish the tarmac would swallow me up. We then set off for a patch of pine forest a few miles from the Institute. Here we pitched up our tents, and wandered to a nearby crag for the start of our climbing and ropework skills. It was a beautiful, bouldered paradise, the air thick with the scent of pine and jasmine, sunbeams shining through the trees, backlighting the golden wings of mayflies as they bounced up and down in their nuptial flights. Swifts and martins would scythe in between the trees to snatch them from the air, crying out 'sree sree' as they went. Occasionally the aquamarine flash of wings from an Indian roller, or the neon dazzle of a purple sunbird would glint as they swept about the conifers.

These first few days were all about basic ropework skills. And I mean basic. That afternoon on day one was devoted to tying eight knots and putting on a harness, things that I had learned over a decade ago. Though my natural inclination as a Brit is not to make a fuss, something had to be done. I approached one of the staff who I knew spoke English.

'I'm terribly sorry, sir,' I said, 'but I have a feeling I shouldn't be on this course . . . Is there any way you could consider moving me up to advanced?'

The commanding officer eyed me with practised disdain. 'You have acquired an A grade in your basic course?' he asked.

'Er, no, but I've been mountaineering for years, I've done all these things many times.'

'So you think you are better than these recruits?' he said loudly, gesturing around him.

Some of the other recruits had overheard and were starting to pay attention. I was wishing the ground would swallow me up.

'You are an "expert" mountaineer? You do not think we can teach you anything?' he demanded, twisting his luxuriant moustache between his fingertips.

'No, sir,' I began, 'it's not that at all—'

'The best mountaineers in India have been through this school and done the Basic course, but it is beneath you?' He was warming to his task now. The whole assembly had stopped climbing to watch me getting publicly humiliated.

'No, sir, forgive me, not at all, it's just that Mr Wangyal said I should be on the advanced course, and he is such an exceptional man . . .'

Jackpot. The CO was still twisting his moustache, but his demeanour had softened, his head tipped to one side in a gesture of interest.

'Mr Wangyal you say? Mr Sonam Wangyal?'

'Yes, sir. I was on an expedition with Mr Sonam Wangyal and Colonel Nath two years ago in Ladakh. To Stok Kangri.' (I didn't of course mention that we hadn't got much above base camp.)

'Colonel Nath and I served together before he took on the IMF,' the CO replied. 'A good man, strong. And Stok Kangri, you say? A good peak. So you have been above 6,000 metres?'

How to respond to that? Did flying count? I opted to obfuscate rather than tell an outright lie: 'It was a superb trip, we certainly achieved our objectives.' I avoided mentioning that the main objective had been clearing frozen-poo Cornettos off the mountainside.

'Then report to Major Rana back at NIM,' the CO responded. 'We can give you your exam now. If you pass with an A grade, you can start on advanced course.'

I thanked him warmly, and ran the few miles back to NIM to go in search of Major Rana, the notoriously stern officer who was in charge of the Institute. The corridors of the main building were empty. Standing waiting outside Major Rana's office door, I felt exactly like a naughty schoolboy who'd been sent to the headmaster's office. Giant butterflies wriggled in my stomach. When at last I heard a voice from within intone 'Enter,' I pushed open the door and stepped into his office. Rana was younger than I expected, in his early thirties, and incredibly dashing. He looked like a young Omar Sharif, with a classic moustache that suggested he should be taken seriously but might spontaneously burst into a Bollywood song, whilst dancing under an apple tree.

'What can we do for you, Mr Backshall?' he enquired, barely looking up from the papers in front of him. He didn't invite me to sit, so I stood before him, took a deep breath, and poured out my story. I told him of the big peaks I'd summited in the Alps, of technical winter mountaineering routes in Scotland. After ten minutes, he nodded sagely and picked up the phone. An hour later I was standing in front of the artificial climbing wall in the gym with one of the trainers. The test required me to set up a range of different rope rescue systems, for people who'd got trapped on climbs or fallen into crevasses. Then I had to climb a strenuous route on the wall, which obviously had to be conquered while making it look like a breeze, despite the fact that the holds were all shiny from years of use, and twisting and spinning from not being screwed in properly.

The nasty surprise, though, came in the form of a written exam paper. I have a freakish memory, so have always excelled at exams, and turned over the paper with confidence. And then stared at the words on the pages. They might as well have been written in Urdu. Angles of slope, international alarm channels, critical loading factors for various items of gear, and then the killer: the top ten highest mountains in India. I managed one. Kanchenjunga (the third highest peak on Earth) then drew a spectacular blank. After half an hour I had to turn the paper back over, and sit shell-shocked. I knew I'd failed. This was going to be mortifying.

Back in Major Rana's office, I sat squirming while he ran down my answers in grim silence, twirling his moustaches between his fingertips like Poirot. He then took a deep breath and paused for dramatic effect. I felt as if I had been swept into a David Lean movie and was about to be sent to the gulags for my impertinence.

'Well, your practical skills were exemplary,' he began. The mother of all 'buts' was to follow.

'But your written exam is all wrong.' He shook his head. 'You have got literally nothing right.' Again the pause. Now I was in an *X Factor* audition, waiting for Simon Cowell to send me back to working in MacDonald's.

'I'm going to give you a chance,' he said, and my heart leapt. 'But this –' shaking the paper – 'this is no good. I need you to get 100 per cent in your final exam, or you will be letting me down ...' he paused, leaned forward and looked at me with piercing eyes '... personally.'

The point was made. Assuring him that I would not be letting him down, promising I would work like a dog, I reversed out of the room, not wanting to turn my back, as if he was royalty and me a grovelling serf.

That same afternoon I was back out at the forest, but this time to be introduced to my new colleagues on the advanced course. There were only fifteen of us, and everyone was already a competent, self-sufficient mountaineer. We even had one Nepalese Sherpa who had summited Everest, though he himself was too humble ever to talk about it. There were two other Westerners on the advanced course: Anthony (pronounced with a 'th' in the middle) was an American, from Colorado, I think. He was the oldest and most experienced among us, and a rock climber of evident quality. He exuded a kind of hippie surfer-dude calm, but in actuality millimetres beneath he was actually quite uptight; a pressure cooker ready to blow. David Tuck, on the other hand, was the most genuinely calm, laid back and gentle man I'd ever met. Over the course of the next month I found out almost by osmosis the extraordinary things he'd achieved, but he was so devoid of ego his grand tales had to be extracted from him by force. He was living in India and spoke fluent Hindi. He'd totally embraced the culture, had studied the Hindu and Buddhist religions and understood it all better than our Indian colleagues. I liked him enormously, and we became firm friends instantly. Along with his climbing partner, Dave had taken a huge fall off Mount Cook in New Zealand, and they had both been very lucky to escape with their lives. It was clear that coming to the Himalayas had an element of catharsis about it for Dave, and there were hints throughout that he was battling to keep the lid on nerves and fears of which he would not speak.

Of the others, the next sure-fire friend was Sidi, short for Siddharta. Sidi was Bangladeshi, and had set up the Bangladeshi mountaineering association, which is not as major an achievement as it sounds, as 80 per cent of the country is only ten metres above sea level. Sidi, though, was as enthusiastic as I was about this big adventure, and had a laugh that reminded me of the asthmatic rescue donkey who'd lived on my family's smallholding when I was a child. Imran was high-born Brahmin Indian, good-looking and suave, but again easy to be around. Together we formed a famous four who barely spent a minute apart for the entirety of the expedition.

From minute one, the advanced course was a different ball game. The first skill we studied was an emergency rescue technique, which involved climbing a vertical rope. So far so easy; this is a basic skill when using modern aluminium ascenders with teeth that bite into the rope and allow you to travel upwards with minimum effort and decent speed. Here, though, we were only allowed to use the rope itself as an ascending device. It's a skill I've not seen used before or since. Essentially you take the dead rope from below you, then with a few complicated and convoluted knots, you tie the extra cord into a gripping 'prussic' knot above you, and shunt it up the climbing rope. It travels upwards fine when it's released and not under pressure, but when you load it with your weight it grips the rope. If you've tied it right, you can haul yourself skywards with surprisingly little effort. If you tie it wrong, you could find yourself spidering over space with literally nothing holding you on. Within hours, we were learning how to replace all of our fancy modern kit with simple rope. Harnesses were shed, then belay plates, I wouldn't have been surprised if they'd got us to abandon our trousers and weave new ones out of hemp.

The expectation was that we all knew a bamboozlement of tricky knots and were expert on quite serious terrain. We four musketeers were all pretty similar in ability, but had enough different experiences and expertise that we could communally bluff our way through most things. Our first rock climb was on a pitch that was right at the edge of my ability, but obviously as the new kid I had to look utterly nonchalant while doing it. Annoyingly, Anthony managed this trick with utter aplomb, swinging up the crack like a chimp on the jungle gym, only pausing to put in protection when the leaders below shouted at him. He'd stop, look about with a disdain that said, 'Why would I want to put any protection in here? I could climb this with my hands quite literally tied behind my back.' He was starting to get on my nerves.

The forest was utterly beautiful, a blissful place to camp, and with blood thickening and lungs finding their strength it soon felt like home. We could all have cheerfully stayed there the whole month. Sadly, as soon as basic skills were honed and we'd acclimatised to the altitude, the expedition proper began. The team tramped back to NIM in order to gather our equipment to begin the trek up into the high Himalaya. Next day we were outside the buildings yawning with our kitbags, ready to go at 5 a.m. Once aboard the battered old public bus, we sang songs and told terrible jokes as we headed up the mountain roads, the westerners laughing at the many memorable signs put up by the military: 'Don't race, don't rally, enjoy beauty of valley', 'After whisky, driving risky', 'No tobacco to miners – smoking and spitting act of 1997 bans the sale of tobacco to miners' (I'd like to see them tell a six-foot coal-smeared Welshman his Capstan Full Strength are against the law), and on a more serious note: 'Girl or boy I'm created by God, don't kill me in mother's womb just because I am a girl – Sex Determination of Foetus is against the law'.

Eventually we rolled into a seedy-looking hotel in the town of Gangotri at around midnight. Outside, the streets were saturated with human faeces from overflowing public latrines. In fact the latrines were so overrun with excrement that pilgrims had given up bothering to go inside and were squatting in the streets. Our hotel rooms stank of urine, dozens of cockroaches scuttled off to safety when we turned the lights on, and cracks in the walls were encrusted with black dried blood – a sure-fire sign of bedbugs. These nasty insects hide in crevices during the day, come out at night for a feed, stabbing their beak or rostrum into your skin to suck your blood. They then creep back home again, bloated, and a little blood gets squeezed out and coagulates at the edge of the crack. They're vectors of many diseases, and leave bites that can fester for weeks. While the others snuggled beneath flea-ridden blankets, I tied myself into my sleeping bag with nothing but my nose showing. It was too hot for me to get a wink of sleep, but it was worth it the next morning when my miserable room mates woke with itchy train-tracks of bedbug bites running in ugly red welts across their legs and backs. I'd stayed in a thousand places like this in my years as a travel writer, and was relieved it wasn't in the tropical steam of sea level, where all the smells would have been a thousand times worse, and we could have added the whine of mosquitos to our insomniac hell.

Gangotri marks the beginning of one of the most important pilgrimages in India. The town nestles in a pine forest in a steep-sided gully cut by a ferocious churning river, whose roaring white-green waters kept us from sleep in our grotty hotel, and thundered us into consciousness the next morning. This is the mighty Bhagirathi River, which eventually flows on to become the Ganga (Ganges), India's lifeblood and mystical icon. Gangotri is two days' walk from the Gamuk glacier, which creaks its way down off some of the most special mountains imaginable. Hardly surprising then that the pilgrimage to the source is so important. During the high season saffron-robed Hindu holymen and other pilgrims make the trek up in their thousands to bathe at this most sacred of places. Above and around these cliffs are thick deciduous forests, bound together with creepers and parasitic vines. Banyan and pipal trees with their many-fingered twisted roots are reminiscent of witches' trees from a Roald Dahl novel, and cactus-like branched trees hang precariously to the rockfaces. Often the trees sit on a ridge, silhouetted against the blue sky. At other points, the hillsides are stacked one in front of another, each one progressively lighter and lighter in hue as they disappear into the distance. Flocks of rock pigeons or cormorants fly in stark silhouettes against the hazy background, and golden light ripples over the churning waters.

Away from the power of the rapids, the water itself has its own beauty. With so few settlements between here and the glaciers that create the river, the waters are icy-clear in the shallows, but the main stream is the colour of a fine green gemstone. The sheer amount of water flowing through channels that are rarely more than 70 metres across creates a maelstrom of currents; the water seems to boil and fizz as the churned and pressurised depths pop to the surface.

Even in late October, with the trekking and pilgrimage seasons well over, the way up and down was thronged with pilgrims and saffron-robed, dreadlocked babas or sardhus; holy Hindu ascetics who have forsaken the trappings of the world and are undertaking a quest towards spiritual enlightenment in an effort to release themselves from the cycle of death and reincarnation and move to a higher plane. On the road up to Gangotri we passed groups of barefoot babas carrying poles with covered buckets at either end. They were returning to their own regions with bottles of water taken from the source as a blessing for their parishes. One such baba we stopped and quizzed was only beginning a 3,000-kilometre walk with his water; we didn't ask how he'd got here in the first place, but certainly many hundreds of people walk both ways – and some travel even further than him. In the high season it's sometimes not possible to drive this road, as the entire 200-kilometre stretch is thronged with pilgrims walking thousands of kilometres with water collected from the source.

Because Gangotri is such an important Hindu sanctuary, it is forbidden to bring any meat into the area. So for the duration of our expedition, the diet would be vegetarian. Food would be carried and cooked by an army of porters who seem to excel at carrying. . . and suck at cooking. It's potentially the world's finest 'fat-camp'; if you had a porky teenager with a discipline problem, it would be the answer to all your prayers! In the morning we had an egg fried with onion, a piece of toast and as much cardamom-flavoured chai tea as we could drink. If we were out and moving during the day we would skip lunch. In the evening it would be rice and dhal (lentil curry), with chapattis. This was fine for the first three or four days, but then the dhal started to taste strongly of the fuel it was cooked with. The smell and flavour instantly made me feel nauseous, and it was a real struggle to force it down. I had bought a few chocolate bars in the town near NIM, and eked those out to a single precious square a day. We'd occasionally get bananas as a treat, but the food wasn't even close to enough for a hefty like me.

As a non-believer, I was most interested in the trek's physical beauty, and in the purpose of those around me. It was impressive, though, how people of Indian faiths welcomed me into their religious observances. They included me as an outsider in sacred pujas, welcomed me into their temples to watch and gawp, and allowed, even encouraged me, to photograph them at work, rest and prayer. In my experience, most other religions around the world are not so amenable.

The walk ascends steadily towards Gamuk, from around 3,100 metres above sea level at Gangotri to around 4,000 metres at the glacier itself. As you follow the gorge the entire way, you are always within sight of the torrential river, twisting and turning below, and each bend offers a new vista of different and spectacular peaks, many of them over 6,000 metres in height. While many parts of the high Himalaya are barren desert, this part of the Garwhal Himalaya has lush alpine scenery, with forests of cedar, spruce and pine. The pilgrims' path is lined with juniper bushes smelling pungently of temples, and surrounded by vibrantly coloured red-, scarlet- and yellow-leafed trees. Grassy verges are dotted with flowers whose petals seem impossibly delicate. Appearances can be deceptive, though, as they have to endure evenings that fall below freezing, and winters buried under metres of snow.

*

We were no more than a few hours up the gorge when Sidi called me back to meet someone I'd walked straight past, too intent on staring at the view. Sitting under a shade constructed of a hessian blanket was a sadhu, clothed only in a saffron-coloured loin cloth, his hair piled on top of his head in thick dreadlocks, and his white beard grown down to his chest. He beckoned me over, and I went and sat next to him, saying the greeting reserved for sadhus: '*Ram ram Babaji*'. The man began to gesticulate in exaggerated movements, then took out a pen and notepad from inside a small handbag that seemed to be filled with cigarettes.

'This is Moni Baba,' said Sidi, 'the silent baba. He hasn't spoken a word in fourteen years.'

I had heard much about hard-core babas who undertake some form of physical constraint as a focus for their yoga and path of self-enlightenment. There was the rolling baba, who laid down and rolled from one side of India to the other . . . and then back again. And the standing sadhu, who stood in one place on one leg for around fifteen years. There was even a baba who held his right arm in the air for over a decade, until it became as blackened and wasted as a mummified chicken leg, fused into its socket. It had always seemed to me an unusually self-obsessed and pointless practice, not unlike cycling naked up Everest or eating a hundred kilos of blancmange to get into the *Guinness Book of Records* . . . until I met the Moni Baba. He was probably the most transfixing man I have ever encountered, with an air of tranquillity and peace that was infectious, and though he often looked like he was just about to speak, he never made a sound.

Any conversation with the Moni Baba was obviously a slow and complicated process, but with Sidi as interpreter, and his notepad as a medium, we managed to get quite chatty. Silence, said the Baba, is godliness. He spent his days sitting beside Mother Ganga and meditating, trying to find synthesis with the five elements. To emphasise this, he gave me a dilak of ash, symbolising fire. (A dilak is the spot, usually of rice and vermillion, that Hindus wear on their forehead to mark the seat of the soul.) He told us that to begin with he'd found the lack of speech frustrating, but now it came as naturally to him as the environment he had chosen. He slept in a cave down by the river, and everything he needed was provided by the faithful making their pilgrimage to Gamuk. He hadn't eaten anything but fruit and water for twelve years. Taking this as a cue, I proffered a small bunch of bananas. The Moni Baba smiled, then tore the bunch apart and gave us each one, urging us eat them, leaving himself with only a half a banana.

We were with the Moni Baba for well over an hour. He had an entrancing face, and smiling was clearly his first language. When we asked if he would ever speak again, he replied that he planned to talk in two years' time, on a date he had in his head but wouldn't divulge. We all wondered whether he'd still have the power to speak, but he seemed confident that he did.

As our mystical meeting concluded, he touched the top of my head in blessing. Miserable old rationalist that I am, at that exact moment I felt a flood of wellbeing, power and peace coursing through me, and I had an overpowering urge to cry like a baby.

It's easy to see how babas pick up foreigners as disciples, and why you occasionally see sadhus walking around with feral Europeans, Israelis or Americans in trail, who've ditched the modern world and decided to give up their days to follow a Holy Man. In our own god-less worlds, spirituality has become tainted by politics and history. We associate religious fervour with so much negativity: fanaticism, intolerance, hypocrisy, abuse of power, greed. Here, though, aco-lytes can follow people whose sacrifice and devotion is genuine. They can shed much of the furore, confusion and complexity of modern life, and find simplicity. Smoking marijuana, practising yoga and meditating, surrounded by the most beautiful landscapes on the planet, they are relieved of the stress caused by excess of choice, relieved of the burden of attachment to possessions. There are parts of their lifestyle choices I deeply envy. Although I have embraced rationalism in my adult years, biology has become my religion and evolution my creed, people who are close to me (my mum particularly) would still call me a spiritual person. Many religious people claim those who lack belief are missing out on the real wonders of the universe, but I think they have things backwards. Reality and science *is* wonder. We human beings have described around two million species that inhabit this planet; there will be at least ten times that amount out there. Take the tiniest animal known to science, the magnificently named Dumbledore-winged fairy fly; it has as complex an anatomy and biology as the blue whale. You could study that one insect for the rest of your life and still not know everything there is to know about it. That minute wasp (not actually a fly at all) can fit on the sharp end of a pin and only be seen properly with a powerful microscope, yet there are mysteries about its biology that will be astounding the scientists of my grandchildren's generation. The infinite numbers of miracles in the real world, and how it came to be, make a mockery of the two small chapters in Genesis that describe how the world was magicked out of nothing. I think it's important in life to be rational and scientific, but not cynical. To remain open to the possibilities of the metaphysical, of things beyond this corporal form. I do not believe in ghosts because I have never seen one, nor any evidence of one. I do not believe in God, because my knowledge tells me He is a human construct, born out of our own weakness, our own desire to be important in a universe that is oblivious to our presence. But for all that, I hope that should I ever see a ghost, or should a god ever reveal itself to me, I'll be open-minded enough to see and wonder. Thus with my heart full of hope and wellbeing, I took my leave of this beautiful man and carried on upstream.

The early part of our trek up towards the glacier was a dream, carried out under blue skies and baking sunshine. It was genuinely like a nice warm walk in alpine meadows in summer, which meant you didn't notice the altitude. Until I woke up in my tent on the second morning with the world's most horrific headache. After hitchhiking across the United States in the mid nineties, I met some friends in a California youth hostel and ended up drinking an entire bottle of tequila. I was found unconscious, naked under a cold dorm shower at sunrise, and couldn't eat or drink anything for two days. This high-altitude migraine felt much the same. A searing pain behind the eyes that made you want to lie down with a pillow wrapped round your head while waiting for death to take you. In all my mountaineering exploits, even when I've ventured into the 'Death Zone' above 8,000 metres, my altitude sickness has always been most profound in this 4,000–5,000-metre zone on the way up. Not surprising then that so many people suffer and even die on Africa's highest peak, Kilimanjaro; it's a technically easy peak trekking-wise, but takes walkers from near sea level to 6,000 metres in about five days.

I did have the luxury of taking my time getting up, though. While the basic course students were frogmarched up in crocodile file, told when to rest, when to drink and how fast to walk, the privileged on the advanced course were simply given a set of latitude and longitude coordinates and told to be there before sundown. That gave us the opportunity to stop and chat with several other babas along the way. The one who will last longest in my memory was one who called himself the linga baba. The ling, linga or lingum in Hindi is the male genitals, specifically the phallus. This particular baba was one of the masters of linga yoga. When I asked him to explain this, he offered to show me. He went into his tent and emerged completely naked, at 4,000 metres above sea level, with ash smeared on his forehead and penis, and a long straight stick in his hands.

He then proceeded to wrap the end of his penis around the horizontal stick. Cranking it around with a series of sharp turns of his wrist as if he was revving up a motorbike, he coiled his penis perhaps six or seven times around the stick. He then turned the stick in a complete circle, helicopter fashion, as if trying to rip his member off at the root. After this, he held the stick horizontally again, and stepped one leg over it, and then the other; so that his entire genitalia – still coiled around the stick like a frightened millipede – was pulled up behind his backside. It was like the psychotic version of what little boys do in the football changing rooms when pretending that they have vaginas. As if this wasn't enough, he proceeded to do a series of squats and other exercises, still with his family jewels tied up his bum.

Next, the linga baba took a boulder the size of a basketball, tied a rope around it, and proceeded to swing it from his penis. The other lads later told me of linga babas who'd appeared at the big Khum Mela gatherings and perform with five grown men standing on their erect penises. Which is just showing off.

Once the linga baba had finished his display, he tied a shawl around his waist and sat down, smoking ganja from a chillum pipe, with a strange smile on his face, as though he had performed some mystical act that we should all be revering. But unlike the Moni Baba, this conjurer of cheap tricks had no effect on me other than to leave me a little disillusioned with the whole thing. He seemed so keen to show us his stunts, was completely stoned, and no matter how you dress it up in religious significance, it's still comes down to a man trying to impress with his schlong. While many of the other babas we met seemed to be inspirational people with genuine missions and abilities, this particular linga baba came across more like an X-rated circus sideshow.

I should add at this point that both the public exhibition of powers and smoking of ganja are facets of Hinduism. As Sidi explained it, the god Shiva once swallowed the most powerful poison in the world in order to save the Earth from being destroyed, and the only thing that would ease his pain was smoking ganja. This worked, though it did turn him blue. Sadhus therefore smoke ganja like taking a Eucharist in order to be closer to Shiva. Showing your powers, on the other hand, is essential in order to gain disciples, and for the sadhus, their efforts are useless unless they are passed on to others.

We continued our trek up to the glacier with two babas in tow to perform a puja ceremony at the source itself. The vast amphitheatre that houses the source is so dramatic a setting that it beggars belief. To one side Bhagirathi's many peaks loom like the arched back of a primeval dragon. To the other is the majesty of Shivling. The name means the penis of Shiva, and while the imagery is perhaps unflattering it is a singularly dramatic, horn-like peak, often described as the Matterhorn of the Garwhal Himalaya. (Every pointed peak that stands alone and dominates its immediate environment tends to be known as the Matterhorn of somewhere, be it Ama Damblam, Khan Tengri, Alpamayo – why does something as stunning as one of these peaks need to be compared to anything else?)

And then in the middle of these thrones of the gods is the glacier itself. Currently 30 kilometres in length and in places 2.5 kilometres wide, the Gangotri glacier is up there with the biggest glaciers in the Himalayas (though tiny compared with Arctic and Antarctic monsters). Being comparatively close to the Equator, it has suffered more than most as a result of climate change. Since the industrial revolution, the glacier has been in rapid retreat, with the decline quickening after 1971. Over the last twenty-five years it has retreated almost a kilometre. Looking at early photos of the region, it is unrecognisable, but even though it has retreated practically as far as the base of Bhagirathi, it still maintains an aura of ancient, timeless majesty. It's a vast creaking tangle of ice and boulders that has cut a swathe between the lofty summits, and at its snout is a vast cave called Gomukh, 'the cow's mouth'. Out of this cave pours an already formed and rampaging river. A few miles downstream it will drop its suspended sediments and turn emerald green, but up here it is still charged with fine-ground sediment and runs brown as chocolate milkshake. Nowhere have I ever seen a more dramatic or obvious source of a river, and this is the source of the world's most sacred waterway, in the world's most spiritual country. No wonder then that this is considered to be a site every Hindu should visit once in their lifetime. A hundred metres from where the meltwater streams off the blue-grey cliffs of the glacier, we bathed in the raging river while a chanting sardhu took us through the ritual of purification. To bathe at the source of the Ganges is said to cleanse seven generations of your family from sin.

Again, I was amazed at the willingness of these devoutly religious people to involve an atheist foreigner in such a precious ceremony. I was given a dilak of vermilion and taught the sacred mantras, then we threw marigolds and coconuts into the river as an offering to Mother Ganga, before stepping into the waters. A thin crust of ice clung to the slower-moving parts of the river and the sides were lined with icicles and frozen rivulets. I had been standing barefoot on the snowy rocks for about fifteen minutes before we stepped in, so my feet were already too numb to feel much, but when the sadhu threw water over my back and head, I felt as if I was having an aneurism.

The world's most evil ice-cream headache passed and left me invigorated and piercingly awake throughout the chanting and quiet contemplation of deities I had never heard of, and incantations I didn't understand. Nevertheless, though the vast majority of the puja did a twenty-one-gun salute way over my head, the majesty of the location, and the primal beauty of the ceremony was incredibly touching. There was even a vague sense that I was missing out, that all this wonderful pageantry had no meaning for me, and I secretly hoped that it would still work . . . even if I didn't believe in it.

To conclude the puja, we placed a banana leaf with some rice, red Hibiscus petals, jasmine and a candle on to the waters. Our offerings were carried downstream, taking our dreams with them along the lengths of the world's most sacred river, across the whole Indian subcontinent, before being washed out to the infinite vastness of the ocean.

The glacier itself held a special challenge for us as recruits: ice. As the frozen river works its way downwards, it occasionally finds steeper ground it needs to travel over and forms icefalls, the glacial equivalent of waterfalls. These are the most dramatic and potentially dangerous sections of the glacier, as it moves fastest here, therefore is most unstable and unpredictable. Also, because the ice is under such pressure, large crevasses open up like sapphire throats capable of swallowing a man, even if he was riding an elephant. The icefalls also create vertical towers and faces of hard ice, and if you can find a stable one, these make perfect training grounds for ice-climbing. Finally we'd come upon an area of expertise where I was far more experienced than anyone else on the course. My ice-climbing is far better than my rock climbing, and I try to fit in at least one big trip to the frozen falls of the Alps or Rockies every year. The deep, deep blue ice in the glacier was stone hard, but the routes were very short. I've led ice climbs several hundred metres high, these were no more than ten, and nothing like as steep or technically challenging. I strode across the glacier in my fancy new hi-tech mountaineering boots and sharpened crampons, flexed my perfectly weighted modern ice axes, stepped over the looming crevasse at its base, then swung my axe, ready to make a big impression. To my delight, the senior instructor chose this moment to show up and watch the master class I was about to put on.

It was instantly more awkward than I had expected. NIM protocol required the use of a pair of rope 'cow's tail' leashes that you tie to each axe and then to your harness. If you wish, you can hang off them, hands free, to take a rest or while putting in a titanium ice screw for protection. It was an old-fashioned method, but I was playing by their rules. Unfortunately, I'd tied my cow tail ropes slightly too short, so every time I made to swing an axe, it would pull up short, looking limp wristed and a bit like the stereotypical 'girl's throw' (sorry to all the girls that throw perfectly well – especially my pal Carol, who can spin pass a rugby ball further than I can). This was further complicated by the fact that I'd left my own modern leash system on the axes as well, so every time I stopped to put in a screw, I had to take those off as well. It was all thoroughly awkward, the sun was beating down into the windless bowl of the icefall, and as I had probably got one too many clothing layers on, I started to sweat. And my cheap Indian sunblock began leaking. It was like having neat vinegar poured into my eyes. Within seconds, I was totally blind. I tried to remove my sunglasses to wipe my eyes clean, but immediately there was a shout from below.

'Leave your glasses on!' barked the senior instructor. 'Lose those and you will go snowblind!'

So I hacked away blindly, failing to find a single axe placement. Alongside me, one of the non-English speaking recruits merrily walked up the ice wall, sitting back on his leashes as if it was the easiest and most natural thing in the world. By the time he had crested the wall and another had taken his place, I had progressed no more than a few metres. The harder I whacked my axes, the more I sweated, the blinder I got. I slipped and scraped down the easy ice back to standing again, teetering on the edge of the looming crevasse. This was pathetic! Turning to face the gathering crowd, I saw the senior instructor frowning and shaking his head. Now I was gripped by the panic of humiliation. I tore off my own leashes and stuffed them into my pockets, wiped my eyes clear with my T-shirt, and set off up the face. This time, I was up it in a flash, and at the top looked back down. The instructor had gone. Later that day, my favourite instructor took me aside and in broken English asked, 'Mr Steve, you have not done the ice climb before, no?' He sounded disappointed in me. I was kicking myself for days afterwards.

After making camp near the snout, we were to cross over the glacier itself and head up into the high meadows beyond, where the pilgrims rarely strayed. Until this point the path had been carpeted with donkey and mule dung of varying freshness, and every kilometre or so there'd be a kiosk where you could get a mug of chai, sticky sweetmeats, or take rest on worryingly flea-ridden blankets in the dark and dingy lean-tos alongside. Once we started our march up and over the glacier, the snow began to fall, and then to hammer down. From here on in it was moun-taineer's territory, and we were not to see another human being for several weeks. Well, other than the basic course recruits we'd occasionally see snaking up a distant trail in their yellow-and-black onesies.

Pretty soon we were peppered with icy blizzard bullets, snow drifting across the trail filling footsteps almost instantly. A Him-alayan griffon vulture soared right over our heads so close that its finger-like primary wing tips seemed to graze our cheeks, skim-ming along the length of the line as if checking out what was on the menu. Despite the sinister sensation of being scouted by such a vast and dominant bird, the truth is that vultures in the Himalayas are some of the most threatened creatures on the planet. This is down to a common anti-inflammatory drug called Diclofenac. It's routinely given by farmers to their cattle as a way of shortcutting a variety of ailments, and when those animals die their corpses remain saturated with the drug, which is passed on to the vultures that feed on them. While most animals suffer no ill effects from the drug, it is lethal to vultures, causing kidney failure. During the 1980s the white-rumped vulture was so omnipresent in India that it was probably the most common large bird on Earth – it's estimated there were as many as 80 million. Today there are only a few thousand.

After days of altitude headaches, not to mention being eternally chilled to the bone, with everything we owned soaked through, our spirits lifted when the clouds blew away to reveal a sky so blue it was almost jet black, ice-blasted clean of clouds. The views remain some of the most extraordinary I have ever seen. In an Alpine valley you walk along with 3000m peaks at most a thousand metres above you. In the Himalayas the valleys themselves are higher than those summit tops, yet the rock faces rise 2000m, even 4000m above you! The scale is impossible to put into words. You feel dwarfed, insignificant, fragile. It reminds us of our proper place on Earth, of how this ancient timeless world ticks on oblivious to our petty dreams. Some might find this overwhelming, but for me it is liberating. It awakens in me the finest existential fantasties. As a student of literature, I was obsessed with the works of Sartre, Camus, Nietzche, Malraux, writers who struggle to tackle the dilemma of our being and existence. If I'm honest, those studies were initially done because I wanted to sound like an intellectual, but they have had a long-lasting impression on me and my perception of life. We are nothing, a speck of flotsam in an ambivalent universe. There is no fate or rules binding our actions, confining the way we behave. There is no deity or afterlife as a safety net. Life is what we make it, no more.

My metaphysical euphoria was tempered by the reality of clear skies in thin air. The second the shadows burnt off each morning, temperatures soared, and the skin began to fry on our faces. Some of the boys began to look as if they had leprosy and smell as if they were decomposing.

At night, all fifteen of us shared a single old-fashioned bell tent. It was made out of white canvas, and no matter how many rocks you pegged around the bottom of it, the wind would still whip through it leaving cricked necks and red-tipped noses. If you needed to pee in the night, you had to slip gingerly out of your sleeping bag, tiptoe over the snuffling, slumbering corpses and out into the chill. Toilet etiquette dictated you then traipse at least a hundred metres from camp before letting rip. By the time you got back into your bag, you were wide awake. On the plus side my nocturnal pee trips meant I got to see the moon rise behind the black silhouettes of the mountains, casting moonbeams into the sky and turning the snow ghostly white. One night I had the remarkable luck of coming out into the darkness to see a perfect black circle evolving over the almost full moon: a lunar eclipse! I sat and watched for half an hour, trying desperately and forlornly to take photos. Eventually, though, it got so cold I had no choice but to scuttle indoors before my eyeballs froze over. Not a single one of us had had the foresight to bring a specific pee bottle, but I know for certain a few of the lads resorted to using their water bottle and then washed it out the following morning. Grim, but when it was hammering down with snow outside and it was a choice of that or lying awake with a full bladder, there was no contest.

Some of my tent mates had snores that would have woken a stone troll, and a few of them suffered from sleep apnoea. This condition is one that seems to show up at high altitudes, and manifests itself in the sleeper suddenly ceasing to breathe. This part is freaky, but nothing like as sinister as when they all of a sudden drag in one huge sucking, almost screaming breath to supply their oxygen-starved brains. As I was the only one of the entire crew who'd had the foresight to bring earplugs, there were many who suffered terribly from sleep deprivation. Annoyingly, there were also a few young recruits who would be asleep and snoring before I could even get the earplugs in.

By this time I was getting to know my tent mates, even the ones who didn't speak English. They had names like Chunder, Lovesong, Peanut and Imp. (This is nothing; on a tiger-filming trip in India my cameraman asked our guide what his children's names were. He replied, 'Shittage and Idiota.' We had to stuff our fingers into our mouths to stop ourselves exploding.) Though they might have been on the small side, they were as hard as Geordie panel-beaters. When the course began, I'd had concerns for teenage Peanut, who was desperately failing to grow a spidery moustache and had the physique of a pre-pubescent girl. This concern was short-lived; on day two Peanut and I each had to carry one of our fifteen-person tents. While I tottered around helplessly like Bambi on ice, he threw his over his shoulder nonchalantly, and sprinted up off the hill.

The next week was taken up ferrying loads to higher-altitude camps. In the afternoons we'd sit down to lectures on meteorology, avalanches, mountain terms and mountain medicine while sitting in the snow in the world's most beautiful classroom. In the background were the magical Bhagirathi peaks, a similar shape to the Black Cuillens on the Isle of Skye, but approximately seven times higher, their sheer rockfaces and snow walls shining white whether in sun or moonlight. I was a less appealing sight; by this point the sun and wind had flayed my face and my beard had small colonies of mice taking up residence. It looked as if I'd been dipped in fur and deep-fried, with my sunglasses held together with sticky tape.

While our time here is designed to create recruits who can plan and execute expeditions into the high Himalaya themselves, there is no doubt that, for every one of us, the real goal is the final summit. Advanced course trainees get to make an attempt on a serious mountain, and most of the course builds towards this final push. Using ancient maps, we planned a route through the valleys to get to a promising site from which to commence our ascent. We trekked past beautiful pointy peaks towards our chosen spot: Kedar Dome, an intimidating shiny massif of snow and ice.

One stunning blue-sky morning, we'd barely finished our breakfast before the officers clamoured around, ushering us to get up and out. We were going to do a quick march before the day began. No need to bring water or food, we had to go as we were. Having grown accustomed to our officers' strange orders, we leapt to our feet, pulled on our boots and set off. The route took a line straight across the moraine, a teetering, unstable morass of dumped glacial rocks, then on to the glacier itself. Nobody had brought crampons, so we picked our way across carefully, finding a path that avoided steep ground and keeping well clear of crevasses. After an hour or so, we were all starting to get thirsty, and Anthony, Dave and I were much regretting not having taken the time to put on sunblock. I made a nose panel out of the cardboard from a Milky Bar wrapper and stuck it over my nose with gaffer tape.

By lunchtime, we were still going hard. This was by far the hottest, steamiest day we'd had so far, not a cloud in the sky, but the officers hadn't let us rest even for a few minutes. We were parched with thirst and stomachs were audibly grumbling. It was immediately noticeable how much better the Indians from humble backgrounds were faring. They were used to working all day without water or food, and hence didn't see what the fuss was about, whereas the Westerners and Indians from more privileged backgrounds were accustomed to modern training regimens which stress the importance of keeping hydrated and getting calories on board when undertaking strenuous activity. Doubtless, this is sound advice . . . until you find yourself in a survival situation and your body expects its regular intake of fluids and fuel. I've seen this many times on expeditions, but also in races. Some of the fiercest competitors in fell-running races in the Alps are local farmers, who run up the mountains in their welly boots, keeping pace with the ultra runners and their power bars.

By late afternoon, the escapade had taken on a serious feel. We were crossing a steep, icy mountainside covered in loose rock, unroped and without crampons. None of us had drunk anything except the odd broken icicle all day long. Some of the boys were moaning with fatigue, others were gripped with fear as we teetered unprotected over cavernous drop-offs. Every time anyone got up the courage to ask one of the officers what the plan was, or when we might head back to camp, the answer was the same: 'It will be some time yet.'

Eventually the sun set, the temperature dropped, and bodies that had been cooking in high-altitude UV were suddenly chilled to the bone. Now it was the turn of the Westerners to have the edge. Poor Sidi lived at sea level in steamy Bangladesh, his lips and nose turned blue, and his teeth chattered noisily like a cartoon character caught in a deep freeze. The chill was followed by dusk and then darkness, and now we faced the further complication of navigating back over the moraine without torches, the sole consolation being that we could no longer see the drop-offs and contemplate the consequences should we unseat one of the boulders as we half crawled over the rubble.

It was pitch-black by the time we got back to camp. The reaction from the educated Indians and the Westerners was bemused. How had the logistics failed so terribly? How could we have been left out in such danger for so long? Had we got lost? Why were we so unprepared? The army boys and lower-caste Indians were much more philosophical about it. They were back now, there was water and tea to guzzle, there was freshly cooked rice and dhal ready to eat. Their sole concern was to fill their bellies and then sleep like dead men.

Next morning after breakfast we were called into our square file so the officers could talk us through our next assignment. Before the major could begin his lecture, Anthony stepped out of line and interrupted him.

'I've been mountaineering for twenty years,' Anthony began, 'and what happened yesterday was totally unacceptable. You sent us out for a fourteen-hour day without food, water or the right clothing. You put us on dangerous ground without protection, you endangered our lives, and I for one am not going to have my life put at risk because you don't know what you're doing.'

The boys all froze in horror. Some squirmed with embarrassment; they would never have considered challenging authority in this way. This Westerner had no understanding of Indian and army culture, no respect, no knowledge of the chain of command. It was horrible. I studied the major, trying to gauge his reaction to Anthony's outburst. Would he yell at him, put him in his place, send him home? Or worse, would he apologise, admit that they'd made a mistake, promise not to do anything like it again?

The major did none of these things. Instead, he looked at Anthony keenly, as if assessing him. He nodded his head. Then he continued with his lecture.

Afterwards, all the talk was of Anthony and his rebellion. The army boys were scandalised and wanted him sent home. Dave and Sidi agreed with much of what he'd said, but thought he'd gone about it the wrong way; he should have addressed the major in private to avoid making a scene. My take on the whole thing was totally different.

For me, the previous day had been brutal, punishing . . . and exactly what I had been expecting the course to be all about. Far from having cocked up, got lost, or sent us out on a fool's errand, I had no doubt whatsoever that the officers knew exactly what they were doing. The NIM prospectus clearly states that the purpose of the course is 'to introduce recruits to the realities of Himalayan moun-taineering by exposing them to hardship, hunger, physical exertion and extremes of temperature'.

The reason they'd sent us out unprepared was, ironically, to pre-pare us for situations where this would happen by accident. The three rules of mountaineering are: 'It's always further than it looks. It's always taller than it looks. And it's always harder than it looks.' It's not possible for a mountaineer to be prepared for every even-tuality. If you tried, your backpack would be the size of a house and you wouldn't be able to move. And then of course there are all those times when you get it wrong. Go out in the hills and run out of water or food. Get way up high and realise you've forgotten sunblock or your down jacket, or come across unexpectedly diffi-cult terrain when you haven't got the gear to deal with it safely. The officers were perhaps imprinting in our heads that we needed to be as ready as possible for anything, but were also deliberately putting us in the big hills at our most vulnerable. To develop confidence in our own skills, to learn to compromise and make the best of what we had.

There was also a vital psychological lesson to be learned. When it comes to endurance, you bite off manageable chunks. If you're rowing the Atlantic, you don't power away from the start-line saying, 'Right, three thousand miles, here we go!' That's too much for the brain to compute, and too slow to chip away at. Instead, you break it down, set yourself bite-size targets: an hour on the clock, the next meal, the next rest stop, the next time a pal will be there cheering you on. This is essential and it works. But at the same time it's dangerous to rely too much on the boost to morale this repre-sents. The mountains are far too unpredictable for that, and this is something the army knows better than anyone.

The Israeli paratrooper's selection course I mentioned earlier had been an old-school beasting that gave every single applicant a good hiding, no matter what their abilities were, and the psychological tricks were identical to those used here at NIM. That course had culminated in a run where we set off at night, carrying a huge pack. At about 1 a.m., the officers stopped us and gave us a massive cheer, delivering a rousing lecture about how there was 'just ten kilometres more to go'. Our spirits soared. Ten kilometres? We were almost there! You could sense the boys dropping their guard, starting to relax, aiming at that meagre ten kilometres, an hour and a half or so to go! After two more brutal hours, the officers stopped us and gave us the exact same lecture, again finishing with 'just ten kilometres more to go'! You could see the soldiers wilting, their spirits crushed, the tangible goal snatched away from them. The officers repeated this over and again throughout the night, and then finally, when we genuinely were ten kilometres from the finish line, stretchers were produced. For the final push uphill into Jerusalem we would have to carry the recruits who had not been able to finish on our shoulders. It broke each and every one of us. Nobody finished that day with anything left to give.

Mountaineering breaks your spirit like this over and again. False summits are something of a cliché, but very real. You battle for hours for the obvious peak above you, crest it, only to gaze on to another peak even higher above. Or you walk several hours down a glacier, only to find your way blocked by a gaping crevasse, leaving you no option but to backtrack all the way up again.

In the mountains, everything is about what you've prepared yourself to do. There are five-hour walking days where you get to the end and feel like you couldn't take another step. Yet on summit days I have managed to keep going for over thirty hours. There is no doubt that the mind is the most powerful organ in the body, but the brain is not a sessile or sedentary entity. It can be trained, and it can be tricked, and that's half the battle.

*

I'd half expected to get up the following morning to another day of unspecified punishment, but instead we were taken to a nearby snow slope to concentrate on our snow skills. Learning to move safely on steep snow and ice is the main skill that sets climbers and mountaineers apart. Rock climbers are used to having protection as they climb. Most of the time, as you climb steep rock, you press gear into cracks and crevices to catch you if you fall. For mountaineers on steep snow, you might rope up, tying yourself by a length of line to your climbing partners or team mates, but you very rarely have the opportunity to protect yourselves. Occasionally you might make a belay, shoving a stake down into the snow, or perhaps burying an axe or a bag and belaying off that. That belay will only be lodged in snow, so is only as good as the medium itself. Often, it is worse than useless, as it lulls you into a false sense of security.

Our steep slope had a gentle run-off at the bottom, and was a good place for us to get a safe sense of how effective the safety measures could be, and what to do in the event of a slip or fall. For several days we clambered up the slope then threw ourselves off it without warning, seeing if our comrades could stop our slide, or practising 'ice-axe arrests' where you roll mid-toboggan into a strong position, then try to halt your slide with a combination of crampons and ice axe. I'd learned all these techniques in the past, but never had I put so much time into trying them out. There were some valuable lessons: on a slope as steep as 60 or even 70 degrees, one man stood an excellent chance of catching his falling partner provided he was beneath him and their ropes were well-managed. However, if it was the leader that fell, it was more of a lottery. As the heaviest member of the team, I could catch my rope mates every time. Even the smallest guy could catch me, but only if he was well prepared and got a decent bracing stance super quick. Several times over the training period I threw myself off, only to find my weight and rope would whip my partner clean off his feet. The two of us would then gather speed, plunging downwards in a Nantucket sleigh ride with snow spray blinding us. We were banned from using an ice-axe arrest, and it wouldn't have worked anyway. I'd guestimate we were travelling at thirty miles per hour, thundering downhill like a giant snowball. As the slope petered out, we'd eventually slow, coming to a halt in a discombobulated heap, peppered white from head to toe, tied up in our ropes, battered, and giggling uncontrollably. The levity of the situation was somewhat tempered by the knowledge that, if this had been the real thing instead of a dry run, death would have been the certain end.

By now we were at a camp in the high-altitude meadows. As our camp had progressed up the mountain, we'd been followed by flocks of Himalayan chough: jet-black crows that bank and weave about the food tent – the prettiest rats on the planet. They'd take the chapattis right out of your mess tin (which wasn't such a bad thing). Even they didn't care for the dhal, though. Prints of snow fox and hare were everywhere and at one point we saw an Asiatic black bear at a distance. He was dark in colour apart from a white crescent on his chest. He lifted his nose and sniffed us on the meagre breeze, then turned tail and shambled off over a ridgeline. He remains the only bear I've seen in the Himalayas. The primary threat to them is the utterly barbaric process of collecting them so they can be kept in tiny metal cages with catheters into their gall bladders, draining the fluids for Chinese traditional medicines. Anyone who wants evidence of quite how low we humans can stoop in our treatment of fellow mammals need look no further.

One of the benefits of the course was the bonds formed with teammates. My rope-fellows were the most modest, generous, caring group of people I've ever met, and the easiest people in the world to be stranded in a tent with. Which was as well, as we had zero time to ourselves, let alone privacy. Sleeping was cosy, to say the least. Believe me, you'd take body warmth from anyone up

Above left Climbing inside a moulin, the whirlpool that drains an Alaskan glacier

Above right In front of Shivling while with the Nehru Institute of Mountaineering

Vertical ice climbing, Toubkal, Morocco

Above Sunrise up high over
the Matterhorn in the Alps

Left On the Dent du Géant
in the Mont Blanc massif

Top right The ridgeline of
L'Evêque in the Swiss Alps

Right Classic exposed ridge
climbing on Mont Blanc de
Cheilon in the Pennine Alps

Advanced base camp with the Nehru Institute of Mountaineering; Kedar Nath behind

With Stuart on the Marathon Des Sables

Top Cholatse seen from base camp

Above Me, Ro, Dave and Tarx at base camp

Left The snowy ridgeline leading towards Cholatse summit

Top Tarx struggling on the headwall of horror

Right Dave and Ro battling an icy rib towards the snow col

Above With Tarx at Cholatse base camp

Above Ro leads on hard roc[k]
above the snow headwall

Left Heading up through
the icefall

there. Whereas for the first few days we'd all selected spots away from the centre of the tent so that it at least felt as if you had your own private bed, as we got higher everyone moved away from the draughty corners, and ended up clustered closer and closer together, until we were all rolled together in one big sleeping bag slug-fest. The morning 'number two area' was like a local café. First thing after our fried egg brekkie we would dig a narrow trench a suitable distance from camp, then the boys lined up shoulder to shoulder with their bums in the wind, chatting about the night's sleep whilst enjoying a poo with a view. The toilet roll was passed up and down the line, and we'd discuss the quality of our bowel movements, and laugh uproariously at the loudest farty sounds, while staring up at Kedar Nath Dome. It was unimaginably huge. There were two gargantuan smooth slabs of rock where hanging glaciers had calved off, taking everything with them, and several technical rock ridges, but otherwise it was a vast bald head of glinting ice. The snow had kept on falling, especially at night, and avalanches were constantly roaring down nearby slopes.

The birdlife was stunning, with vultures and golden eagles seeking thermals way above us around the clifftops, noisy chough and ravens cawing and diving around our ears. We also came across groups of noisy partridge called snowcock, their silvery flanks streaked with chestnut and black barcodes so that it looked as if you could pick the dumpy little birds up and scan them through the self-service checkout. Not that you'd ever catch them; if anyone so much as wandered by they would scarper for the bushes with a panicked upright gait. Closely related, but much more dramatic, were the Satyr Tragopan, lurid crimson pheasants with white dappling, like the reflections of light bouncing off rippling water. In stark contrast, their faces were cobalt-blue, lending glorious focus to their beady black eyes. Their 'gwaah gwaah gwaah' call would rise in volume until it became incessant, sounding like a human baby swiftly going from 'D'you know what, I'm a bit peckish', to 'I'm about to die of hunger'. The prize of the birds to be found on the ground, though, was the Himalayan Monal. The males of the species are ornate in the extreme, scampering through rhododendron forests like oversized Fabergé brooches. Their call is the piercing whistle of the shepherd ordering his dog to 'come by'. It's almost pointless trying to describe their colouration, as every sheen and shade is represented on their dazzling plumage. The quills above the male's crown appear as a crest of laurels, giving them the air of an ancient Olympian. In the late afternoons we saw herds of Himalayan blue sheep, a kind of mountain goat that wanders lazily over the slopes munching grasses. Clearly the naturalist that named them was not having a creative day; blue sheep is a plain and functional moniker that does no justice to the spectacle of these mountain goats. The males are bedecked with dramatic curved horns, huge dark bananas protruding from their rock-solid craniums. During the rut, they crash headlong into other male challengers with an earth-shuddering clatter that gives you whiplash even looking at it.

Two days before summit day the blue sky gave way to very high cirrus clouds, those wisps of ice on the edge of the troposphere that usually herald a change in weather. We made a stunning camp on an upturned wok of snow, and spent two hours stamping the snow as flat as possible to make a passable floor for our tents. It was tough work at this altitude, but utterly vital. As your body heat warms the snow, it melts then turns to ice, setting hard as stone. Any laziness in your floor flattening will be felt a thousand-fold on a freezing sleepless night two days later.

Three in the afternoon of the day we were due to climb, it started to snow hard. Snow which quickly transformed into the mama of all blizzards. If this had been a normal mountaineering expedition, we would have bedded down in our tents, busying ourselves to keep them from being buried under the deluge. No way would we have considered a push for the top. But we were in the army now. Instead the senior instructor sat us down in the main tent and told us that we were going to make for the summit regardless. His justification was that the strictures of the course involved not summiting but gaining height. After all, we were training for situations where we might get caught out by a swift change in weather. You could tell from the faces of many of my colleagues that they didn't share his enthusiasm. Everything was against us. Our camp was at an altitude of 5,300 metres, which would mean a vertical mile's push in foul conditions, zero visibility and thick snow. I don't think they were scared though, it was more that this plan would condemn our long lusted-for summit. Even the most superhuman wouldn't stand a chance against those odds. Nevertheless, we all spent the remainder of the afternoon faffing with our kit, streamlining every single gram so that we would be carrying no excess, trying out every combination of our layers and watching over everyone else's shoulders to see how they were doing it. Even I managed to cram down mouthfuls of dhal, trying to fill up my tank before the big push. The one huge plus point for me was that the fifteen-strong team was split into two summit parties, and I was given lead of the advance party. The senior instructor singled me out as the strongest and fittest of the team, and gave me control of route-finding and breaking trail. I nodded calmly, but couldn't make eye contact with my pals for fear they would see the pride bursting from me. My ice-climbing nightmare was behind me: I had proved myself!

We went to bed early, huddled close to each other and as wide awake as it is possible to be. For the first time, there was no snoring or sputtering. Nobody could sleep for excitement and fear. After a few hours lying in the dark, wearing our boots in the sleeping bag so they wouldn't freeze solid, we roused ourselves at midnight and set off. It instantly became clear why I had been given the honour of trail-breaking. It had nothing to do with prowess and everything to do with the fact I was by far the biggest and heaviest person on the team, and compacted the trail more than anyone else. I sank desperately into the fresh snow, chest deep at times, and fought to make progress, gasping and coughing, but refusing to give up my place at the front. Even working this hard in a down jacket and three pairs of gloves, it was fiercely cold. The going was so slow that the chill spread through us like the Ready Brek boy in reverse. Eventually I simply couldn't lead any more, and with my spirit crushed I dropped to the back of the peleton, suddenly desperately tired. Every footfall was a struggle. My waterbottle was frozen solid, and the chocolate was a distant memory.

After hours of trudging in the dark, the sun finally began to rise, chasing away the blizzards and painting the peaks, all the jewels of the Himalaya laid beneath us in diamond-dust flurries of glinting wind-torn snow. Soon the climbing started to steepen, crevasses and holes dropping under our feet. We set to fixing ropes for our colleagues to follow, which took even longer. By this time there was no response from my feet when I tried to clench my toes.

Mid morning, the sun was beating down on the snow-sodden slopes, generating an high avalanche risk. I couldn't resist taking off my glove to get a look at my altimeter: ten hours' slog and we'd reached 6,600 metres, with a vertical 300 metres remaining. Most of the boys were keen to keep going, but it was no longer our call to make; the instructor stepped in and ordered us to turn around. It was simultaneously a huge relief and a terrible blow, but worse was to come. As soon as we started down, I was hit by a fatigue so potent that it seized my entire body. Robert Service once said, 'Be master of your petty annoyances and conserve your energies for the big, worthwhile things. It isn't the mountain ahead that wears you out — it's the grain of sand in your shoe.' For me those grains of sand were weeks of insufficient calories, muscles starved of glycogen, lack of sleep and general decline. This resulted in a deep, deep tired-ness; it felt as if every muscle had simply turned to blancmange. I'd lost a lot of weight, and exhausted my reserves; I simply didn't have anything left to call on. The trail-breaking had affected me worse than I had realised. As the clock ticked past noon, I could only stagger a few feet then collapse daftly on my backside. Thankfully by then we were off the steep ground, or the outcome could have been disastrous.

Endurance athletes talk about 'hitting the wall'. Classically, it's something that marathon runners experience at mile 20. It's where the muscles cells have used up their supply of available fuel, and turn instead to burning sources like fat and muscle. The term is much overused; if you can take a little break and then carry on running, then you haven't actually hit the wall, you've merely hit a low patch. At this point, though, I was done; left to my own devices I would have had to slide and crawl back to camp. To my humili-ation, one of the instructors took my backpack, and recruits took it in turn to mother me back into camp. On arrival, I collapsed in front of the tents, too exhausted even to make it to my sleeping bag. The boys brought me tea and rice until I could muster the will to at least get inside and sleep.

This long day up high and exposed to the wind was also my first experience of hypothermia. Classified as when your core temper-ature drops below 35°C, the first symptoms are the reduction of motor functions, clumsiness, and shivering so intense that it hurts. The opposite is hyperthermia, where your core temperature goes too high. I've only had this once, and it is far more intense and frightening. It was on the double marathon day of my endurance race in the Sahara; I had been trotting over sand dunes in 50 de-grees temperature all day long, without being in the shade at all. The race continued as the sun set, and on into the night. Gradually I realised that although the night had got seriously chilly, I was not cooling down; in fact I was getting hotter, seemingly heated by a furnace from within. I was pouring sweat, vomiting, hallucinating, feeling like I had the world's worst fever. I collapsed on a rock, and waited for death to take me. Turns out, it was incredibly lucky that my hyperthermia didn't kick in until so late in the day. If it had come on during the midday scorch, there would have been precious little they could do. Out there in the middle of the Sahara, chances were the results would have been very serious indeed.

Hypothermia is nothing like as scary or intense as hyper. It is, though, every bit as insidious, and dangerous. In later years, I was to make a programme on extreme environments with the help of Portsmouth University's sport science lab. To deliberately make me hypothermic, they lowered me into a bath filled with water chilled to 10°C, with an internal rectal thermometer and a range of high-tech gadgets to measure my body changes. The triumph of the mammalian machine is its ability to regulate temperature, to be warm-blooded regardless of the external environment. But your core temperature has only to change two degrees either way in order for the body to spiral rapidly and scarily out of control as it battles to constrict the blood vessels that run close to the skin and carry the warming blood to your core. The thermal-imaging camera showed how in no time at all my skin was the same temperature as the water. Without warming blood, my extremities started to shut down, leaving me totally incapable of performing the simplest of tasks. Within minutes I'd started to shiver. Within half an hour, the shivering was so intense that my entire body was convulsed, burning off huge amounts of calories to power the shakes. The next day, all my muscles ached from the effort.

They took me out of the cold water after forty-five minutes, when my core temperature had dropped a mere two degrees. This was when the really interesting stuff began. Human organ and brain functions have evolved over millions of years to function in that spectrum of a couple of degrees of core temperature. Once your equilibrium has been thrown, your systems go haywire, and it is almost impossible to recover. I was in laboratory conditions, and was put into a warm bath, which they gradually started to make hotter. After a bit, I was feeling pretty good and tried to get out and carry on filming. I was pushed firmly back into the hot water. The rectal thermometer showed that my core temperature had dropped another degree and a half! All that warming blood that had retreated to protect my core had now flooded back out to my peripheries. I was dangerously hypothermic, but totally unaware of it. According to the scientist who was observing me, if I'd got out of the bath, I would probably have fallen unconscious. It was at least another half an hour, in a hot bath, in a lab with a team of people looking after me before I recovered.

This is why hypothermia is so scary. Hyper is obvious, you know instantly you've got it and can at least do something about it – even if that amounts to nothing more than panic. But hypo is impossible to differentiate from having the shivers when you've been cold. I would say I've been badly hypo three times, and each time I've only realised afterwards when I've tried to warm myself up and can't. This was exactly how I felt on Kedar Dome. I fumbled my way into my minus-thirty-rated sleeping bag, fully clothed, in the middle of the day when the sun was up and temperature nice and warm. And yet I was still shivering uncontrollably for at least five hours. The boys brought me hot drinks, but I mostly just shook them all over myself. I always fantasise about what a total hero I would be if I was trapped in a high-altitude storm, carrying my colleagues out over my shoulder like sacks of potatoes. Utter nonsense. Had I still been out in the cold after this drop in body temperature, I would have simply curled up out of the wind and waited for death to take me.

The following morning it also became clear that I'd got my first case of frostnip. Frostnip is the very early stages of frostbite, sometimes classified as first-degree frostbite, and is a superficial freezing of the skin. Both little toes and my little finger on my right hand were purple, and totally without feeling. I lost the two toe-nails, which makes me think it was probably due to my boots being a bit too tight there, further restricting the circulation to these, my most extreme of extremities. One toe and the finger recovered in about three months, but the other little toe was still without feeling a year and a half later.

I got lucky. When I did my first 8,000-metre mountain, I borrowed my down suit from Tom Clowes, who with his brother Ben had recently returned from summiting Everest. They're delightful boys, with boundless enthusiasm, but when I went to collect the suit, Ben was in very low spirits. He'd suffered a nasty case of frost-bite to fingers and toes, and was facing many months off work. The affected fingers and toes looked like the black shrivelled extremities of the ancient mummified corpses I've seen in tribal villages in Papua New Guinea.

As strength started to return, so the deep sense of accomplish-ment and wellbeing started to swell inside of us. There is no doubt that it is good for the soul to suffer every now and again. Perhaps that's one of the reasons people choose to row across the Pacific, swim great distances, or walk the entire length of the Amazon. Suf-fering is seen as a badge of honour, and by choosing to endure the agonies one can prove oneself, perhaps even make history, though it's a field where the bar is continually being set higher and higher. For many, however, these feats of ultra-endurance serve much the same purpose as the pilgrimages, fasts and extravagant physical ex-ploits of the ascetic. Pushing your body to the limit can bring very intense physical and psychological rewards, even if you don't share the ascetics' belief that it will get you closer to nirvana or whichever deity you worship.

Not that I haven't ventured down the ascetic path myself. As an eighteen-year-old, I spent a week in a Buddhist retreat in Southern Thailand. We were forbidden from reading, writing, speaking, from making eye contact with the other initiates. All we did all day long was meditate, in the hope that we would find our way to enlightenment. The meditating itself was called Vipasana – 'mindfulness with breathing' – and the technique was so simple it was taught to us in half an hour. You had to concentrate on breathing in and out, and any time a thought or image came into your mind, you would drive it away and try to return to a state of empty mindedness. That's it. Chanting mantras and various physical positions are alternative means to attain the same goal. It turned out to be the most frustrating and difficult thing I'd ever done. The first couple of days my mind screamed out for input. I was replaying entire movies in my brain, doing anything to keep my frantic consciousness entertained. By the end of the week, I could sustain an empty mind for longer and longer periods until I was getting close to an entire minute without thoughts. Then one night as I was sitting by candlelight, meditating, I managed to drive away all thoughts for a minute or so and was suddenly flooded with a warm calm feeling like a golden light that overwhelmed my mind and suffused every fibre of my body with total ecstasy. This was it! This was the sensation they'd been talking about! In my impatience, I grabbed out for the enlightenment and it shrank away from me, darkness flooding the light, which disappeared, leaving me shaking as I sat in front of my candle. I have never experienced that enlightenment since.

The closest I've ever come to it has been through exercise. When I'm out on my bike or running, there's a precise level of training where I'm comfortable yet stretched enough that all I can concentrate on is my breathing. There is nothing in my brain; nothing at all. I am experiencing mindfulness through breathing! These periods of solitude and thoughtlessness have become vital to my wellbeing. If I go without them for a few days I become irritable, claustrophobic. And though I have never experienced that sense of nirvana again, many marathon runners describe 'runner's high': a sudden euphoric burst of energy and intense feeling of wellbeing. Chemists have shown that this is due to the presence of endorphins such as endo-cannabanoids (exactly what they sound like: cannabis-like chemicals that originate in the body's hormone secretion system). It's been suggested that this response evolved in the days humans practised persistence hunting, singling out a weak animal and running it down over many hours, keeping it on the move until it collapsed with exhaustion.

Cheated of our treasured goal, the team couldn't wait to pack up our skeleton camp and descend to the bigger, better-stocked camps lower down the valley. We completed our qualifications with an orienteering challenge below the glacier at Gamukh. Our blood was so saturated with oxygen that we sprinted around like mountain goats. The much-feared written paper was this time an absolute doddle, allowing me to gain the grades I needed to repay Major Rana's faith in me. Having achieved the highest grade pass, I was now qualified to lead expeditions into the high Himalaya. When I finally returned to civilisation, I didn't recognise the ginger-bearded skinny freak in the mirror. I had lost two and a half stone (over 11 kilos). This may sound like a dream to some, but my body fat percentage was actually higher than before I left, as my system had gone into starvation mode and protected its valuable emergency fat stores. It was muscle that had wasted away, and I was so weak I couldn't do a single chin-up.

Before we slogged down the valley, we were given the privilege of raiding the supplies to cook our own dinner. The boys turned out to be remarkable chefs and very particular about their cooking, and as they came from all over the subcontinent we feasted on West Bengalese aubergines, Rajesthani dhal, a Goan fire curry . . . it was like a high-altitude version of *MasterChef*. As they squabbled over the salt, we used our mess tins and cooking pots as percussion instruments, singing Hindi folk songs to the accompaniment of hissing pressure cookers. Behind us the jagged summits of Mount Meru seemed to be blossoming red clouds as the sun began to set. It looked as if the mountain was on fire.

CHOLATSE

'There have been joys too great to be described in words, and there have been griefs upon which I have not dared to dwell, and with these in mind I say, climb if you will, but remember that courage and strength are naught without prudence, and that a momentary negligence may destroy the happiness of a lifetime. Do nothing in haste, look well to each step, and from the beginning think what may be the end.'

Edward Whymper

As we descend through the icefall, rapier sunrays pierce the twisted cold sculptures, glinting crystalline faces, old ice the shade of azure Mediterranean seas, towering white trolls lumbering over us with their chilly paws poised to snatch us up. Far behind us, the imposing vertical headwall sneers at our retreat, the summit far beyond it clear of clouds and so close you could reach out and stroke its snowy cap. The icefall on Cholatse has been compared to the Khumbu icefall on Everest. Vast blocks of ice hang like upturned skyscrapers over chasms that drop into sickening darkness. The ice creaks and cracks as it slowly moves, and there is the constant sound

*both near and far of tumbling slush, rolling rocks and collapsing ice
blocks.*

*Knowing that this is the most dangerous part of any glacier, Tarx
and I are short-roped together, trying to cover the lethal ground as fast
as we possibly can. I am in the lead, picking a path across the snow
bridges, crampons skittering over the hard surface. Two loose loops of
rope hang from my right hand; I'm keeping the tether between us tight
because the last thing Tarx needs is loose rope trailing in the snow in
front of him, snagging in his crampon front points.*

*Suddenly the toe of ice I've been following disappears and I'm facing
a neat crevasse, perhaps a metre and a half across, directly across my
path. I don't even break stride; dropping the two coils in my hand in
order not to pull Tarx off his feet, I leap across, landing on one foot
on the other side. Then I walk on with caution, not wanting to tug
my ropemate along. But then I hear a cry of fear, and a moment later
I'm ripped off my feet and land flat on my backpack. I can feel myself
sliding backwards towards the crevasse. Tarx has fallen into darkness,
and his weight on the rope is dragging me into the abyss . . .*

When I am in the mountains I am a different person, content, with
my senses heightened, permanently zinging with a kind of zeal it's
hard to express in words. As I look around me, I'm mentally picking
a route up every peak, wishing I could summit them all. If I have
to go a few months without a trip to the mountains, I start to feel
homesick, nagged by a constant sense that I'm not where I'm supposed to be.

Three years into my stint on the *Really Wild Show* I was still
something of a nomad, sleeping on people's floors, not ready to
set down roots. Moreover there were big chunks of my year that
weren't taken up with filming, which left me with a tremendous
opportunity for adventure. Sensing that my brain needed challenge and my body needed punishment, I knew I had to set myself

some big goals that would get me out of my rut and back into the hills.

The first goal was to run the Marathon Des Sables in the spring of 2005. Known as the 'Toughest Race on Earth', it entailed 160 miles of running across the Sahara desert and mountains of Morocco, carrying everything you needed on your own back.

My preparations began with my housemate Nick jumping on my bed at 7 a.m. on a Sunday morning and dragging me out to run my local half-marathon. In a hailstorm. I was overtaken by a woman in her seventies as I walked up the steepest hill, had a group of schoolkids trot past me chatting easily, had to stop halfway to vomit noisily in a bush and finished, humbled and horrified, in an hour and fifty-four minutes. I was so exhausted it was all I could do to walk back to the car. I knew then I had a lot of work ahead of me.

Again it was the mountains that came to my aid. On Friday evenings after work I'd drive from Bristol to the Brecon Beacons in the little black mini Metro I'd bought off my mum for £200, and pitch up at a pub on the outskirts of Brecon town. I'd avidly read Andy McNab's books about going through SAS selection, where he described how, the night before each big yomp, he'd stock up with a bag of chips and two pints of Guinness. If it was good enough for him, I figured, it should be good enough for me. I'd sit on my own in a lounge bar that hadn't been decorated since the 1970s, nursing my Guinness and a huge portion of pie and chips. No one would talk to me: they could tell I was English (I have, without a word of exaggeration, walked into pubs in this part of Wales and had everyone turn round to look, then switch from speaking English to speaking Welsh). I wasn't too fussed, because I didn't want any probing questions into where I would be sleeping that night. At closing time I'd go out to the car park and drop the back seats on the Metro, which left a surprisingly large flat section where I could roll out a mattress. If I lay diagonally in my sleeping bag, and slept on my side, I could just about squeeze in with the boot closed. I'd take care to be up and running not long after dawn, so I didn't get in trouble for vagrancy. My day's run would take me over all the mountains in the Brecon Beacons, and bring me back to the Metro around nightfall. I'd change out of my soaking clothes behind the open car door and get straight on the road, only stopping off at a chippy on the way home to get yet more chips. A few hours later, I'd be at the pub in my local Home Counties town, drinking with my oblivious pals, most of whom had spent the day playing rugby.

One of the benefits of putting yourself into a race that scares you, and even more one that you are using as a fundraiser, is that fear and guilt are the best motivators. Even now when someone asks me for tips on getting fit or losing weight, my advice is to sign up for a race you're not capable of doing, and get loads of friends to sponsor you for it. On winter weekends when you're not feeling up for it, or when the weather reports look grim, you somehow find the impetus, because of all the people you'll be letting down, and because of the fear of how badly and publicly you'll fail if you don't train. And it works. On winter days with howling rain and pizzling dreek, I'd still drag myself out to the mountains for a thirty-mile run. And once I was out there, the Welsh hills would always pay back my allegiance. On every one of those runs, the sky would clear for at least a few hours and I'd be rewarded with views of the snow-capped Beacons, sometimes even blue skies and sunshine. Often I'd have the place entirely to myself. Sometimes there'd be a solitary dog-walker or hardy seventy-year-old rambler high up on Pen Y Fan, and we'd exchange a knowing nod but keep moving, fellow members of an elite club of hardy hill-freaks. There was no need to stop to chat. No one who yomps this ridgeline alone on a sodden February day is doing it in search of companionship.

The miles, though, were starting to have their effect on me. As the winter dwindled away to spring, I'd be doing those thirty milers without stopping, and almost every weekend the times would get five or ten minutes quicker. I was ready.

The Marathon Des Sables probably sounds like the worst kind of sado-masochism to the uninitiated, and I can understand why. There are endless horror stories from the race, and I've witnessed a few first-hand. On day one, my running partner Stuart and I were overtaken by a sturdy blonde nineteen-year-old called Amy, running in tiny white hotpants and with a large cuddly teddy bear sticking out of her rucksack. She beat us both again on day two. And then the soles of her feet fell off. In their entirety. 'Amy Feet', as she was thereafter known, lost every inch of skin from the underside of her feet, not just once, but several times. She was being pumped full of morphine, bandaged up so she was pretty much running on bleeding raw stumps . . . yet she carried on going. And she ran an extra five marathons, crying and shuffling along like an old woman, through temperatures that exceeded 50 degrees, over sand dunes, rocky mountainsides, and carrying everything she needed on her back.

My own experience of the MDS was very different. It wasn't life-changing because of the level of agony I went through, but because it was the most uplifting and joyous event of that period of my life. We raced over treacherous mountain climbs, through timeless scenery of rusty red and charred black rocky peaks, almost Martian in its colourful barren bleakness. Camp was an other-worldly blend of heaven and hell. The military types I met there said it was very much like being at war; people might be afraid and hurting, but they displayed extraordinary selflessness and humbling courage. The friendships forged in those conditions very quickly felt like family ties. To begin with, everyone was a little sheepish about the lack of privacy inherent in 777 people living under crude tents on open desert, and would wander miles off into the distance to find a tiny bush to squat behind when they needed to make their ablutions. After the second day that went out the window; no one was going to walk even one step further than they had to. After the Berbers had taken our tents off our heads and left us shivering in the open, people would wander a couple of metres from their beds and drop their lycra. Some took to shouting advice to their running mates, even counting the results out loud as they plopped on to the sand. Everyone was farting, belching and liberally and publicly lubing up their bits to prevent chafing – often all at once in mid-conversation. It was not a place for the sensitive.

The field was a pick-and-mix of the superhuman and the eccentric. The European and North American contingent were mostly skinny ultra-runners with physiques like pubescent boys and school-lunchbox-sized rucksacks to match. The fastest were two farmers from Morocco: the Ahansal brothers. They ate handfuls of dry rice every night, allowing it to swell inside their stomachs, and when they ran past me were going at a steady pace I could have kept up for a mile tops. Then there were the Brits; a mix of military, trust-fund types, sturdy girls who looked as if they could eat the elite runners whole, fell-running tough nuts, barrow boys and a trio of hairdressers from Cardiff. If you came across an unprepared, slightly distracted, possibly tubby-looking person who clearly shouldn't have been there, chances were they'd be British.

Some of the tents were deadly dull places to be, with their inhabitants talking solely about troop movements in the various military campaigns of the late 1990s. Others were deadly because one of their number had been forced to withdraw but had to remain with the race until its conclusion, being dragged along in the tent trucks. That tended to put a bit of a dampener on things. Others were sparkling chuckle-fests, and my favourite times of the day were tramping round to the tents of running pals to find out how everyone was doing; we'd compare foot barbarism, who'd had the most vivid hallucinations, and see if anyone had spare food or drugs on them. There was a thriving black market in painkillers, sleeping tablets and anti-inflammatories, and you could buy pretty much any prescription drug for a couple of wet wipes and a bag of wine gums.

The whole process did seem a bit bizarre to me; charging through some of the most startlingly beautiful mountains and desert I've ever seen, ignoring the scuttling lizards and endless marine fossils because your eyes were fixed on the square-metre of sand in front of you. Rather than gazing in wonder at the mountains around you, the focus was on your breathing, fluid and calorie consumption, and the endless battle to get some aggravating tune out of your head. For all that, it was a dazzling yomp through one of the most beautiful deserts on Earth. Every evening, as the sun started to set, it would stain the world with the most ludicrous colours, the worst of the heat would melt away, and it would feel like an insane paradise. Then night would fall. Nothing can compare with the desert by night. You are so far away from the rest of the planet. The sky is free of light pollution and it seems you could reach up and buff the stars.

That race gave me some of the most uplifting moments of my life. I forged friendships that will endure to my dying day. With Kes, the gentle giant who stopped in the middle of running a double marathon to help local villagers clear boulders off a patch of sand they wanted to turn into a football field. And Rob, who ran with me for long hours, chatting about any old nonsense to take our minds off how far we had left to run. But most of all with Stuart, who I ran over a hundred miles with. On the double marathon day I staggered in long after dark, suffering from heat exhaustion having been vomiting and hallucinating, to find him at the finish line waiting out to clap me in. He took my pack, cooked my dinner, dressed my feet for me – and all after having run 54 miles himself. He's been my best friend ever since. I was best man at his wedding, and hope he will one day return the favour.

Despite the ridiculousness of stampeding across the desert with 800 other crazy fools, the MDS was an experience that deeply affected everyone who took part. It was a baptism of pain in the wilderness. Everyone bonded in a way I've never seen before or since. I guess it's mostly because, aside from the ten or so ludicrous ultra runners who are competing to win, everyone else is there to finish. You know what your fellow runners are going through, and would give anything to drag them over the finish line. Stuart and I ran the half-marathon on the last day faster than I'd done my local half the year before, crossing the finish line hand in hand like conquering athletes. Despite the fact that overall I had come 228th, and taken nearly forty hours to finish. The next few hours were spent watching people crossing the line. I have never cried so much in my entire life. Seeing people accomplish their dreams, having dragged themselves through places too dark for me to even contemplate . . . it was quite something. Amy Feet got a particularly big cheer, although I don't think she was too aware of where she was or what was happening. And she was only one of hundreds – it was so humbling.

There were moments when the level of suffering had you wondering if it was all worth it. At the airport afterwards, banks of wheelchairs had to be provided, and a hush fell over the crowds of cheering loved ones as the stumbling zombies lurched out, shoeless and displaying their mangled feet. Watching the customs officers look travellers up and down, and then stay looking down, staring gobsmacked at the feet was a Pythonesque comedy moment.

The MDS had a big effect on me, but somehow I got through it without losing any of my muscle bulk and was thus no closer to my ambition of improving my technical climbing skills. I still looked nothing like a climber, and still huffed and puffed my way up vertical routes that a twelve-year-old would sneer at.

So my next expedition wasn't going to be a vertiginous technical climb. Instead I decided on an ultra-endurance run in the mountains. This was something I could do solo, it wouldn't require much in the way of organisation or expense, but it would sate my desire for challenge, adventure and exploration. Plus it had a purity about it that appealed to me. But when I sat down with maps and tried to decide which mountain range to run across, it was as if the stars suddenly aligned to guide me. Ever since returning from India the previous spring, I had been desperate to return to the Himalayas. David Tuck, too, had developed a thirst for the mountains that needed to be slaked, and the two of us kept in constant communication, emailing grand plans – many of them preposterous – to each other from opposite sides of the globe. Finally Dave and his climbing partner Rowan, plus me and Tarx (my journalist climbing partner), all found ourselves free in the same six-week period in October 2005. The four of us had a hankering for Nepal, but wanted to take on something unusual and technically challenging. We plundered the libraries of the Alpine Club, contacted mountaineers who knew the area well, and finally settled on a peak called Cholatse in the Khumbu region of Nepal. The peak had been first climbed in the 1980s, but there had been very few repeats.

Legendary American mountaineer Conrad Anker, who had led an assault on Cholatse the previous year, kindly gave us guidance and advice on how to approach and attack the mountain. When we applied to the Nepalese Mountaineering Foundation for a permit, we learned that ours would be the only attempt that year, so we would have the peak entirely to ourselves. It was exactly the adventure we had been praying for.

On the flight in from Kathmandu airport I read Joe Simpson's latest book, in which he details climbing a nearby peak, and mentions our mountain in passing: 'I looked across at Cholatse, a frightening mountain draped in flutings, wild mushroom cornices and chaotic ridge lines – a route just as serious as we had climbed in Peru ... just as dangerous as Siula Grande.' Siula Grande was the Andean peak that Simpson attempted with Simon Yates, as recorded in his book *Touching the Void*. It's probably the best-known mountain book of our times, detailing the horror that ensued when he tumbled off the peak. Yates was forced to cut the rope that held the two of them together, and Joe fell, smashing his leg, but still managed to drag himself to safety over several tortuous days. In this new book, Simpson decided Cholatse was too challenging for him, and instead took on another nearby peak ... and fell 1,000 feet, smashing up his other leg and nearly dying ... again. The thought occurred to me that Joe Simpson should probably take up a new hobby. Also that anyone thinking of getting into the mountains, but nervous at the prospect, should steer clear of Joe's (excellent) books!

Tarx and I had travelled in together from the UK. Our flight's course took us along mountain valleys towards the iconic Lukla, one of the most spectacular landing strips on Earth. As you come in towards the runway, the valley floor still a mile below you, it feels as if the wings are going to graze the mountainsides. The runway is on the short shoulder of a big peak and seems painfully short, with a vertical drop-off at one end, and a vertical cliff at the other.

My two Antipodean climbing buddies (both full-time climbing bums) had spent a month up high, topping several summits for acclimatisation, and Tarx and I were to meet them there at Cholatse base camp. Though we had left ourselves plenty of time to make the trek up, we were eager to begin. So we hired a young porter at the airport and started walking. We had food for five weeks, climbing and mountaineering gear, tents, sleeping bags, etc, so even with a porter in tow we were laden, but the path was well worn, and there were tea shops serving pizzas and banana pancakes every half mile. We were in Namche bazaar in two easy days. Namche is predominantly a trekking centre from which people prepare for Everest base camp and Gokyo Ri hikes. It would have been a delightful place to spend a few days, lounging and wandering, but Tarx and I had the bit between our teeth and were keen to get ahead of the game.

I first met Tarx when interviewing him for an adventure series I'd been doing for National Geographic five years previously. He's the same age as me, and crucially very similar in abilities and ambition. We instantly got on like a house on fire. Apparently his father had given him his impossibly posh name 'Tarquin' as a means of toughening him against the bullies. His sister was probably tougher. Her name is Alice. Their surname is Cooper. Tarx is a journalist by profession, but mostly writes about the outdoors. He's terrific value on any climbing trip, because he is the world's most spectacular adventure nerd. He can relate any story from the annals of mountaineering history, and he does it with such enthusiasm and vigour you'd think he was there to witness it first-hand. He also has opinions on everyone in the adventure world, and the dark secrets of every drama, cheat and scandal. It's like having the adventure world's version of *Heat* magazine in your tent. And if that weren't enough he's a geek who knows every new bit of kit and technique before the guides do.

The base camp at Cholatse was a dream: acres of flat meadow, with rivulets of fresh water running through the flower-rich grasses. The peak and our route lumbered directly above it, so you could sit and stare at the mountain, dream and plot. We arrived there to see a red tent already erected, but no one around. It was evening when our climbing partners finally returned from their day's exploits. Tarx and I were expecting two altitude-hardened mountain men with walnut skin and steely eyes. We were in for a nasty surprise. Dave and Rowan were so skinny they could have had rickets. Both wore immense beards, their skin was chafed raw, and their hacking coughs echoed round the valley. They resembled two tuberculosis sufferers who'd been deep-fried in batter and pocket fluff. Nevertheless, their morale soared upon seeing us. Especially when they went through our massive food bag and found fresh cheese, chocolate, and the huge lump of chorizo that I'd brought all the way from home. Ro declared that it looked like donkey penis, and thus it was christened. For the remainder of the trip, every dish was enlivened with 'donk'. Eventually we got so sick of it that it was three years before I could eat chorizo.

Dave was every bit as delightful as when I last saw him, on that magical mission to the Indian Himalaya. Rowan was like a ginger version of Dave, boundlessly positive and enthusiastic, but much more dry and droll, and so laid back you could fall asleep during a single sentence. He was by far our most competent climber: genuinely talented, experienced, and instantly the unspoken team leader. On some expeditions you can do nothing but struggle to escape the awful people you've been saddled with. The four of us could have been locked in a Portaloo, and we'd still have had laughed ourselves to death.

Cholatse is a very special mountain indeed. It's very pointy, looks like it's leaning over to one side, and every potential route to the summit offers considerable challenges and lashings of danger. The route Conrad Anker had told us about was impassable due to huge overhanging seracs or ice cliffs looming over the pitches he'd described to us. We would therefore need to find our own route up the 6,440-metre mountain. My one triumphant addition to the team kit was my fancy bird-watching binoculars, and we sat for hours in base camp, studying the ridges and faces above us, and talking through what we thought the attack route should be.

As the only group at base camp, we attracted a lot of attention from the local wildlife. We had to shoo off a big brown yak who stuck his nose into our food sack and threatened to stomp all over our tents with his clumsy hooves. Hooded crows, ravens and chough pecked at our rubbish, and were a constant screaming presence wherever we went. Anything that appeared even vaguely edible would be thoroughly investigated by these inquisitive crows. Their keen intelligence was initially fascinating, until they started to get a wee bit too bold. After a while, any bag that was left in the open would be ransacked and torn to shreds by busy beaks. One week in we acquired a mascot in the form of a hungry little pika who scampered in and out of the rocks of my camp kitchen. We christened him Boris. Pikas or mouse hares are related to rabbits, but look more like little guinea pigs. They're super inquisitive, and are well known for gathering hay piles which they dry out and then store in their burrows for the winter. Boris was a cheerful visitor, and totally unafraid of us. He'd sit chomping a single oat, looking at us as if he was listening to our conversations. When his cheeks were moving, Ro would give him a voice, high-pitched in tone, stupid in character. We'd scold Boris for talking with his mouth full, and laugh at his stupidity, and pretty soon he became a treasured member of the team. If we surprised him with too sudden movements and sent him scampering for safety, we'd apologise profusely to him, and then sit motionless until he returned. Then one morning as I headed to the kitchen to make our morning cuppas, I stopped dead. The lithe serpentine shape of a weasel was practically flowing in and out of the stone walls like a russet slinky. In all my years as a naturalist in the British countryside, every sighting of a stoat or weasel has been fleeting, a flash of red-brown to be ever-treasured. My longest sighting was one swimming across a canal in front of my kayak before bounding off across the bank like a nuclear-powered red knee sock. I'd never had the privilege of sitting mere metres away as a weasel scampered around like this. It never stopped moving for a second; a hyperactive, hyper-stimulated, stretched piece of reddy-brown wonder, that lives in a non-stop world of action we cannot even contemplate. Weasels are smaller than their stoat cousins, but can take prey that's far bigger than they are. The males have even been known to take rabbits, which blows my mind. They don't hibernate during the coldest months, are active by day and night, and feed almost constantly to appease their voracious appetite. When I quietly retreated to get my camera, he disappeared, and we didn't see him again. Unfortunately, his appearance also coincided with the last sighting of Boris. We watched every morning with growing anxiety, but it soon became clear that he had met a horrible end, at the pointy teeth of one of the most ruthless predators known in these lands.

Despite their physical condition, Dave and Ro were well acclimatised to the altitude. Tarx and I, on the other hand, still needed to build up our levels of red blood cells. Over the course of several days we load-carried food, tents and climbing equipment up to an advanced base camp at the base of the Cholatse icefall. Each time the climb would become a little easier, and we'd feel a bit stronger. Our carotid bodies were sensing the lack of oxygen, and that was prompting an increase in our breathing rate. Our hearts were beating faster, and non-essential body functions were suppressed. This reduction of digestive function is a real struggle on high-altitude expeditions, resulting in lack of appetite, nausea and loss of energy as what little food you feel like eating is not digested as efficiently. Though it feels as if your systems are shutting down, your body is ensuring your survival by frantically doing all it can to ensure that you don't asphyxiate. Eventually the red blood cell level will plateau and your plasma levels will decrease, thickening your blood into oxygen-rich treacle. Once you're fully acclimatised, there'll be an increase in your levels of myoglobin (this is like haemoglobin, but works inside the muscle fibres) and mitochondria – the energy burners inside your cells. The capillaries in your skeletal muscle and your pulmonary artery pressure will also increase, and the walls of the right side of your heart will thicken. However, to fully acclimatise would take 45.6 days – and that's only to 4,000 metres, which was the altitude of our base camp. Few people without special genetics can ever properly adapt to altitude much higher than this. This means your body is always struggling to catch up.

There's an obvious reason for this. Human beings evolved in Africa, mostly at sea level, and headed out over several migration events to colonise the planet. Almost all of the world's present population still lives at low altitudes with dense oxygen, and has never needed the 'thick' blood necessary for life at high altitude. There are, of course, exceptions: peoples who have lived at altitude for millennia and exhibit inheritable genetic characteristics that favour life in thin air. Put simply, they have evolved to be more efficient in hypoxic (oxygen-poor) environments. Tibetan women whose families have lived for generations above 4,000 metres on the Tibetan plateau, give birth to babies that are 500 grams heavier than the Chinese women who have recently joined them. They're born with blood-oxygen levels that are way higher. Tibetan adults, however, do not exhibit raised haemoglobin levels such as outsiders develop when they travel to the Tibetan plateau. This, it seems, is too stressful and demanding on the body's systems; thicker blood means the heart and circulatory system have to work much harder, leading to shorter lifespans and heart problems. Instead Tibetans have bigger lungs, they inhale deeper breaths, and take more breaths a minute than lowland counterparts. They also have double the levels of nitric oxide in their blood, which is believed to help blood vessels to dilate and thus improve circulation. These remarkable traits allow Tibetan people to be comfortable at altitudes that would make a lowlander instantly sick, and they can continue to function at extreme altitudes that would kill lowlanders without acclimatisation. These adaptations are believed to be due to the preservation of the gene EPAS1 from an extinct hominid, the Denisovan peoples, who lived between 400,000 and 40,000 years ago.

Tarx and I do not have gene EPAS1, and we were far from acclimatised even to base camp. These yomps up the mountainside scorched the lungs. We'd have to stop every few hundred metres and sit on a boulder, puffing, our hearts trying to thump their way out of our ears. We were low on tents, so would all be sharing one small dome tent on the climb, which was probably only comfy for two. On the plus side, we wouldn't have to worry about finding a sizable flat space to camp on, on what appeared to be a knife-edged ridge high above us.

Finally, after several runs, we had a well-stocked camp on a stunning sloping shoulder, from which we would launch our attack. The four of us had our last supper – actually a big breakfast consisting of our remaining supply of bread, cheese, porridge and fried 'donk'. From here on in it would be freeze-dried food, carefully selected to give us exactly 2,500 calories a day.

People who know me in normal life will be flabbergasted to read this account. I generally have a thousand things going on in my head at any given time and therefore come across as a bit slapdash, easily distracted and disorganised. My home in the UK is chaotic – except for the loft, which is an Aladdin's cave of adventure equipment, neatly stacked and labelled by activity. My kitchen is a joke of cracked plates encrusted with the remains of scrambled eggs, and cupboards filled with food ten years past its sell-by date; if I cook at all, it's likely to be a ready meal. On expedition, I am the polar opposite, thinking through every meal to the ounce and the nearest hundred calories. I insist on setting up the camp kitchen, and it is a military operation, everything in its place, an exquisitely built rock wall around the outside to deflect the wind, foodstuffs packed in rodent-proof containers, pans and implements hung on improvised hooks. The stoves and meal preparation are my preserve and mine alone. Anyone who even sniffs around the kitchen while I'm preparing dinner receives a guttural lupine snarl, and is sent whimpering off with their tail between their legs.

I should point out there's a practical reason for this behaviour. The multi-fuel MSR stoves we use on expeditions are superb if you care for them properly, but if you misuse them, they can clog up and leave you scuppered. But there's more to it than efficiency. I adore the simplicity of base camp. In the jungle, I get an insane amount of pleasure out of thatching a roof for the camp toilet, or improvising tools, or setting up the perfect hammock. Partly it's satisfaction in your own resourcefulness, your own self-sufficiency, but it's also having a little world you can totally take charge of, and make exactly as you want it. It's nesting instinct. In normal life in the 'real' world, there are too many elements at play, and too many distractions. I can't put any time into making things exactly as I would want them. Here, without those distractions, I can have a place for everything and everything in its place. Maybe it's another manifestation of me being a total and utter control freak.

One thing that even the greatest control freak can never influence is the weather. We'd chosen October for our trip because the monsoon was supposed to be long gone, leaving dry and settled conditions on these high peaks. We needed fine skies, as here on the high mountain we were particularly exposed. Without sat phones or radio we had no connection with the outside world, so no access to weather reports. We had to rely on looking at the sky and trying to figure it out. We failed. First night in advanced base camp, a blizzard began in the middle of the night. We had to take it in turns to go out and shake the tent free of snow so that it didn't collapse around our ears. It led to a sleepless night for all, but this wasn't as big an issue as expected, because we were to get plenty of rest. The blizzard lasted three days, and while it calmed enough that we didn't have to constantly panic about the roof collapsing on our Chicken Littles, it did mean we were not going anywhere. Instead, the four of us huddled in our two-man tent playing endless card and word games. We'd play 'Random Fact of the Day', where you had to come up with something interesting the others hadn't heard of (mine, not surprisingly, were all animal facts). You'd think four people crammed into a small tent for three days with only a single pack of cards for distraction would be like some terrible reality TV show, where the contestants end up killing each other. But the four of us never exchanged a single cross word. I have never laughed so much in my entire life. I laughed until my diaphragm ached with exertion – not hard to do at 5,200 metres above sea level. Every time we laughed ourselves stupid, we would lapse into ten-minute wheezing fits, until we had to lurch out of the tent into the snow to suck up some clean air.

To make matters worse, all four of us were struck down. Thankfully not by HACE (High Altitude Cerebral Edema) or HAPE (High Altitude Pulmonary Edema), but by HABE (High Altitude Bottom Evils). The tent was like the beans scene in *Blazing Saddles*. It's tempting to think this was due to eating pot poodle and chorizo donk for a month, but I've suffered with something similar on every altitude expedition, whatever my diet. It may well be something to do with the digestive system being compromised as your body fights to adjust to the thin air. Either way, breathing air that was mostly methane can't have helped our acclimatisation.

And then one night I went out for a pee and was confronted by a scene of breathtaking clarity. There wasn't a cloud in the black, black sky, and the moon smiled down on me beatifically. The next morning we emerged from our four-man down snuggle to blue-rinsed skies, searing sun and temperatures that jumped twenty degrees the second the sun peeked out from behind the hills. We took the opportunity to scamper down to base camp to regroup and allow the snow to consolidate and the avalanche risk to abate.

The next few days were the best holiday I've ever had. We went from smog-breathing, down-wrapped Michelin men to Costa del Sky sunbathers, sitting around in our grotty unchanged pants, with pasty white bodies and creosoted heads. All our stinky clothes and sleeping bags were draped out over rocks to air and dry out in the glare. There was an epic game of cricket, using our ice axes as stumps, the snow shovel as a bat, and some rolled-up socks for a ball. We sought out the big boulders around camp, and set each other climbing problems, starting with conventional bouldering, then using our ice axes in 'dry tooling' style. This was the hardest and most technical climbing I'd ever done with my ice axes. Ro was extraordinary, moving round the overhangs with axe tips teasing tiny nubbins of rock, hanging to rest in a figure-of-eight position, his leg looped over his arm. I was less adept. On my second climb, my ice axe popped off and I hit myself in the head with it, giving myself a Harry Potter wound on my forehead, and leaving myself open to ceaseless teasing from my colleagues.

The snow at base camp melted away in a day. Higher up we could see big avalanches hammering down over the faces and through the gullies. It felt as if you could reach up and touch the summit, but this was an optical illusion – it was actually a vertical mile above us. What was still obvious, though, was that Conrad Anker's route was out of the question for the season. As we stared up at it through binoculars there was no escaping the fact that the rib was menaced by vast skyscraper seracs and unstable ice towers. It was an identical scenario to the horrific disaster on K2 in 2008, when seracs collapsed above climbers, killing eleven people – the worst single accident in the history of the world's most dangerous mountain. No climber would have been stupid enough to attempt this route. Our second choice – Ro's favourite – was a steep ice couloir to the side of the south-west ridge. After the snowfall this too was out of the question, as constant spindrift avalanches blew down it, and occasionally a tumultuous proper avalanche would rumble the entire valley with its thunder, channelling down the couloir like a bobsleigh run.

Instead, we turned our attention to the steep, blank snow wall at the top of the icefall. I was against it, as this route would be difficult to protect. Roping up would be for peace of mind alone, as no snow stakes or ice screws would have any real effect in the near vertical snow. If anyone fell, it would be impossible to halt their fall, and they would slide all the way down the slope. And waiting at the bottom was the bergschrund. From the German for 'mountain cleft', the schrund is a gaping crevasse at the very end of the glacier, where moving ice breaks away from the stagnant ice or firn above. These schrunds extend all the way down to the bedrock, and are the deepest and most dangerous of all crevasses. Mountaineers avoid them at all costs, and even if we didn't fall off the vertical face and end up in it, crossing the schrund would be deadly dangerous.

Looking through the bins, I favoured the rock to the right side of the snowy headwall.

'I reckon we could freeclimb that face,' I pushed. 'At least we'd be able to protect it.'

'You're kidding yourself, Steve,' was Ro's judgement. 'That rock is going to be hardcore, way out of your league.'

'It might be out of your league, Ro,' I replied. 'I'll have it for breakfast.'

'Random fact of the day, Backshall: you are more full of shit than a large intestine!' That was Tarx's wise contribution.

Ever the peace-maker, Dave cut in: 'Guys, guys, I reckon the snow slope's the answer. It's no harder than the approach on Mount Cook.'

Tarx and I looked at each other, incredulous. 'Er, Dave, I don't like to be an arse, but didn't you fall off Mount Cook and nearly die?'

Dave and Ro looked sheepish. They had both taken an epic tumble off New Zealand's highest peak together, and been very lucky to escape with their lives.

'You feckers can do whatever you want, I'm hacking up the snow,' Ro retorted in bullish form.

'You can try,' Tarx replied, 'but wearing those antique welly boots, you probably won't even make it through the icefall.' (Ro hadn't been able to afford mountaineering boots, so he was wearing a twenty-year-old pair of plastic boots, so clunky and heavy it would be like climbing with a toddler clinging to each foot.)

'And if you get there,' Tarx added, 'that cough of yours will probably avalanche the whole thing down on our heads.'

'At least we'll get a sky burial,' I concluded, 'and the vultures can pick over our bones.'

Despite the banter, the tide was changing. Everyone was plumping for Ro's option.

The rest of the day was spent sharpening ice-axe tips and crampon front points with a file, and packing and repacking a dozen times over. In an attempt to save weight I tried to snap the handle off my toothbrush, and then looked stunned as it broke right in the middle of the head, leaving me with a few useless bristles. I cleaned my teeth with my fingers from then on. Every time I was sure I had my pack completely sorted, I'd see that Tarx had his ice axes arranged slightly differently, or that Dave was taking chocolate bars instead of nuts, and it would be back to the drawing board. This frantic organising and packing is a classic sign of nerves. It's wanting to have control over some small part of the unknown that lies ahead, which of course is totally out of your hands. Finally, there was nothing more we could do. It was time.

We trekked up together to advanced base camp, and dropped our bags at our tent. As we hiked higher, Tibetan woodcock (a kind of grouse) flashed their tail feathers at us like musty plucked peacocks, and laughed at us sweating our way up the slopes. Once we were unburdened, we set into the icefall, trying to find a way through. The Cholatse icefall is a steep hanging glacier of huge, tangled ice sculptures, riddled with evil bottomless crevasses, leading up towards the south-west ridge. It's a serious proposition, but at this stage we were only route finding and knew we would be returning to advanced base camp that evening. We were not yet committed, and thus could enjoy our first real climbing since getting to the Himalaya.

The following day, we packed our tent and returned to the icefall to pick our way through, except this time we were laden with packs weighing about 20 kilos each. The further we got into the ice, the more committed we became, and the more the sense of vulnerability closed in on us. We were all scared, you could hear it in our voices, and in the way we nervily picked our way around ice climbs that were well within our limits. We overprotected every possible fall, proceeding with too much caution, desperate that nothing should go wrong. As we began moving early in the morning, the sun started to melt ice high up, releasing the boulders that had been bound into it. At around 10 a.m. there was a noise like cracking thunderbolts, and the world seemed to shake. A cavalcade of huge boulders had come loose and started to bounce down the rockface to the side of the icefall – the route I had suggested we take when looking up through the binoculars back at base camp. The rocks seemed to be the size of pebbles, and they were bouncing in slow motion, but we knew this phenomenon was a trick of the light and clarity of the air. What we were looking at were vast, house-sized boulders. There was no way anyone on that rockface would have survived. And this was only the first of a dozen such falls we

MOUNTAIN: A LIFE ON THE ROCKS

witnessed during the climb. Ro merely looked at me with a steady gaze that said, 'Random fact of the day: "I told you so".'

Finally, as the sun began to set, we reached solid, snow-covered ice at the top of the glacier. Big gaping crevasses ran in from both the left and the right, but they were open and obvious, and there was a flat area of snow between them. Ro probed the snow with a tent pole to make sure there weren't any slots hiding from view. The environment felt exposed but stable. With no danger of avalanche from above, it was as good a campsite as we were going to find. Camp camaraderie was in full force that evening as everyone fought to be the one to flatten the most snow for our tent-site, to melt the most snow for drinking water. Earplugs and eye shades were vital that night, as pre-match nerves had someone getting up every hour or so to pop out for a frightened wee. It was an alpine start, waking before dawn, preparing breakfast and unpacking camp in the dark, then setting off the second we had enough half-purple light to perceive the yawning crevasses.

Our plan was to get past the horror of the snowy headwall while it was still icy, the snow still bound by the night's freeze, and before the sun had a chance to turn it to slush. Dave and Ro set off together, with Tarx and I on a separate rope fifteen minutes later. Ro had come up with all kinds of convincing reasons as to why this was an efficacious method of us moving over the terrain ahead, but I sensed it was more down to him not wanting to be at the end of a rope if I were to take a whipper. I did after all weigh about the same as him and Dave combined.

Crossing the bergschrund was easier than we anticipated. It was mostly filled with old snow, and we managed to find a decent step across it. Above us, the headwall towered like the concrete face of the Hoover Dam. To begin with, our plan paid dividends. The snow was firm and crusty, and took our crampon points like a bread-knife into crisp watermelon. But once the sun rose – even though it would be many hours before the warming rays would fall on to the face – the rise in temperature of a degree or two began to have a noticeable effect on the snow. At first it started to soften, then an obvious gradient began to form between the crunchy crust on top and slushier snow beneath. It was like a Crunchie in reverse, with the soft chocolate on the inside and a coating of brittle honeycomb on top. The only way to protect your fellow climber was to cut out a seat in the snow, bury your axe straight down behind you, and belay them using your body as ballast. This was pretty safe when the leader brought up the second from below. Provided you kept the rope taut, any slip or slide could be balanced out from a tug on the rope. But in order to achieve this the leader would end up with fifty metres of slack rope between them and the belayer below, which meant they were as good as soloing. At least we were bouncing leads (swapping who climbed first), so you spent half the time safe, and half being one mis-step away from a slippery death.

On future hard Alpine routes, Ro and I have had our only dis-agreements about climbing style. Sometimes on the hardest terrain Ro will want to take the rope off, and climb solo, saying that a fall would result in both climbers being pulled to their death. My disagreement stems not from the fact that I am the lesser climber and much more likely to be the one that tumbles. Instead, I believe passionately in the rule of the rope. When I climb with someone, I take their life in my hands and ask them to take mine. If they fall, there is always a chance that I might be able to somehow hold them. And if they do go, then I would rather go with them. I could not live with myself otherwise. To ditch the lifeline and suddenly shout 'every man for himself' at the critical moment is anathema. If someone is concerned I might be the weak link, then I genuinely have not even a hint of a problem with them refusing to climb with me. But once we have started together, we must finish the same way, whatever the consequences.

It was several hundred metres of ascent, and the final five metres was the hardest, leading up on to a saddle above. The top was vertical with a slight overhanging lip, and Ro had taken the first lead, getting over it with delicate movements accompanied by the sound of distant rampant cursing. Tarx was to lead our pitch, but I could see he was having difficulty, his feet slipping around in the vertical sludge, getting more and more worked up. Eventually Ro tossed a section of rope down to help him up to the top. When I reached the final pitch, it was very clear why he had struggled, and also that it had been very fortunate Ro had been first. Pulling myself over the lip and on to the ridgeline was not only a tremendous relief, the staggering vista that opened out almost made me forget what we'd just been through. From our sun-stroked chunk of snow, with its steepening sweep leading towards a rocky buttress and the south-west ridge beyond, we were afforded a breathtaking view that encompassed 8,200-metre Cho Oyu to the north, as well as Taboche towering above us, seemingly so close we could have leapt out and landed on its face.

After a few minutes' rest, to the sound of Dave and Ro coughing as if they were trying to expel chunks of their lungs, we progressed up the snow ridge, and from there on to the rock buttress that guarded the way towards the summit. This was where things started to fall apart. We'd anticipated a route made up of snow and ice, and that's what we'd prepared for. All the photos of people climbing this section had shown the rock covered with snow and ice that we could happily have attacked with axes and crampons. Instead we found ourselves facing bare rock that would have been difficult at sea level without packs, and certainly without crampons on our feet. It was like trying to climb in ice skates, at near 6,000 metres, with sphincter-clenching drops to spiky boulders thousands of feet below. To say we scared ourselves witless would be an understatement. Ro as the best climber started fidgeting around with his ice axes on some simply terrifying-looking exposed rock. Tarx strad-dled the snow ridge like it was a skinny white horse and plunged his ice axe into the slush to provide a belay that could offer nothing more than the illusion of reassurance. I decided to take a different tack, and climbed as high as possible on the snow before taking off my crampons, leaving behind my ice axes, and starting up the rock. Even without my crampons on, it was clunky and clumsy trying to find meagre footholds in my heavy mountaineering boots. How Ro was managing in his huge plastic monstrosities was beyond me.

Acrophobia – the *irrational* fear of heights – derives from the Greek *acro* meaning peak, and *phobos* meaning fear, and it affects about 5 per cent of the populace. They can find themselves having panic attacks when they are in no danger whatsoever, standing on balconies or windows in not especially tall buildings. (Vertigo, the term often used to describe this fear, is in reality a symptom of inner-ear and balance disorders that result in sensations of spin-ning, wobbling, dizziness and feeling sick, but have nothing to do with height.) There is nothing irrational about being gripped by fear of falling when you are somewhere like this, and the risk of a tumble is very real. Scientists have carried out experiments where they placed infants on the ground, with a glass floor and the ap-pearance of a vast chasm evident beneath it. Only 3 out of 36 would crawl across the glass to get to their mothers; most cried and would not venture out over the glass gap no matter what. They tried the same experiment with dog puppies, kittens, kids, chicks and lambs, and the results were the same. Beyond demonstrating that scientists will torture pretty much anything for kicks, this proves that fear of falling is something we're born with, that seems to come from deep in our primal consciousness. An innate cautiousness where great heights are concerned would obviously have been beneficial for our survival, and thus it has been preserved in humans as in other species through time.

According to Sigmund Freud's *Interpretation of Dreams*, the sensation of falling is a 'typical dream', i.e. 'dreams which almost everyone has dreamt alike and which we are accustomed to assume must have the same meaning for everyone'. Modern studies have shown that 79 per cent of people across the planet have such dreams regularly. It's thought this can relate to loss of control, loss of consciousness, a real sense of danger, recollection of falling in the past, or of genuinely traumatic experiences. I know I'm not the only person who will dream they're falling and wake up with a terrified sleep twitch. Falling is a sensation that is linked to fear more than anything else in our subconscious mind.

The intriguing counterpoint to this has been studied by Florida State University and dubbed 'high-place phenomena'. This is the urge, on reaching a high place, to hurl yourself off. The study, entitled 'An Urge to Jump, Affirms the Urge to Live', showed that about 33 per cent of those interviewed had experienced the phenomenon, and of those about 50 per cent had been suicidal. But what of the other 50 per cent? Well, the study hypothesised that it was all a trick of the mind: if someone leans towards the edge of a precipice, primal survival instinct immediately kicks in and pulls them back. Afterwards they reassess the situation and wonder what made them shrink from the edge when there was no danger of falling. The brain then offers the solution that there must have been an urge to jump. Thus people were misinterpreting the survival urge as the urge to jump. Psychologist Pauline Wallin offers an alternative explanation, positing that we fantasise about 'leaping from high places for the same reason 13-year-girls like going to Halloween haunted houses – for the thrill, and as practice for not buckling under to fear.'

I'm one of those non-suicidal 15 per cent who regularly pulls themselves back from cliff edges because my mind is wondering:

'What if you were to jump now? How would that feel?' So I prefer Pauline's elegant solution. I think it's a challenge to yourself, a tester, a shot of adrenalin to set your pulse racing. Here on Cholatse, faced with genuine fear and danger, I did not have an urge to jump. And there never is when I'm truly at risk; it only hits me when I'm safe. Instead I just wanted to hug the rock, close my eyes and plant my face against it to make the fear go away.

My initial reticence at picking my way up a virgin rockface was eased when I found a tatty piece of rope crammed into a crack above the snow ridge.

'This is the way, Tarx! Come here and set up a proper belay!'

Tarx shuffled carefully from his seated position, turned towards the rockface, and stood up. This was a seriously sketchy position to be in. Neither of us had any protection whatsoever. To our right was a steep snow slide ending in a drop-off. To our left was a vertical drop of at least 300 metres. Any mistakes from either of us and we would both have died.

Taking care not to snag himself on my ropes, Tarx edged up towards a flake of rock to his left. 'I reckon I can get a cam in behind this.'

Still teetering on my toe tips, I reached round on my harness, took off three cams in different sizes, and clipped them to my rope. They slid down towards my climbing partner like soldiers on a zip wire.

Taking a cam in one hand, he pinched it tight to slide into the gap behind the door of rock. The whole thing peeled forward with a horrific rasping sound. Tarx shrieked like a barn owl chick calling out to be fed, then we held our breath. The rock settled. But there was no way we could put any protection behind it. All of a sudden it was too much for us. I can't honestly remember who called it, only the initial relief quickly being subsumed by crushing disappointment as we trudged back down the snow ridge to the saddle, where we found Ro and Dave already rigging up an abseil to descend the snow slope.

I've gone through those few hours when we retreated from Cholatse thousands of times more than I can calculate. The answer was simple: I should have pressured Ro to go back up to where I was climbing, had him take off his big plastic boots and put on the rock-climbing shoes he had in his pack. He could have led the pitches above us. Then the rest of us could have seconded our way through to the top of the buttress. It would then have been a nerve-racking, dangerous, but technically achievable snow teeter to the summit. We had blue skies and sunshine, and no clouds at all, suggesting at least a few days of settled weather. At the very least, we could have set up camp there on the saddle and talked things through, made a plan. But we were scared. We felt vulnerable, exposed, a million miles away from anyone and from help. Every one of us had run through what would happen if someone fell. It would be three or four days before any of us could sprint back to the nearest place where you could call for help. There were no helicopters within a hundred miles, a rescue up here was not an option. The only people who'd be able to get up here to help would be technical climbers. It would be weeks before you'd be able to even think of a rescue, by which time the weather could have changed. It was no wonder we were all overwhelmed with doubt and fear. Dave and Ro were ill, the altitude had intensified their coughing and spluttering, and they had lost every ounce of morale. They wanted to be back in a café in Namche bazaar drinking chai and Benylin. I was the one with the most drive and energy left, but as the least capable climber I didn't have the confidence or ability to push forward. So we bailed.

It was not over yet, though. The next morning, Tarx and I trawled slowly down the glacier filming everything as we went. Tarx had a camera attached to his helmet which was perfect for catching action shots as we leapt with ice tools flailing over crevasses, and teetered precariously over ice bridges. Minutes after executing a particularly unnecessary bound and slide over a gaping chasm, I was wrenched off my feet as the rope snapped tight behind me, and I heard a strangled expletive squealed by Tarx. In blind panic, I hauled on the slipping rope, dumped my pack, and thrashed around trying to put an anchor into the snow. The crevasse had obviously been partially covered by snow and invisible to Tarx – it had suddenly collapsed under him, sending him tumbling ten feet or so into the darkness, where he was now hanging upside down, with his heavy rucksack towing him down into the cold black. In my desperation to secure him, I tried bashing an aluminium snow stake into the slope, and hammered it so hard with my hand I bent it in half. It was totally useless. We thrashed around for the best part of half an hour, before I managed to reel him in a little, and eventually he was able to release his pack and climb out using his ice axes. We lay panting in the snow giggling like nervous schoolgirls until we got ourselves together, and grabbed the head camera to take a look at the award-winning footage we had captured. The tape had run out two minutes before he fell.

Six years after our debacle on Cholatse, the first guided expedition on to the peak was launched. It's now guided every other year, with a one-to-one Sherpa to climber ratio, and with fixed ropes through the technical sections. It saddens me that our wild peak can now be conquered this way; it seems cheapened. I suppose in part it's because it makes our failure seem all the more abject, but at the same time it does genuinely concern me. The objective danger on Cholatse was in a different league to most of the other Himalayan routes I've been on since. There's so much that can go wrong, with rock and icefall, slopes and ridges that are difficult to fully protect even with the manpower and logistics of the big adventure outfits. I know I am not the world-class mountaineer that guides on

Cholatse are, but I still don't see how they can guarantee a client's safety on it. Maybe that's sour grapes on my part.

I have a beautiful photo of Ro and Dave as tiny dots on the snow ridge leading up to the rock that beat us. Skies so blue they speak of infinity, intense white, the finger of the ridge beckoning us ever onwards towards the summit, looming at the top as a shimmering promise. It has been on my bedroom wall since we returned over a decade ago. It is the first thing I see when I wake in the morning, and the last thing I see before I fall asleep at night. To begin with, I put it there to take me to the Himalayas, because it is a beautiful picture, reminds me of the grandeur of the mountains, of how small we seemed in the face of that majesty. It was a happy, halcyon image of one of my fondest expeditions, with very special friends, when we were young and strong and full of ambitions beyond our skills. Over time, though, my relationship with that picture has changed. I've lain in bed looking at it, running through in my head the ways we could and should have done it differently. It has become a taunt, a reminder of the fear we felt. A prick of shame at the way we psyched ourselves out of what would have been my most treasured summit. It's a thorn deliberately lodged in my heel to make me run faster.

HEART OF DARKNESS

'But risks must be taken because the greatest hazard in life is to risk nothing. The person who risks nothing, does nothing, has nothing, is nothing. He may avoid suffering and sorrow, but he cannot learn, feel, change, grow or live. Chained by his servitude he is a slave who has forfeited all freedom. Only a person who risks is free. The pessimist complains about the wind; the optimist expects it to change; and the realist adjusts the sails.'   *William Arthur Ward*

The whooping songs of gibbons resound over the valley far below me, singing duets of ever-increasing cadence and tone. They lollop branch to branch, hand over hand, travelling through the canopy as fast as a bird flies. A tissue of long clouds extend smoky tendrils through the vast treetops; some of the ironwood giants here are among the world's tallest trees. Hornbills fly sorties across the gaping divide, their ludicrous head ornaments weighing them down. Grasping the flaky limestone beneath my feet, I tug the rope up from below me, so I can turn, sit and rest. Puffing with exertion, I wipe the slick of sweat and grime from my eyes, wait for my breath to settle, and enjoy my first open sky and open view in over a week. Above me, white vertical rock walls, streaked with orange and grey, and strung through with vegetation, glower in defiance. Below, there's nothing but an unbroken mantle of Bornean rainforest; pristine, unlogged, little known but as yet unprotected. There can be absolutely no doubt that I am the first human being to touch this rock, and see this view. Below me, my partner shouts up, anxious to find out why I have stopped. I scan the luxuriant canyon one last time, trying to imprint its beauty of my mind for ever, then turn back to the rock, and set my jaw to ascending slowly upwards.

So many times in my life, events that have seemed to be cataclysmic endings have led to new beginnings springing Phoenix-like from the ashes. One of these moments came as *The Really Wild Show* drew to an end after twenty years on British TV screens. Luckily, I didn't have to wait long for the next opportunity. Series producer Steve Greenwood had been charged with making expedition films for the BBC's Natural History Unit, the first of which was going to be Borneo. He had heard from several sources that this part of the world was my specialty from my Rough Guides days, and so involved me early on in the process of planning and preparing the expedition. Originally, he agreed to take me on as an assistant producer, which was a step backwards from where I'd been on *The Really Wild Show*, and offered no guaranteed screen presence. He then set about constructing a team of biologists and wildlife filmmakers to provide the narrative to the show.

As the spring of 2006 approached, Steve and I journeyed out to Borneo several times to recce locations for our base camp, and come up with conservation stories to give the series its drive and purpose. From the start, the two of us got on like a blazing building. The project was perfect for both of us, its key ingredients being adventure, storytelling, wilderness and wildlife, and we shared the same childlike enthusiasm. It was as if we'd been teleported back into the greatest ever *Boy's Own* annual, and given the chance to become proper explorers in the Heart of Darkness. I still consider Borneo, and the other expedition series I made with Steve, to be the highlight of my career, even of my life.

You'd never take Steve for an intrepid adventurer if you came across him in the UK. He's tall and rangy, dresses smartly in waist-coats and pressed shirts, and wears round John Lennon specs that give him a studious, almost professorial air. He looks the type to be directing the *South Bank Show*, not gritty nature documenta-ries filmed on location at the ends of the Earth. But I've never seen him more at home, or more enthused, than when he is poring over maps, or with his face pressed up against a moth sheet, gazing in wonder at the array of tropical bugs.

The island of Borneo is divided between Malaysia, Indonesia and Brunei, and we were searching for evidence that would eventually help pave the way for the Heart of Borneo – a huge national park that would span the international borders. The reasons for this grand park were manifold and truly frightening. The plight of the Amazon rainforest is well known and for sheer scale is more hor-rific. But deforestation has happened faster and on more complete levels in Borneo than anywhere else on Earth, at any time in human history. More than half of the world's tropical timber comes from here, but not for much longer; 80 per cent of the island's forests have gone for ever.

I'd been to Borneo several times, and had seen the place change with my own eyes. On my first solo trip in 1992, I'd gone up in a light aircraft and flown for hours, looking out of the window at the endless rainforest below, covering the island in every direction all the way to the horizon. It was the most exciting jungle island I'd ever visited. But then Malaysian logging companies, international mining organisations and oil palm companies started to hack and burn their way through those seemingly infinite forests. In 1997, the whole of Southeast Asia was brought to a standstill throughout the summer by a thick smog formed by the burning of Borneo's ancient forests. From July to October, the haze covered an area of 1,200,000 square miles over Malaysia, Thailand and Indonesia. In Singapore, hospital attendance went up by 30 per cent, mostly due to respiratory-based ailments. Average visibility across the area was less than a kilometre, but I was there at the time, and in places you couldn't see a hundred metres in front of you. Slash and burn was the culprit: a technique where forests are hacked down, the expensive trees taken, and the more minor stuff burnt away. Fire was also controversially used by those looking to make land claims; after burning out a landowner's forest or crops, the interloper would plant their own and lay claim to the land.

Costs to the region of the burning were said to be around 4.5 billion dollars, but it's not possible to judge the true cost. Much of the burnt land was taken over by oil palm plantations. Oil palm is a crop used in a huge variety of products, from soaps to foodstuffs. Now, when you fly over Borneo, the landscape below is still green, but the vegetation is formed into the neat, symmetrical lines of oil palm plantations. This probably doesn't seem like too much of a problem, until you get down into the plantations themselves. A rainforest is a place that reverberates with the life that inhabits it: frogs calling, cicadas with their 110-decibel whinings, hornbill wings beating like a helicopter overhead, and the far-off mournful song of gibbons resounding through the valleys. At dusk, you have to shout to be heard. And then you step into an oil palm plantation, and it is totally silent. Eerily silent. Nothing lives there except rats. Monoculture – the farming of one single item at the expense of diversity – is one of the biggest evils facing the healthy future of our planet. My memories of Borneo are of the orang utan hiding from the rain under a banana palm leaf, the scamper of unknown species of bugs, proboscis monkeys with weird flapping noses stooping from emerald boughs to drink the brown water of rivers where colossal saltwater crocodiles lurk. But we have so much more to gain from biodiversity than simple beauty. Huge parks like Heart of Borneo are vital not just to safeguard rare species, but to protect our planet and ensure the future of the human race.

Natural systems are so much more complex and occasionally fragile than we will ever understand. An example would be the catastrophic decline of bees around the world. In America at the beginning of 2008 more than a third of honeybees mysteriously died; around a million colonies. The death rate in France was over 60 per cent, and in Britain the government farming minister warned that bees could be extinct within a decade. There are many reasons why bees are disappearing. Neonicotinoids (a relatively new kind of pesticide) have a role to play, as does the spread of the bee parasite the varroa mite. It is, though, convincingly argued that monoculture is an even more potent force. Bees evolved from a wasp-like ancestor over 100 million years ago, and have survived ever since by gathering pollen and nectar, feeding from a variety of different food plants in every single foraging session. Bees that are bred to specifically pollinate monoculture crops exhibit stress, suffer greater and more intense infections, and are more likely to suffer from Colony Collapse Disorder. And the cost of losing bees? In Southern Sichuan in China, thousands of people with sticks ending in a chicken feather clamber among the apple trees, pollinating the trees themselves, as they have done for two decades since all the bees disappeared. To do this in the United States would cost £64 billion a year. We cannot begin to calculate the effects of environmental change on the scale that is occurring here in Borneo; bees are only one infinitesimally small part of an infinitely complex problem.

The environmental devastation in Borneo had another complicating factor. To apply for permission to film in Sabah, Steve and

I went along to the Yayasan Sabah building in Kota Kinabalu, the capital of Malaysian Borneo. It was the flashiest, most opulent building in the nation, and we travelled up in the elevator to the penthouse office of the government minister for the environment. It turned out he was also the minister for logging. Obviously we kept our mouths shut about this, as we needed his help to obtain permits to film in far-flung and unprotected areas of Bornean forest. But it stuck in the throat that the man responsible for protecting the dwindling forests stood to gain the most from cutting them down, given that all the huge multinational companies lobbying for logging concessions had to go through him. Not surprisingly, over the years this relationship has been the focus of major scandals as colossal multibillion-dollar corruption has been exposed throughout the system.

Protected reserves were at this stage the only realistic option to preserve Borneo's forests, and we were confident that one particular location could be perfect. Imbak Canyon was relatively close to the existing reserve of Maliau Basin; although unprotected at that time, its remoteness and geographical ruggedness meant that it had not yet been exploited. Just outside the walls of the canyon, though, the loggers had moved in and obliterated nearly everything in their path.

Imbak was perfect for us. We set up our base camp in the most accessible part of the canyon, in order to make it easier to carry in all our tonnes of gear. On helicopter recces, I'd discovered that the canyon's southern rim rose with vertical cliff walls to a summit at 1,500 metres called Gunung (Mount) Kuli. The north face had exposed limestone escarpments of uncertain height; from the heli they looked challenging, but climbable. The summit appeared to be covered in dense forest, which would potentially be home to different species of plants and animals to the ones found in the lowland forests below our base camp. In rising excitement, I contacted all the local rangers asking for information about the peak. Did they know of anyone who had climbed it? I asked. Again and again the response was a definite no; no one had ever climbed any part of the canyon walls, and we would have to be fools to try. I then contacted the government and park authorities, only to be told the same thing. Scrutinising the maps, and with a knowledge of mountainous jungle gained over months and months of expeditions, I surmised they were probably right. The rock itself would be the safe and easy bit. The approach to the base through steep, apparently impenetrable forest would be the real challenge. By this time I was blind to the folly of undertaking such an enterprise, all I could think of was what a terrific adventure it would make: a virgin peak, deep inside the heart of the jungle where no man had ever set foot. It seemed to me exactly the kind of thing our expedition had been created for.

The venture was fraught with difficulty from the outset. We'd insisted that not a single tree would be felled in order to make our base camp, which was all very commendable, but as a result we had neither the light, space or mud-free zones to organise the technical kit needed. We also had advice from our ex-military base camp manager, who kept looking at our rope systems, tutting and shaking his head, saying, 'I wouldn't do it like that.' He insisted that we take a backpack trauma kit and heavy military HF radio kit – those two items alone were a full load for one man. By the time we'd got three kilometres from camp we'd ditched the trauma kit for a more realistic first-aid kit and the radio had stopped working. On our return, we learned that someone had put a machete through the aerial of the receiver in camp. The sat phones never worked as we so rarely had a clear view of the sky. Depressingly, the best contact we had from camp was with my mobile phone. It connected with a signal from an unseen but nearby logging camp. I would call the office back home in Bristol, and then pass on messages that they would phone through to the sat phone in base camp!

My feeling about teams has always been that, as with equipment, streamlined is the only way to go. Every extra person is one more variable to worry about, an injury or illness waiting to happen or possibly a klutz you can't count on. Far better to have a small team of people you know and trust implicitly. You need to be able to rely on them to have their own shit together, so you can get on with worrying about your own job. For the Kuli trip I put together a three-man dream team. I would be joined by cameraman Johnny Rogers, a tough and resourceful Irishman who was an old hand at keeping the equipment working in the most challenging of conditions; and climbing supremo Tim Fogg, my utter hero, and probably the safest pair of hands I've ever worked with. Tim was officially our multi-purpose safety expert, but the truth was the whole thing would be a team effort, with all of us chipping in regardless of job description. We were an unstoppable, experienced and enthused unit, all bursting with excitement at going somewhere no one had ever been before.

We set off with a couple of hundred metres of rope, ten day's worth of Pot Noodles and one pair of pants each. With the overall ambience of the Borneo jungle being akin to a mudfight in a Turkish steambath, we condemned ourselves to levels of squalor no human should ever sink to. The unbreakable rule with jungle expeditions is that you have two sets of clothes: your 'wets' and your 'drys'. The drys are for sleeping in only, the wets for every other situation in the almost permanently soaking rainforest. It's so tempting at the end of a hard day to change out of your vile wet kit, but the second your drys are soggy is the second you cannot escape the soak, and that's when things become unbearable. There was unlikely to be any standing or running water on the knife-edge ridge leading up to the rockface. The bedrock was ancient and porous, so rainwater would immediately drain away. This meant that most of our load was made up of ropes and water. I began the climb up the steep slope with fifteen litres of water, and one of the heaviest packs I've ever carried.

The dangers of life in the rainforest are never what outsiders expect. It's not venomous snakes, spiders or scorpions (I've gone weeks in the jungle without seeing any); it's the simple things – like getting lost. Finding your way around when you have no extended view and everything looks the same is a serious concern. On one of my jungle trips, a researcher wandered away from camp to take a comfort break, and we didn't find her again for three hours. She had probably been no more than a kilometre from camp, had been shouting and yelling, and we had been out in organised search sweeps, yet it took that long to find her. Even the latest equipment can't overcome the challenges of jungle navigation: the forest canopy blocks GPS signals.

In fine visibility, finding your way in the mountains is easy. You can see where you're going from many miles away, and rarely need to refer to the map. When a whiteout starts to descend or when, as here in the jungle, it's impossible see any landmarks, and micro-navigation can mean the difference between life and death. A good navigator can look at the contours of a two-dimensional map and 'see' the three-dimensional landscape come to life in their heads. They can walk a mile looking solely at their compass in a jungle where every metre looks exactly the same, in whiteout and total darkness, and end up on a precise one-metre square of land. Without the ability to walk off a minutely accurate compass bearing and count your steps to judge distance to within metres, in a whiteout up high you might as well roll up into a ball and wait for the snow to stop. An illustration would be the Welsh 1,000 metres peaks marathon, which is my favourite mountain race. It runs from the coast at Aber in the north, up and over the four 1,000-metre peaks in Snowdonia, to finish on the summit of Snowdon, and is one of the most beautiful and iconic fell runs in the British Isles.

If you're not carrying a full map of the area and a compass, you won't be allowed to take part. The first time I did the race, it was a glorious spring day and I never took the map out of my pack. Not even once. I could see the top of every peak, and the runners ahead of me, so I just headed for them, cursing the weight of the navigation kit in my back. The second time I did the race, thick clouds covered the peak tops, and I had to walk the whole thing with face screwed up, compass pressed to map for almost every second. My nav is pretty solid, but it took me an extra hour, and my brain was spent by the end. Throughout the race, I kept bumping into wide-eyed endurance athletes shivering in their Ronhill track tights, stumbling around lost. Within an hour I had a retinue of fell-runners trotting along behind me, all stopping to do up their shoelaces every time I stopped! Eventually, I came across someone who was a better map-reader than I was, and we nonchalantly followed him, like a bunch of sweat- and drizzle-drenched rats following a map-wielding Pied Piper. Half the field didn't even finish; most stumbled their way to the nearest road, flagged down a passing motorist and hitch-hiked out to safety, vowing never to run in the mountains again!

Generally speaking, if you are moving quickly using a map, you use techniques like continuous map reading, ticking off features on the map as you pass them, making note of pylons, fences, cliffs that should be turning up in an estimated amount of time. If they don't turn up, you stop, and backtrack to the last place you knew for certain where you were. When nav is tricky, you rarely take the quickest routes; it's better to take a big detour if it means you can take advantage of good 'attack points', easily identifiable landmarks from which you can recalibrate yourself to your true destination. Even better are 'handrails', which are very obvious unchangeable features that you can follow for long distances without thinking. I've gone hours out of my way in order to keep alongside a fence-line or the banks of a river, knowing I don't have to think about my nav and cannot get lost. It saves you time in the long run.

The early part of this trek up towards the north face of Kuli was a serious navigation challenge. There were numerous ridgelines leading up towards the rock, but they were encased in forest, making it difficult to determine which one to take. And the last thing we wanted was to end up in one of the gullies between the ridgelines. In 1994 a British army team ended up in Low's gully, which comes off one side of Mount Kinabalu right here in Borneo. Their fate is detailed in the appropriately named book *Descent into Chaos*, and the movie *The Place of the Dead*. The trained military team abseiled into the gully, but once inside couldn't negotiate the horrific terrain and couldn't get out again. There were falls and several nasty injuries, and they were extremely lucky to escape with their lives. Extended court martials followed in an effort to establish who was responsible for pitching them into that nightmare environment in the first place. And Low's gully was on the north face of Mount Kinabalu, which has a well-worn tourist path that I wandered up in the early 1990s alongside a bunch of Korean schoolkids. It is only a stone's throw from the capital city of Sabah, but, regardless, in a steep rainforest gully there is no contact with the outside world, and zero chance of rescue. Once you're in, you have to get yourself out. Here in Imbak, we were far more exposed, and even more reliant on our own abilities. There could not, MUST not be any mistakes in our route-finding.

It's difficult to get across, or even to truly remember quite how horrid our trek to the rock was. The terrain was steep, muddy, slippery, and made all the more arduous by the fact we were carrying a phenomenal weight. Halfway through the first day, the slope started to thin from both sides until it became a ridgeline. At least this meant there was no longer any doubt where to go: the only way was on and up. As the light began to dwindle, we faced the fact that we were already running out of level ground and trees to construct a hammock camp, so we stopped at the first viable spot. It was a pinch at best, our three hammocks strung out between trees that were too close together or far apart, and hanging on silly inclines. We had the strong feeling, though, that it was the best we were going to get.

As expected, there was no water nearby to wash away the sweat of an evil day straining uphill in near 100 per cent humidity. Wanting to preserve our water for cooking and drinking, we gave up on washing. In order to keep our dry set of clothes dry, we wandered around camp naked. It would have made a very strange sight indeed had anyone happened upon us – three pasty white Brits tiptoeing around a vile jungle ridge with their tackle out. With no shelter other than the insides of our hammocks and no light, we retired to bed shortly after dark and sat huddled up like swinging bananas while Tim played mournful Celtic tunes on his tin whistle. It would have been even more amusing to see us the next morning as we squeezed into our soaking, stinking sewer suits, our faces contorted in impressions of gummy grandmas sucking on lemons.

Our first challenge was to get close to the rockface. Beyond our camp the ridgeline steepened and the vegetation began to get more and more dense. From here on in, I'd take the lead, hacking a thin path with my machete through the tangle. There are few more arduous and slow environments to move through than this. Over several days, we hacked our way through the forest, ascending from sea level to near a thousand metres where the rock began.

At this altitude the giant trees give way to stumpy moss forest, with every tangled tree root and vine swathed in thick green velvet moss drapes. It turned every glade into a Tolkienesque cavern, and you half expect a giant spider or orc to emerge from the darkness any second. The moss soaks up the endless rain like a green sponge, meaning every time you come in contact it soaks you to the bone. The thousands of pitcher plants (some of them holding two and a half litres of water and capable of capturing rats and birds) tip soggy bug sludge down the back of your neck as you machete through the undergrowth, and the rattan and grasses turn the slashing into death by papercut. In extremis we would have used boiled pitcher plant water to cook with and drink, but by now we were being pounded with constant rainfall, so instead set up a tarpaulin, with one end tipped down towards our pots. They filled in a matter of minutes. The vegetation was so thick we proceeded at about ten to twenty metres an hour, and it came as a huge relief every time we broke out on to rock; anything was better than crawling through this sewer.

It's one of the eternal conundrums of expedition television that the more dangerous and harder something is, the less chance there is of it looking that way on camera. It is easy to make a rock climb in Yosemite look gnarly; you can set cameras filming from every angle, and be sure that you're filming at the crux. You can be dangling off overhanging rock, which looks horribly dangerous to non-climbers, but can be protected and made 100 per cent safe. Steep, slimy, overgrown rock on the other hand looks messy and terminally unimpressive, even though it carries infinitely more danger of a fall. People who make adrenalised rock-climbing films have it easy! When you're in situations where life and death genuinely hangs in the balance, it's all hands on deck. Nobody is thinking about filming, because they are so busy making sure none of their friends die. Plus, in all likelihood, the situation will be too challenging for the cameras to even come out of their bags.

The classic situation would arise later in this same Borneo expedition, when we were exploring a giant sinkhole in the Mulu mountains. The terrain was very similar to what we found ourselves on now. Steep, muddy, slippery, treacherous, with massive drop offs. One night as we were rigging at the sinkhole rim, an electric storm hit us. The tropical downpour was so fierce we were forced to retreat to lower ground, slithering down ludicrously steep slimy slopes among the spindly trees. I remember looking up through the tumultuous cloudburst and seeing my comrade's head torches sweeping the darkness like light sabres, raindrops and splashes illuminated into backlit baubles, dark silhouettes scrabbling down in terror. 'This would make the most jaw-dropping sequence ever,' I remember thinking. Obviously, in those conditions the camera was safely in its protective cover; it would have been flooded instantly otherwise. At that moment one of our team got into serious difficulties. He had taken a load that was much too heavy, and had glasses on which had steamed up so he couldn't see. He staggered over a traverse with a fatal drop-off, clinging on to a rope handrail for grim death. And then he lost it; no strength left, unable to keep his feet, he was going to fall and knew it. Camerawoman Justine Evans and I dropped our loads and scrabbled in to help, catching his arms, taking his pack, dragging him physically back to solid ground. We saved his life, the terror in his eyes behind the steamy specs told that with certainty. The storyteller in me obviously wishes we could have captured all that on camera. But it simply wasn't possible. Perhaps in the near future, as helmet cams get smaller, have better performance in low light, and are at least nominally waterproof . . . But back then there was no chance.

In all the years that I've been making expedition programmes, this ascent of Mount Kuli has been the most dangerous, but on camera it was perhaps the least impressive. There was no way Johnny could get alongside or above me when I was leading, so most of the shots are of my backside above him, and then only when he himself could get on to safe ground. But it was the ridgeline itself that offered the real horrors. On camera, it looks like a green mess; you're enclosed by vegetation most of the time and rarely catch a glimpse of the view, but the reality was that to either side of you the ground fell away at least the height of the Eiffel Tower.

The closest we came in all of these expeditions to an actual death was on the ascent of Kuli, and yet again it could never have been caught on camera. I had been leading the way up the side of a short steep section, unroped and unprotected. I should probably have put in a handrail, but had nothing decent to secure it to. Johnny was close on my heels, and as he came to the top of the steep bit he grabbed a root to haul himself up. It came clean out in his hand, he overbalanced, and pitched back into space. Everything went into slow motion. I saw his face open in horror, his hands flailing, army windmilling. I had time to register spiky treetops like spears hundreds of metres below. I even saw myself telling his widow and small child the news that Johnny had died on my watch, and facing a lifetime of guilt because of it – all in less than a second. As if somehow disconnected from my body, I saw my hand stretch out and grab the front of Johnny's T-shirt. Then his hand swept up to grip my wrist. It was like a moment in a Hollywood movie, two joined hands the only thing keeping my friend from spiralling out into the abyss. A moment later Johnny crawled up alongside me, hugging the rock, then looked behind him at the empty space – and laughed maniacally for about half an hour.

The second night we simply couldn't find anywhere to pitch our hammocks, leaving us with no choice but to return to the previous night's campsite. It was morale-busting to retrace our steps, but it was the only hope we had of getting any sleep. Thankfully on the third night we found a better campsite much higher up the ridge-line. This one was more exposed, and for the first time we had a decent view of the canyon as a whole. It was shaped like a mossy gutter, with a slightly flattened 'U' shape three kilometres across, twenty-five kilometres east to west in the portion we could see, stretching off as far as the eye could see. The rain hammered down on our hammock canopies all through the night, but we woke in the morning to extraordinary clarity. We could see mist seething through the trees, growing and receding like smoke from a witch's cauldron. The songs of gibbons resounded the length of the canyon; whoop, whoop, whoop calls getting louder and more insistent, responded to by other equally vocal friends and rivals. We watched the distant black shapes of hornbills flapping over the canopy in squadrons, seeming to struggle with the weight of their own cumbersome beaks.

Eager to make the most of the weather window, we started early, and pushed hard that morning to finally reach the vertical rock. We had carried around forty kilos of ropes and climbing kit all the way up the ridgeline to attack this virgin rock, and prepared ourselves with building excitement. First ascents of rock routes are always treasured. First ascents of entire mountains are a rare privilege. Johnny filmed frantically, Tim fussed around, trying not to frighten me with the dire consequences should I take a fall.

'Don't attempt anything that's even close to your limits, Stevie; remember where you are. This is only telly, it's not worth dying for.'

I slapped chalk on to my fingers, wiped the grime from the soles of my climbing shoes, and levered myself off the ground. Within metres a short overhang took me beyond the eye of Johnny's lens. I was on open warm rock, fabulous views stretching off in every direction, the world at my feet, not merely a climber but an explorer, pushing the boundaries of human knowledge. For about ten metres. After scrabbling up an easy rock ledge, the route plunged back into our favourite tangled, tearing vegetation, where we were to remain for the rest of a horribly frustrating day. The terrain was steep and sketchy, and after the previous day's lucky escape Tim or I had to stop every few metres to fix lines to make the ascent and descent safe. I reckon during that entire day, we pushed on no more than a hundred metres.

Wildlife was hard to come by up here in the moss forest. A vast black rhino beetle the size of a baby's fist with extended head ornaments wandered along one of the green boughs. These accoutrements are used in battles between males, where they try to overthrow each other in order to win the right to mate. Scientists have tested the strength of beetles of this kind, and found they can resist a force equal to 850 times their own weight, making them officially the strongest animals on Earth. My next weird find was a hammerhead flatworm. This is a true weirdo. A broad planarian worm about as long as my handspan from little finger to thumbtip. Its head is shaped exactly like that of a hammerhead shark. Even weirder is the fact these worms are predatory, tracking earthworms, slugs and snails. The flatworm envelops worms, and extends its pharynx out through its mouth on to its prey, then secretes digestive enzymes to dissolve its meal while it's still alive. It'll then suck up the remains when they're good and slimy.

With the route cut and lines in place, it took us only twenty minutes to return to our base camp that night. This time, though, it was with a sense of real excitement. We had been given a glimpse of a proper rock cliff at the top of our endless ridge, and it seemed that would lead us to the top of Mount Kuli. Tomorrow we would surely summit.

The following morning we slogged back up through the tattered tunnel I'd hacked with my trusty machete. We were keeping our eyes on the ground in front of us, because we really didn't want to look up at the skies. Steve Greenwood had organised a helicopter to fly in while we were on the rock walls, getting the wide shots that would finally show this climb in all its majesty. It was the only thing that would give our mission its background and scale, and was costing thousands of pounds. But in order for them to even approach to our level, they needed clear skies. And the cloud cover started about 500 metres below us. We had no contact with the heli or with base. Our only hope was that the cloud would clear, and that they would see us there, our helmets bright unnatural-coloured flecks on the huge blank expanse of rock.

When we finally reached rock, it was horrible: friable sandstone overgrown with vegetation and impossibly brittle. It felt like climbing in a shrubbery, with the added attraction that your handhold was liable to come off in your hand. We were, however, extraordinarily lucky with the severity of the rock. As I've said before, I am not a world-beating rock climber, but an average slogger at best. If the rock had been too easy, the whole thing would have felt like a damp squib. Too hard, and we wouldn't have been able to make the top. What we found was right at the limit of my abilities, enough to give me a serious challenge. The helicopter had been hovering below us, desperately trying to find us, but unable to pierce the clouds. We couldn't wait any longer, we'd have to push on.

On the hardest section of the climb very near the summit, I grabbed hold with both hands on to a vertical slab of rock, bracing myself backwards against it in a move climbers call a 'layback'. Alarmingly, the whole slab shifted with a rasping noise, and I barely had time to leap sideways before the whole thing came away from the face and a half-ton chunk of rock slid right off, skidded past my feet over the top of my ropes, then slid past Tim with a metre or so to spare. I had a matter of seconds to catch my breath, still my beating heart, realise I was alive, then to look down to Johnny, who would have got the shot that would surely justify our whole expedition and feature in all the trailers for the series. He was staring up at me in dismay. The camera was fogged up with humidity. There was nothing he could do.

It was then, hanging on by my very fingertips, that I saw it. Skittering around on the rock in front of me was a huge bright-red ant, the size of a 9-amp fuse. Something about the way it was moving caught my attention; scampering forward at speed, then stopping dead, tapping around with its sensory antenna before speeding off again. Not the movements of an ant at all, but something familiar, something I watched often at home in the UK . . . but what was it? Then as I looked at it closer, I noticed that what appeared to be the characteristic narrow waist or pedicel of this monster ant wasn't actually there – it was fake; merely an hourglass narrowing of the abdomen. As I watched, fascinated, I realised the 'ant' was not working with his smaller black cousins, he was hunting them. The shape of the cephallum, the way it was moving . . . there was no doubt in my mind: this wasn't an ant, it was a tiger beetle of the family Cincindelidae. This was mostly down to the way they run. Tiger beetles can get up to 5mph, 120 body lengths a second. If you scale Usain Bolt up to those proportions, he'd be running 480mph! This is so fast, that the tiger beetle's vision becomes blurred, its brain unable to catch up with the world around it. As it's sprinting, the antenna are held out in front of it stiffly, functioning like a blind man's white stick. It frequently stops in order to allow the smudge of its vision to clarify, and its prey to come into focus. The staccato motion is unmistakeable. It was definitely a tiger beetle, but one pretending to be an ant.

This in itself is nothing unusual. Mimicry is a commonplace oc-currence in biology. The best-known examples are probably Latin American snakes. While the vast majority of snakes are camou-flaged to blend in with their environment, some come in bright, lurid colours. Coral snakes, for example, are members of the cobra family, with short fangs at the front of their mouths, and lethal venom; the bands of red, white and black along their bodies adver-tises their presence by what's known as aposematic colouration or 'honest signalling'. The bright colours are a warning to predators to leave them well alone. 15–20 per cent of snake species in the region also have these colours . . . but not the venom! They gain protection against predators, who see the bright bands and think danger, but they don't have to manufacture venom, which burns up an extremely high amount of energy. This kind of con trick is called Batesian mimicry, named after the naturalist who first described it.

In Borneo, the creatures that cause the most misery to every other animal are not snakes but ants. This may seem bonkers when you're accustomed to British ants that are at worst a mild annoyance at a picnic, but in the forests of Borneo ants inflict vicious bites and stings, and can gang up on other animals in extreme numbers. Because of this, many birds and mammals will give ants a wide berth. Thus it is of benefit to be a Batesian mimic of an ant. Many other invertebrates have become convincing ant-mimics; hundreds of species of mantids, stick and leaf insects, spiders, flies, bugs and other beetles have gained protection from evolving to look like ants. Indeed, one of the expedition's biggest triumphs came when Dr George McGavin, our resident entomologist, discovered a completely new species of ant-mimicking jumping spider. I'd done my research ahead of the climb, but had never heard of an ant-mimicking tiger beetle – let alone one that was the size of a baby's finger and the colour of glowing red molten lava. I started to sweat with anticipation, I could almost taste the glory. I envisioned myself wowing the ladies at dinner parties with tales of how I found a new species while hanging off a cliff face by my fingernails, in my head I heard the applause as I accepted lifetime fellowship of the Royal Entomological Society . . . OK, I was getting a bit carried away there!

But I had something of a conundrum. You can't identify a new species without a 'halotype', that is a specimen that you preserve so it can be kept in a museum. George had given me strict instructions to bring back anything interesting, but all my collecting pots were in my bag at the bottom of the face. I had no camera, it was starting to rain, and the week-awaited summit was no more than ten metres away from me. My fingers and forearms were starting to vibrate with the effort of clinging on, and I couldn't hold my position much longer. I briefly considered catching it in my hand, but knew I would have to use that hand between there and the top. Squished tiger beetle was even less use than no beetle at all. There was a moment where I considered popping it into my mouth and trying to keep it alive till the top, but that was crazy talk. I could probably have down-climbed and retrieved a collecting tin, but the top was so close, and it had been so risky getting here . . . Teeth grinding in agitation, I hung there looking at my prize, hunting those he was so elegantly imitating. There was no doubting his true identity: with their scuttling gait, massive jaws and huge compound eyes for visual hunting, tiger beetles are one of the most easily identifiable of all the coleoptera. Eventually, though, there was no evading the issue any longer. I either had to go down or up. I gingerly reset myself, and continued upwards.

A few metres above me, the rock ran into a dangling brush of tree branches and foliage, hanging like a fringe over the forehead of the rockface. Without my machete, I yanked and pulled my way through the vegetation, tying off my climbing ropes to the sturdiest-looking tree roots. Within metres, and it levelled out – flat ground! We were on the top, I was the first man ever to scale the north face of Mount Kuli, and the first person ever to stand on top!

Not wanting to waste my excitement, and desperate that Johnny and Tim should share in the glory, I fixed a rope that they could ascend, and drew them up. Tim's first reaction was to punch me in the arm with a look of severity. 'I told you not to climb anything that hard!' he scolded, before his face broke out into the Tim smile I value most of all. Johnny was not far behind, camera rolling, sweat pouring down his face but full of joy and excitement. Instead of the bare rock we'd expected, the summit was covered in spindly forest, cut through with game trails from mouse deer and pig that obviously foraged up here. But that was not all.

'What's this?' blurted an incredulous Belfast voice. 'Oh God, this is not good, this is not good.'

Tim and I turned to see Johnny standing up on a rock which seemed to be the highest point on Kuli, with a bewildered look on his face.

'Stevo, look at this, man!'

I looked down at Johnny's feet. There was a crushed cigarette packet in the mud. Looking up and around us in confusion, we fought to find an explanation for the conundrum. Maybe it had fallen from a helicopter? Perhaps it had blown up here on the wind? But then we saw it. Alongside the boulder, tied to a cut stick, was a mouldy old red sock. It was an improvised flag.

'This is a bad do,' said Tim with characteristic calmness.

'I'll tell ya what this is,' said Johnny. 'It's a load of old ballacks!'

We were not the first people to conquer this summit. In fact, looking around, it seemed that people often came up here. When we finally got to see the footage from the helicopter, it was clear why. From inside the canyon, Mount Kuli was the vile north face that we had broached. From either side, it was a knife-edged ridge-line that would have been even worse. But from the south side, the mountain sloped off relatively easily. Our maps and satellite images showed that this side was covered with virgin forest, stretching for miles, with no human settlements of any kind. However, in this fast-changing environment those maps were already outdated. The mobile signal my phone picked up on the ascent should have been a hint. Illegal logging camps had already made their way to within a few miles of Imbak. Poachers in pursuit of game had forged trails from those camps into the surrounding forests, and they'd beaten a path all the way to our summit. A summit we'd taken a week to climb, and nearly killed ourselves in the process.

We were all bitterly disappointed, but this soon faded away. There was no question that we'd made the first ascent of the north face, and it had been a grand adventure. Plus, it was real, and the reality of every story is to my mind the most important thing; there's no point pretending the world is still the Garden of Eden; there are truths and lessons to be learned from how things really are. Plus people are more likely to believe you when you do eventually come to a virgin summit and put your hand on your heart and say, 'We are the first people ever to set foot here.' Not everyone at the BBC agreed. The executive in charge said that the finale made not only us, but the whole of the Natural History Unit look foolish. He insisted that the reality of the summit would have to be edited out, and our reactions glossed over. It was the only intentional tinkering with authenticity I witnessed in the course of these (often brutally) honest BBC expeditions.

Days later, when I returned to base camp, my first stop was George's hammock. I described my find in as much detail as possible, eager to learn whether my ant-mimicking tiger beetle may be a new species or not. George is known for his enthusiastic manner, particularly about all things bug, on which he is a worldwide authority. His response was unequivocal: 'Fantastic! That's certainly a new species, maybe even a new group – there's nothing like that in the keys . . . So where's the specimen?' I took a glass of our dollar-a-bottle whisky, which tasted a bit like Windowlene, and had a quick slug. 'Well, George, it's like this . . .'

Ultimately what I took away from the Kuli experience was the consciousness of failure. There is nothing, absolutely nothing more likely to nag eternally at your brain than the sense that you held a miracle of huge potential in your hand, and let it slip away. I know full well that when I'm on my deathbed, I won't be looking back to awards, grand achievements or high moments. I'll be thinking of that damn beetle. Somehow in my mind it's come to represent missed opportunity. Rarely a week goes by, even now, that I don't think about it, and rue the discovery that never was. If anything, it has made me all the more determined to do everything in my power to suck the juice out of every morsel in life. I never want to look back and think 'What if?' No one can hope to achieve every goal they set their heart on and mistakes are inevitable. But you stand a far better chance of achieving big things if you say yes, if you open your heart and mind to exciting ideas and opportunities. In the words of the legendary ice hockey player Wayne Gretsky, 'You miss 100 per cent of the shots you don't take.'

While I may have missed my personal chance with the discovery that never was, the expedition itself had far more broad-reaching successes. When it was over, Steve and I met with the head honcho at Yayasan Sabah and presented him with our findings: the animals we'd filmed, the new species we'd seen, the evidence we'd found that logging and poaching were already encroaching into Imbak, which was potentially one of the jewels of Sabah. On our first meeting he had seemed arrogant, distracted, and barely paid us any attention. He had not even heard of Imbak canyon and certainly didn't seem to be affording it any thought. This time he looked at us with keen eyes, and listened to our words carefully. Now that the documentary had been made it would be broadcast in over a hundred countries around the world, including his own, which meant he was facing a potential public relations disaster . . . or a triumph, if handled correctly.

A month or so later, Imbak Canyon was afforded grade one park protection status, the highest level of protection his nation allowed. In the years that followed, a permanent conservation camp was built on the site of our base camp, alongside the wonderful falls where we used to wash our smalls. Now a steady trickle of Raleigh gap-yah students, undergraduates and even tourists can discover the wonders of Imbak for themselves. The park covers 30,000 hectares or 300,000,000 square metres – an area the size of the Isle of Wight – that will be protected for the future, where orang-utans and clouded leopards can make their home. It seemed pretty significant when we were in amongst it all, but the sad truth is that it is now one of a few remaining islands of vitality in the midst of a growing wasteland. Borneo's forests will only survive in comparatively tiny pockets like this, so protecting national parks is vital. The destruction of such a precious resource is a travesty and a tragedy that makes my heart weep, but I am truly proud to have had a small role in protecting one minuscule part of it.

THE ROOF OF
THE WORLD

'A ship is safest in harbour, but that's not what ships are built for.'   *John. A. Shedd*

My foot is encased in a concrete boot. Lifting it and placing it slightly above the other takes fixed concentration, as if it is no longer a part of me at all. Fatigue, hunger and thirst, combined with the down suit I'm wearing, like some Michelin man fancy-dress costume, have turned me into something resembling an astronaut on a high-gravity spacewalk. I move in slow-motion, as if encased in my own little bubble. The hood encloses my head like a helmet, shutting out sounds. My headlamp throws a small pool of light on the slope in front of me, which is all I can focus on. My oxygen mask covers the lower part of my face. Huge down mitts fumble at the ropes with all the dexterity of a grizzly bear trying to thread a needle. Far above me a dozen tiny fairy lights jink and jangle as if bouncing from the boughs of a swaying Christmas tree – the headlamps of another climbing team a couple of hours ahead of us. The thermometer reads minus thirty, and as we crest the summit plateau we find ourselves battling winds so strong I estimate the wind-speed to be fifty miles an hour. But finally, as the sky turns to blue, the real world emerges into focus, and it's the most beautiful thing I have ever seen. I have never felt so high, looking out to a horizon that extends hundreds of miles in every direction, looking down on peaks that would dwarf the highest on every other continent. Even Everest right next us, seems to be lower. As the sun slowly rises, the mountains around us gain new depth and become three-dimensional. And then across the landscape, seemingly all the way to the edge of the Earth, a dark pyramid begins to grow. It is the shadow of our mountain, its grim and perfect imprint dominating everything, commanding the greatest mountain range on the planet. It is a moment of such awe that I cannot ever hope to repeat its wonder.

It's been said that extreme high-altitude mountaineering is like banging one's head against a brick wall. Kind of cool . . . once you stop. Personally, I would compare it to a month-long absinthe hangover. You spend days longing for sleep the night can never offer; you're ravenously hungry and burning thousands of calories, yet too nauseous to eat; you're irritable, exhausted and the slightest exertion leaves you gasping for breath. Even at base camp, which at 5,885 metres is as high as Kilimanjaro, something as simple as tying your shoelaces can have you puffing like an asthmatic. It seems the most ludicrous folly, even though it's giving you the opportunity to spend long weeks in the most dramatic scenery on Earth.

I'd returned to the UK after my 2006 Borneo expeditions with most of the autumn work-free, but my appetite for adventure not yet sated. As soon as I was home, I began calling everyone I knew in climbing, trying to find someone, anyone, who'd be prepared to come away into the hills with me.

In the past I'd have had plenty of takers, but this time I drew a massive blank. Most of the people I'd been climbing with in previous years were now at that age where they were getting married and having kids, or they had proper jobs that wouldn't allow them to take six weeks off for a trip to the mountains. So I needed an expedition I could do alone, that wouldn't cost the earth, yet could give me a decent achievement, and some proper time in the big mountains.

Most of the commercial trips were too expensive, or the wrong time of year to fit my schedule. But one company's name kept coming up. They specialised in facilitating experienced and self-sufficient mountaineers on expeditions into the greater ranges. Essentially they'd organise your permits and a base camp, and leave you to do the rest. Consequently the costs were low, you'd be climbing along-side a team of ready-made mountain chums, and there was always the option of hiring a porter to help get you into base camp, and Sherpas to help in the final ascent. It was perfect, and the one peak that was on offer for my timeframe was a biggie: Cho Oyu – 8,201 metres above sea level, the sixth-highest peak on Earth, and right next to Everest.

The name Cho Oyu is Tibetan for 'Turquoise Goddess'. It marks the border between Tibet and Nepal, and offers all the challenges you'd expect from an 8,000-metre peak (there are only fourteen on the planet, all of them in the Himalayas). Cho Oyu was first attempted in 1952 by a team led by Eric Shipton and including Edmund Hillary, who was training for his Everest attempt. To this day many climbers use Cho Oyu as a dry run for Everest. This first team was driven back by avalanche danger high up, then forced to flee the area when reports came in of Chinese troops massing across the border. Two years later the peak was finally summited by an Austrian team who climbed the north-west ridge, the same route I would be attempting.

The plan was to start our climb from Tibet, to the north of Cho Oyu, but the journey itself began in Kathmandu, Nepal. This has been the start and finish point for so many expeditions, it's as if the city was built with that in mind. The centre of the 'hippy trail' for travellers across Asia since the 1960s, the centre of Thamel was up there on the traditional backpacker's pantheon with Bangkok's Khaosan Road, Goa and Bali. That means you can stick yourself in a café surrounded by dreadlocked Israelis and vest-wearing Australians, watching rip-off DVDs while eating banana pancakes and swapping torn-out sections of Lonely Planet guidebooks. For me, it's a nostalgic throwback to my days as a professional backpacker. During my time working for Rough Guide I trawled round thousands of cafés rubbing shoulders with the kaftan-clad and clichéd, from terrified white boys fresh out of Heathrow to seasoned nut-brown pros. It's a scene that evokes mixed emotions in me these days. Those years travelling solo in the early and mid 1990s played a vital role in setting my goals in life and giving me the confidence to organise and run expeditions. At the same time, even back then I could see the negative impact that this influx of backpackers was having. It's understandable that developing countries where the inhabitants earn and own very little would fall over themselves to accommodate hordes of middle-class trustafarians driven by the desire to get drunk, stoned and party in ever more exotic and cheap destinations. Unfortunately, in the process these beautiful places are changed irrevocably, their unique culture diluted and degraded, homogenised by the very tourists who've travelled all that way to experience them.

While the abiding memories of my own solo travels involve hacking my way through uncharted rainforests or downing pints of still-warm buffalo blood at a funeral ceremony with a tribe that had never seen white people before, the fact remains I was once a terrified skinny white boy who pitched up in Thailand on his travels (the term 'Gap year' hadn't been invented then) and made straight for Chiang Mai and the famous Full Moon parties along with the rest of the crowd. I spent two months basically on an extended holiday before I got up the confidence to walk away from the madding crowd and go and achieve the things I wanted – learning native languages, living with the real people, making an effort to ignore the guidebooks and visit places nobody else ever got to. Even then, I was still part of the problem. The villages and islands I went to where no one had ever seen a white person before would have been more irrevocably changed by my visit than Kuta Beach in Bali would be transformed by a few Italians sunbathing topless. And after my spells of tough independent travel, I still gravitated back to places like Kathmandu to eat banana pancakes like everyone else. The fact is, the world is changing – and at a terrifying rate. All we can do is take responsibility for ourselves, show sensitivity to local sensibilities and culture, and spend our money with those that need it rather than the big multinational companies that don't.

The backpacker scene in Kathmandu is very much concentrated around Thamel, and the one thing that sets it apart from other travellers' centres is that it is the best place in the world to buy second-hand mountaineering equipment. You can pick up Russian-made titanium ice screws for about a fiver, and Chinese rip-off North Face down jackets for about the cost of a pint back home. As soon as I arrived, the obligatory kid-in-a-candy store melee was under way. I got my old sleeping bag re-stuffed with duck down, my favourite Gore-Tex jacket fixed, and bought a pair of high-altitude mitts that would have set me back a small fortune in the UK, but here were about the same price as breakfast.

Filming commitments meant I'd arrived in Nepal some days after my party had already departed, so I hooked up with members of another expedition in order to head up towards our mountain. The battered bus took us half a day's drive from the city through lush green Nepalese mountains. Early afternoon, as the road curled around steep hillsides, the sun's rays penetrated the precipitous gorge below us and glittered off the raging white waters of the Sun Khosi river. And then a strange concrete monstrosity came into view, spanning the gorge: the so-called 'Friendship Bridge', which links Nepal and Chinese-occupied Tibet. On either side were lines of trucks, some facing a wait of many days before they'd get clearance to cross over. In order to circumvent the red tape, lines of porters formed human chains to hand the entire contents of the lorries across the bridge.

It turned out our bus would face the same red-tape barrier as the lorries, so we all disembarked and sat drinking tea in a café to the side of the bridge for a few hours while our guide greased the wheels with a few hundred dollars in bribes. Then we shouldered our bags and trekked past the white concrete box of the border post, emblazoned with black writing in Mandarin script and red flags. The entrances were lined with stern-faced Chinese soldiers all bristling with automatic weapons.

The bridge itself was like the eye of the storm. There were very few people and no vehicles on its broad road. It was quiet and clean, with a spectacular drop over the side to the river beneath. We had been warned not to linger too long, and under no circumstances to risk taking cameras out to snap the view; apparently the men who seemed to be enjoying a casual smoke while contemplating the vista were plain-clothes Chinese security, ready to pounce on any transgressions. We tried to take mental photos of the weird scene and then, a few minutes later, we were in China. And it felt like it. The display of red military might was in your face from minute one. A huge poster loomed above the bridge, showing three bright-faced Chinese soldiers, two men and one woman, in characteristic high-peaked military hats, weapons held in front of them, beatific faces turned slightly upwards towards some invisible godlike leader. It called to mind Nazi propaganda posters of the 1930s.

Coming from Nepal, which has to be a contender for smiliest place on Earth, it was all the more of a shock to be confronted with one of the most stern and smile-free zones on the planet. Uniforms and rifles were everywhere, and the air rang to the sound of soldiers barking orders at the porters as they scampered across with blue plastic barrels packed full of climbing equipment and food.

We boarded a different bus and set off on China National Highway 318. Known, without a hint of irony, as the 'Friendship Highway', the road travels 800 miles to Lhasa, the capital of Tibet.

Much of the strife in Tibet is due (as are so many problems in the region) to the efforts of my ancestors. In the 1850s, the British embarked on a series of invasions, capturing Nepal, Sikkim, Bhutan and Burma. It was 1904 when Tibet finally fell, thanks to the efforts of Lord Curzon and Colonel Younghusband, and was declared a British protectorate. Over the years, Tibet gained a degree of independence, but this did not sit well with the newly established People's Republic of China. In 1949, Mao Zedong declared his intention to bring Tibet under Communist control, and 7 October 1950 Chinese troops crossed the Yangtze River. The Tibetan nation was barely defended, and what troops they had stood no chance against the million-strong Red Army. The rest of the world was preoccupied with events in Korea, and made little complaint against the invasion. In 1959, when the Chinese captured Lhasa, the Dalai Lama fled to India, where he has been ever since. Amnesty International estimates 1.2 million Tibetans were killed in the years following the invasion, about a fifth of the population. Many more languished in prisons and labour camps. Over six thousand monasteries, temples and historical and cultural sites were razed to the ground. In 1981, Alexander Solzhenitsyn described the Chinese regime in Tibet as 'more brutal and inhumane than any other communist regime in the world'. Opponents to the regime and participants in demonstrations against Chinese rule in Lhasa are 'disappeared', never to be heard of again. Thanks to the huge unregulated influx of Chinese into the fertile regions and cities of Tibet, in many areas they outnumber the natives by two and sometimes three to one.

And while the Chinese flouted the Geneva Convention and denied the Tibetan people the basic freedoms of speech, assembly, self-determination, movement, expression and travel guaranteed under the Universal Declaration of Human Rights, the rest of the world remained silent. Few world leaders were prepared to speak out in defence of a country with few natural resources when to do so would risk offending China.

It's not just the human population of Tibet who've suffered. The high Tibetan plateau is one of the most fragile environments on Earth. Before the invasion, wildlife was so abundant that visitors compared the region to the plains to East Africa with its swarming herds of strange antelope and mountain goats. The Tibetan antelope or chiru resembles the iconic oryx of Africa with its long rapier-shaped horns. They used to roam in herds thousands of animals strong, perhaps a million animals in total, until truckloads of Chinese soldiers took to strafing the herds with automatic gunfire and pretty much wiped them out, along with most of the other native wildlife. The land now appears so barren, so lifeless that it's closer to a Martian landscape than the veldt. In all my travels in the region I've never seen a chiru.

Tibet's forests were once vast, but since the 1950s they have been plundered, with no attempt at reforestation. Potentially even more destructive are the hydro-electric systems required to meet the insatiable energy demands of the most populous nation on Earth. Reporting on the construction of a massive power plant on the sacred lake of Yamdrok Tso, the *Independent* noted: 'environmentalists fear this giant project will create one of China's worst ecological disasters of the 21st century'. Having visited Chinese industrial centres that look like post-apocalyptic dystopian nightmares and national parks that are utterly silent, without even a single bird singing, the prospect of something worse in store is utterly terrifying.

One of my most memorable experiences of traditional Tibetan life was in Thikse Monastery in Ladakh. It sits on a tit of grey rock popping up from the flat glacial valley floor, joined to the fledgling mountainsides by a thin causeway that carries the road up to the base of the monastery, a twelve-storey complex of bright stucco-plastered edifices with delicately carved wooden embellishments. Most of the outer walls are a deep vermillion colour, but some of the buildings have been painted in shades of rusty orange or dirty yellow. In the open-air courtyard of the monastery (against the backdrop of the sun setting behind the leviathan summits), a debating class was going on for about fifty young monks. None was older than eleven years old, they all had their heads shaved and wore dark scarlet robes. They debated in pairs, one sitting on the ground on a plank of wood, while the other stood in front of him and declaimed a series of questions from the teachings of the Buddha. At the end of each question the enquirer would lunge towards his partner and clap his hands in his face. Both questions and responses were yelled with considerable gusto, and the cacophony was so loud as to drown out conversation.

Every Buddhist family aims to send at least one son to a life of religion, seeking enlightenment and further progression on the path to Nirvana. This may seem harsh, until you see how much those boys seem to enjoy what they're doing, living in what would have to rate as one of the most awe-inspiring places I have ever seen. I envied them; I even envied their faith and spirituality.

Around the outside of one level of the monastery runs a line of prayer wheels the size of catering cans of coffee. You walk the perimeter of the building, keeping the wheels on your right, spinning each wheel as you pass it, and chanting 'truth will prevail' (preferably in Tibetan) with each spin. I can't even begin to explain the significance and purpose, but if a confirmed old cynic like me could feel the mystical effect, it had to be something potent.

The peace and simplicity which typifies Tibetan traditional life has been crushed out of existence in much of Tibet itself. It's heartbreaking to think quite how completely this rich and gentle culture has been repressed and destroyed.

We began our journey across the Tibetan plateau, a barren desert with an *average* height above sea level greater than the summits in the Alps. The place seems to suck the moisture and life out of your body, and its deathly dry air had everyone coughing and wheezing. These coughs were in many cases to last for the duration of the expedition, and put an end to summit hopes. The second night we stopped at the town of Nyalam, which translates as 'Hell's Gate'. It lives up to the name, being dusty and arid, with a few forsaken remnants of Tibetan buildings where local people still wear their long black hair wound through vibrant red scarves and cowbells, white teeth flashing against mahogany-tanned skin. These days, however, the town is dominated by modern concrete monstrosities with all the charm of 1960s multistorey car parks. All of the businesses in town are Chinese-owned, and everyone working there is Chinese. Many Tibetans sit out in the streets, a proud and gentle culture driven to begging for scraps.

With no choice but to uphold the status quo, we stayed in the Snow Hotel, stomping its carpets decked out in thousands of pounds' worth of modern mountaineering clothing and giving our money to the Chinese owners. To their credit, every single one of my climbing companions took care to slip a few notes or luxuries to the Tibetan people we saw sitting in the streets outside.

From here, the Friendship Highway headed up to a 5,000-metre-high pass, higher than Mont Blanc, though it turned out to be a vast orange-brown plateau that seemed to go on forever. At the highest point was a metal archway, bedecked with a hundred thousand once-colourful but now sun-bleached prayer flags, fluttering bleakly in the howling wind. Our next stop was the desiccated frontier town of Tingri at 4,300 metres, 60 kilometres from Mount Everest. This place was straight out of the Wild West, the dust road lined on either side by a single row of battered wooden cabins, their paint bleached by fierce high-altitude UV. Flyblown sides of beef and less identifiable carcasses hung outside butchers' shops, while beaten horses dragged wooden traps down the streets. Yet even in this nowhere town in the middle of the desert, the Chinese military maintained a strong presence. A red flag stood proudly above every single building, and army trucks spilled heavily-armed, cigarette-smoking teenagers in uniform.

Eager to escape the depressing realities of Tingri, I took a bottle of water and yomped up a nearby peak to acclimatise my body to the intense altitude, stumbling over hot rock to gaze down on the immensity of the plateau. A few hours' trekking brought me to a point at the same height as Europe's highest peak, Mount Elbrus. Gasping for breath, head thumping from the thin air, I took in the vista of the town below. Tingri's blocky white buildings sprawled over a bigger area of the plateau than I had appreciated; a town of nearly 600 inhabitants, it was dominated by the Chinese garrison to one side. The unassuming curved peaks beyond seemed little more than hills in this landscape, but would surely dwarf the highest peaks on any other continent. The outstanding views, however, lay to the south and east. The day was cloudless, and though a little hazy with windblown dust, I could clearly see the north face of Everest, iconic and instantly recognisable to any mountaineer. I was alone, and had no guide to tell me otherwise, but the peak to the west had to be our mountain, Cho Oyu. As it was closer to us, it appeared far bigger than Everest, and had a majesty about it that sent an excited chill up my spine. Until that point I'd been somewhat underwhelmed by the prospect; Cho Oyu is not renowned as a particularly technical climb and wouldn't normally have been on my radar, I'd ended up here by default because nothing better was on offer. But standing here, gazing at the highest mountains on the planet and knowing I would soon be standing on top of one of them . . . it gave me goosebumps.

Perhaps it was arrogance to be so confident of success – this was after all an 8,000-metre mountain – but I was still flush with the self-belief of (relative) youth and certain I could do anything I set my mind to. I was also in the best physical condition of my life. My success on the Marathon Des Sables had led to a passion for fell-running. After a year or so of doing big mileage it suddenly clicked, and started to feel like I could run forever. There is nothing more joyous and liberating than flying over a mountain track in carpet-slipper-thin fell-running trainers. Theoretically Cho Oyu should have been well within my capabilities . . . as long as I could stay fit and healthy. But as legendary Austrian mountaineer Hermann Buhl once said, 'Mountains have a way of dealing with overconfidence.'

Getting high then sleeping low is one of the keys to acclimatising. You push yourself as much as possible during the daytime, then make sure you have thicker air during the nights. That way the body starts to manufacture more haemoglobin to transport oxygen efficiently. If you rush the process, you run the risk of altitude-related illnesses, which could put an end to your expedition, and possibly your life. The very next day, I paid the price for my over-enthusiasm. Cho Oyu base camp wasn't far but it involved a 1,500-metre ascent, so the wise thing was to take it slow and easy – after all, we had loads of time and would be living at that altitude for a month; there was no point in rushing it. But in my arrogance and over-eagerness I practically sprinted to the campsite while burdened with a full pack, revelling in the strength in my lungs and legs. It was situated in a rather lovely meadow, with ankle-high flowers and semi-permanent fairground-style tents made up of tarpaulins and blankets and equipped with wood-fired stoves. These would provide much-needed refuge from the wind and sun outside. Mahogany-faced Tibetans flashed white teeth at me as I entered, and invited me to put down my pack and join them for yak butter tea and a bowl of soup noodles. As soon as I sat down with them, I realised I'd been hitting it too hard. My shallow breathing and pounding heart rate still hadn't stabilised thirty minutes after sitting down, and I was feeling light-headed. The dazzling white light outside given me a slight headache, but the diffuse white light inside the tent seemed even more unbearable. I wanted nothing more than to lie down and stick my head in a bucket.

Pitching my tent seemed to take an eternity, and not just because the wind seemed intent on blowing the whole thing off over the horizon. The simple act of clicking the poles together took all the concentration I could muster. I was feeling nauseous and the head-ache was thudding behind my eyes. As soon as my tent was up, I collapsed inside with my sleeping bag wrapped around my head. The wind was howling, flapping the tent in an unbearable repeti-tive noise like an old-fashioned prop plane trying to take off. Eyes closed to blot out the intensity of the light, I felt around in my pack for my iPod, slipped the buds into my ears, and prepared to listen to some soothing music. As soon as I pressed the play button, there was a pop and then the winding-down sound of electronics dying. Nothing. I was later to find out that some pieces of technology need a certain amount of air pressure to 'allow the heads to float above the hard drive'. The iPod started working again once the expedition was over and I descended below 3,500 metres, but that was a month later. The one luxury I'd afforded myself, and it didn't even work!

I lay there the entire night without moving, clothing wrapped around my face to ease the migraine. I was beyond tired, but sleep would not take me. Classic acute mountain sickness. Damn me and my stupid over-eagerness! When the morning finally came, I

Top Mount Kuli seen from the south, our face lies behind the peak

Above With Tim Fogg on the grimy hack towards the summit of Kuli

Left Cameraman Johnny Rogers on the ridge that nearly cost him his life

Below With Tim and Johnny on the summit of Kuli, shortly after discovering the sock and cigarette packet

Right Camp Two on Cho Oyu

Below right With Tarx after dragging him out of a crevasse

Top With Sammi and Dave at Camp Three on Cho Oyu

Above The shadow of Cho Oyu cast across Tibet

Top The team: Tim, me, Steve, John, Ivan, Fuco and Keith, with Upuigma behind

Above Waking up on the ledge on top of Upuigma

Left Climbing vertical ropes

Below Shortly before the fall
on one of the crux pitches

Right Waking up with hundreds of
metres of empty air beneath us

Below right Portaledge life

Top Slogging across the summit forest of Upuigma, where every step is the first a human has ever taken. Possibly the most exciting moment of my life!

Middle John Arran dragging himself throug[h] bromeliads shortly after reaching the top

Left The mystery Upuigma frog

got up, puked in front of my tent and dragged myself to the mess tent. Everyone else was in fine spirits. Several of my companions were in their sixties, and having seen me taking such pleasure in my sprint up the mountain the day before there was no doubt a touch of schadenfreude at my predicament.

Though I'd brought with me bottles of the two climber's pills of Dexymethasone and Diamox, I'd promised myself I wouldn't use them. Yet here I was, day one, cracking open the Diamox. I took a half a tablet every day from there on in. Diamox forces the kidneys to excrete bicarbonate, re-acidifying the blood, which acts as a respiratory stimulant. By making you breathe more, it gets more oxygen into your system. One of the side effects is that you need to wee more often. I also got weird pins and needles in my hands, and for weeks everything tasted of sulphur. Fizzy drinks were completely undrinkable.

While the rest of the team headed on up the mountain, I spent the morning feeling very sorry for myself, and not a little stupid. I knew how important it was to be in shape when I made base camp and met up with the guys who would be my climbing companions for the next month, yet here I was, already suffering from altitude sickness like some muppet amateur.

Luckily it wasn't much of a march and I arrived at the crazy colourful trading post that is Cho base camp as a glorious sunset started to burn the mountaintops magenta and gold. The surrounding area is too steep to make camp, so tents have to be pitched amongst the rubble of a glacial moraine. For the next month we would be sleeping on rocks, which meant a never-ending battle to flatten out the floor as much as possible. It was a classic princess and pea situation, except here the pea in the small of your back would turn out to be a rock the size of a melon. The thin inhabitable area ranged from 5,400 metres in elevation to just under 6,000 metres, making it one of the world's highest base camps. The sites at the lower end of the glacier were the most coveted, and had been claimed by the first of the thirty-odd expeditions to arrive on the mountain in the post-monsoon season. These expeditions would have further to walk before they could begin their trudge up the mountain, but that was a small price to pay for the advantage of sleeping half a kilometre lower. These happy campers would suffer fewer altitude-related illnesses and would recover more quickly from their exertions.

Surrounded by munching yaks and scuttling porters stretched for over a mile, the tents occupied every vaguely flat piece of land. Most expeditions tended to have the same tents, so to aid identification each tent was decorated like a colour-coded Mardi Gras float, adorned with washing lines and strings of prayer flags. It hadn't snowed in a good while, and the rocks and hillsides were clear of white but alive with black Himalayan chough that circled and swirled in clouds, feeding off the detritus of several hundred mountaineers in this temporary city above the clouds. Peaks towered over us on all sides, but they were all dwarfed by Cho herself. No matter where you stood on the base camp moraine, your view of the mountain was always framed by lines of fluttering blue, green, red, white and yellow prayer flags, their messages imprisoned in the unseeing winds and blown with restless violence round about the pendant world.

There had already been one death on the mountain that year. German climber Raimund Sprang had summited but then fallen on his descent, sliding seventy metres before hitting his head and tumbling into an ice chasm. He had been buried on Cho Oyu. It was a sobering reminder that mountains don't only give, they often take away.

Finally I found the cluster of tents that belonged to our expedition. They had clearly been the absolute last arrival at the mountain, as we were right at the top of the moraine, as high as it was possible to be and still be in base camp. My altimeter showed our tents were a smidgeon under 6,000 metres – we would be sleeping at the same height as the summit of Kilimanjaro. I took a deep breath. This was going to be harder than I had anticipated. Worse still, our next-door neighbour was the Chinese military camp. While everybody else's tents were hung with Buddhist prayer flags in keeping with Himalayan traditions, their ring of tents was dominated by a central flagpole with a red flag blowing as if it were throwing down a challenge.

I arrived as dinner was being served in the main tent, and my noisy crew were all assembled along trestle tables under a patch of canvas I would soon get to know very well. Having spent ten days together on the jaunt up from Kathmandu, they were now either strong friends or starting to get on each other's nerves. These bonds would become tighter and the annoyances more pronounced with each passing day. Unlike the expensive 'guided' expeditions where porters carry everything and you're pretty much dragged up by a personal Sherpa, our group had no deadwood.

We had fifteen fit, experienced, self-sufficient mountaineers on our team, all determined to climb the mountain. Perhaps the most eye-catching were Sammi and Jere, two very able Finnish mountaineers, physically imposing and beaming confidence. Samuli Mansikka had film-star looks, straight white-blonde hair, ice-blue eyes and ruddy red cheeks. He looked strong enough to hoist a yak on to his shoulder and run up the mountain with it. It was to be his first 8,000er, though he would go on to become one of the world's strongest high-altitude mountaineers, summiting ten times on 8,000-metre peaks, including Everest and K2 without oxygen. His compatriot Jere was taller, with a generous ginger beard. Both did that involuntary sucking in of breath through the teeth to register 'affirmative' that I've come across before in Scandinavians. I didn't have long to contemplate this with Jere, though, as he spent most of his time stooped double with a horrendous hacking cough – and he wasn't the only one afflicted. There are many possible reasons: fine glacial silt in our drinking water, the desert dust carried by the wind from the Tibetan plateau below, or the plummet in temperature at night. Whatever the cause, for many unlucky climbers it develops into HAPE (High-Altitude Pulmonary Edema), which ends all hope of summiting the mountain.

Steve Lawes, Steve Marsh and Lee Farmer were from the UK, and blew my hope of anonymity by unmasking me to the others as a TV presenter. Accomplished adventurers with lengthy expedition CVs, the Steves were both policemen. Even in their high-tech mountain gear, they were unmistakably coppers; their stories were always prefaced with the time and date, then they'd adopt a staccato, fact-based delivery as if they were down the station reporting to the guvnor. They might as well have produced notebook and truncheon before going into the old "Ello, 'ello, 'ello, what 'ave we 'ere then?' comic routine. They were good people, and fun company. Marshy was on the police diving team and told tales of recovering bodies from the weirdest of places, including an industrial-sized vat of yoghurt. He was plagued by 'high-altitude bulimia': everything he ate ended up being noisily vomited out the back of the tent five minutes later. It could well have been a more violent version of my nauseous reaction to Diamox. Or simply the disgusting food. Whatever the reason, Marshy started the trip as a ruddy-faced West Countryman, and by the end looked like a deflated balloon. Steve Lawes was yet another victim of the coughing epidemic and fearful it would scupper his chances of summiting.

Two other tentmates were Jason and Dave. Jason was a ginger American surfer dude with an infectious laugh and upbeat attitude. Under his down jacket, he was dressed for Venice Beach in board shorts and flowery shirts. Dave was an Aussie with close-cropped hair and wasp-like dark glasses that he wore even inside the tent.

When he removed them, he resembled Lance Armstrong, cheek-bones gaunt through pounding pavements and pedals on ironman triathlons. He was even more laid-back than Jason, with a dry, wry sense of humour. Dave was also the only person on the entire expedition who retained his appetite, and ate not only everything that was put in front of him, but all the food the rest of us left. Despite this, he was as skinny as a size-zero supermodel, leading to speculation that he must have an anaconda-sized tapeworm. The three of us would cluster around Jason's tiny travel Scrabble set together every evening. We'd play six or seven games, then one of us would make as if to head to bed and the others would cajole them to play one more game. This would go on for hours and hours.

The day after my arrival was spent sorting out my base camp tent, flattening out the floor, finding the best combination of roll mat and inflatable thermarest, hanging up wash kit and stacking books and belongings in their designated spaces. The following day, our mission proper began. Base camp has half the oxygen present at sea level, or rather a third of the partial pressure of oxygen. Because the air is under less pressure, each breath contains fewer oxygen molecules. The summit of Cho Oyu has only a third of the oxygen you'd find at sea level. If it was possible to be transported up there, you'd be unconscious within minutes, and dead very soon after. So proper acclimatisation is vital at each stage of the journey. How well people acclimatise varies. I've seen first-timers cruise up into the Death Zone oblivious, while experienced climbers who've nailed the highest peaks suddenly go down with altitude sickness. Some super-fit athletes never adapt, while occasionally you'll get overweight forty-a-day smokers who trundle on with no problem. The best you can do is take it slow, go up, come down, go up, come down, and listen to your body as much as possible.

Thus every expedition on the hill was engaged in this ritual of thin-air yoyo, ascending the moraine to the mountain's lower slopes and then heading back down again. As we were a self-supported ex-pedition, we climbed to the high camps carrying backpacks loaded with gear, which we'd drop off for use when we made the final summit attempt. My first push was to Camp 1 at 6,400 metres, and involved a long but pleasant slog through a rocky glacier to a steep shoulder on the mountain proper. From here the trail switchbacked up to a flat promontory with space for about ten tents. We pitched a couple of our spare tents there and dumped a load of climbing gear, plus fuel, stoves and food, before returning to base camp.

Two days later we were back. I made it to Camp 1 in shorts and trainers in a couple of easy hours, feeling like I could carry on to the summit with one of my fellow climbers riding piggyback. Some of us decided to press on and carry a load to Camp 2 at 7,100 metres. This took us on to snow and the first piece of actual climbing on the route, so I had to switch to my big mountaineering boots and crampons. It was nothing major, and all protected by fixed ropes, but I felt that finally the climb proper had begun. I attacked the short roped sections with gusto, and forged on towards Camp 2. Later on in the afternoon, I paid the price: the headache was back. I tried stopping more frequently and guzzling down water in case it was dehydration, but nothing I did had any effect.

It was an intensely hot, windless day, and as the afternoon dragged on my pace slowed until I had to stop and rest after every single step. All I wanted to do was lie down in the snow, dig a hole to plunge my head into like the apocryphal ostrich, hoping the blackness would ease the torment of the white light inside my head. Eventually the pain and fatigue got so intense I could go no further. I lay on my back, still strapped into my pack, with my arms draped across my eyes. It could have been hours later, or maybe only minutes – I was so out of it I couldn't tell – but someone was shaking me into consciousness. I couldn't tell who the climber was behind his heavy glacier glasses and hat, and he seemed to be gabbling in Russian.

'English,' I mumbled to him, pointing to my chest.

'You OK, man?' he replied. 'Don't look so good.'

I could only shake my head. Even talking was too much effort.

'Very close,' he said, taking me firmly by the shoulder. 'One hundred metres more. Very close now.' He was pointing up the trail, and had to be right, it surely couldn't be that far to Camp 2. I nodded my head to show I understood, and he helped me to my feet before heading on his way.

As soon as I rounded the next bend, I could see the flash of colour from the dotted tents at Camp 2. It can only have been ten minutes' walk, but with the flashing fire inside my head and the fatigue in my limbs, it seemed to take hours. A single step, then a stop to steady myself, then another step, another and another. Finally I reached the spot to find that Aussie Dave had erected a tent, with enough room for me to join him. Thank God! I collapsed inside, impervious to the icy cold coming up through the tent floor. It was nightfall before I managed to move and start making myself comfortable. In retrospect, this has to have been one of the scariest things that's happened to me in the mountains. It was an easy section of a mountain I had seen as being almost 'beneath me' in terms of challenge. The weather couldn't have been better. I was well fed, had all the right kit, was in excellent shape; everything was on my side. And yet if the camp had been further away I don't think I could have made it under my own steam. This is the bit you can never get across to non-mountaineers: the sheer commitment required to climb at extreme altitude. When your body says, 'Sorry, buddy, I've had enough,' there's not a lot you can do about it.

After a sleepless night flat out in my sleeping bag, my body seemed to have pressed the reset button. Dave had spent much of the evening gathering and melting snow, so I drank as much as I could, scoffed a few chocolate bars and headed down to dump all my climbing gear, including my big boots, in the tent at Camp 1. The next time I would pass through here would be on the push for the summit itself.

After a day's rest I was firing on all cylinders again, and the prospects looked good. Within ten days of arriving at base camp I'd completed my acclimatisation and felt confident enough to climb alongside Sammi without oxygen. In fact I was so confident I was ready to book an early flight home after my triumph. The plan was to take three or four rest days and then have a pop at the summit. But on rest day two it started to snow. By nightfall it was snowing so heavily that by the time I made it from my tent to the mess tent I looked like Frosty the snowman. And it didn't stop for a week. By then base camp looked like Lapland, buried in a quaint white duvet, with lots of little elves wandering about lost with nothing to do.

I've had some frustrating times on expeditions before, but Cho Oyu was in a class of its own. The snow meant all we could do was sleep and get thin – Marshy's 'bulimia' being the method of choice. We couldn't even get out on to the glacier and do some ice climbing because our gear was buried under six feet of Colombian marching powder up at Camp 1. I'd read every book in camp by day three and played more games of Scrabble than I would choose to in a thousand lifetimes. Far from providing a refuge from tedium, the mess tent was a vision of purgatory: thanks to the Diamox everything tasted as if it had been steamed in rotten eggs (even the huge bar of chocolate I'd brought as a treat had a tang of sulphur), and the tent echoed to the sound of hacking coughs as people sat playing interminable games of cards, retelling the same old expedition stories, or engaging in mindless conversations about sleeplessness and nausea. Hardly surprising that everyone was getting on each other's nerves.

One guy spent the whole time shuffling around with a face like a half-sucked mango; he could have given Marvin the Paranoid

Android a lesson in mindless, self-obsessed negativity. 'I can't believe this is happening to me; we're never going to get up this mountain, never – I've worked so hard for this mountain, and I won't have the chance again – God knows I'm getting older – I could get hit by a bus when I get home and then where would it leave me?' Mute, with a bit of luck.

We also had a Brit who'd lived Stateside for fifteen years and insisted on calling everyone dude and using expressions like 'now THAT's the sh*t I'm talkin' about' and 'you do the math' in a voice that sounded like Jeremy Irons impersonating Robert De Niro. It was all I could do not to point out that he wasn't some hood from Harlem but a skinny white 'dude' from Berkshire. In the end I just kept praying for an extremely localised avalanche.

As you've probably gathered, I don't do boredom. Give me some nice masochistic pain or butt-clenching fear and I'm anybody's, but sitting staring at my tent walls . . . When the high point of your day is having a poo, and the public cogitations thereon, you know things are bad.

It probably seems insane to those who don't do expeditions that those of us who do seem obsessed with having a poo. Truth is, on an expedition it becomes disproportionately important. Imagine wandering out into a snowstorm at minus twenty and trying to find somewhere to go. Or of fighting to manoeuvre yourself into a position on a rock wall without coming out of your harness. It can be the hardest part of the day, but also the most rewarding. Ed Stafford, stranded for two months on a desert island, described his daily poo in detail; for him it became a way of tracking his progress, seeing how his digestive system was coping with the snails and coconut he was feeding it. Flatulent gases can be much the same thing. These are made up of a variety of constituents: methane (which is odourless) and then stinky gases like hydrogen sulphide, and methyl mercaptan. The precise quantities of gas depend on what we've eaten and the health of our digestive system. From an evolutionary perspective, revelling in the smell of our own farts is more than a reminder of a meal, it gives us a running commentary on our own digestive health. This is why we humans are disgusted by the smell of other people's farts, but kind of intrigued by our own!

And there's nothing like a tall toilet tale to relieve the stress of a tense expedition and keep us all amused. On that first mountaineering trip to the Alps I mentioned earlier, we were making our descent when my climbing partner asked me to turn my back then relieved themselves to the side of the slope we were climbing, before wiping then covering it with snow. A moment later one of the Italians coming down behind us appeared and flopped down onto his back in the snow. Without a word, we got our stuff together and headed down the mountain. Another time, on a caving expedition, the only female member of the team went to take a poo break in a side passage then came back to join us in climbing up a tumultuous waterfall. She threw her hood over her head to keep off the water, only to find she'd left something odorous in her hood.

One afternoon I braved the snow and headed down to the camp of legendary mountain guide Kenton Cool and expedition doctor Rob Casserley. Kenton has summited Everest a record-breaking eleven times, including twice in one week, and we had several friends in common. He was working with Russell Brice, the head honcho on these high hills, taking high-paying clients to the summit. While it was a breath of fresh air to meet new people and hear some stories I hadn't already heard a thousand times, sitting in their well-appointed main tent eyeing their hot chocolate, stone-baked pizzas and assorted fine cakes and biscuits left me salivating and horribly jealous. They did, though, have the best and most up-to-date weather forecast, which advised that a high-pressure system was on its way. Our summit window would be with us any day now.

When blue skies did finally appear, many of the expeditions immediately started packing up and heading down the mountain, anxious to get out while the spell of good weather lasted. Some were leaving because their time was up, others took the view that it would be weeks before the avalanche risk abated and decided to cut their losses. My team, bolstered by the report of good weather on the way, were ready to dig in for another fortnight if need be. In the meantime we decided to amuse ourselves with a half-hearted snowball fight. To our horror, a mis-thrown snowball sailed over the head of its target and into the Chinese military camp, landing right in the middle of a group of teenage soldiers who were making tea and knocking their kettle over. The soldiers immediately leapt to their feet, and with a battle cry unleashed a volley of . . . snowballs, pitched with excited teenage glee towards us.

The next hour was spent in an epic battle between our expedition and the massed ranks of the Chinese camp, outnumbering us five to one. It was a snowball fight to end all snowball fights, with our Nepalese Sherpas lending a hand by making piles of snowballs and bringing them to us in their jackets (and yes, I am aware of what a colonialist image this is!). A senior officer in old-fashioned glacier glasses sat in a camp chair barking orders at the young Chinese soldiers, directing their attacks. After an hour, they stepped up the intensity by taking hostages. I was the first to be captured; about eight Chinese soldiers overwhelmed me, then carried me kicking and screaming to their camp, where they rolled me around in snow, then solemnly gave me a cup of hot chai before allowing me to return to the fray. We upped the ante even further by seizing a table and a broken tea flask, to much hilarity on both sides. We launched guerrilla raids – or rather Jason the surfer did; wearing a shiny red climbing helmet and carrying a bag loaded with fresh ammunition he shot past us with a blood-curdling battle cry. Sadly he'd failed to warn us, and we were all so busy laughing that he was absolutely buried by the opposition. It was a joyous afternoon, with the universal language of slapstick and silliness breaking down boundaries. Finally, after two hours of chucking snowballs at altitude, every one of us was destroyed. We just about managed to drag ourselves back to the mess tent, where we collapsed breathless and red-faced, barely able to speak for the rest of the evening.

A few days later, however, we were to see our opponents and the 'Autonomous Region of Tibet' in a very different light. Our little frontier town in the clouds was about to become the site of an international incident, and the focus of the outside world.

When at last the clouds cleared, after what the experienced guides described as the worst storm in Cho Oyu's recent climbing history, the peak looked like a big Mr Whippy, sugar-frosted in deep snow, which spelled avalanche and trail-breaking hell. Many of the expedition teams on the mountain had already packed up their yaks and headed for home, but those of us who'd remained felt a surge of optimism at weather reports promising a sustained period of high pressure. Some of the other teams stopped packing and everyone left in camp began making preparations to get back up on to the mountain.

On a big peak it's usually illness that takes out the lion's share of combatants. Only seven of our fifteen-strong team even got a chance to summit: two went down with HACE (High Altitude Cerebral Edema) a type of altitude-induced stroke. Fluid in the lungs, or High Altitude Pulmonary Edema took out another three. One guy didn't sleep a wink in three weeks and went mental; another couldn't get within ten metres of food without projectile vomiting; and the coughs took the rest. One night Jere had such a fierce coughing fit he broke two ribs, ending his chances of summiting. Sammi suffered a terrible case of high altitude flatulence and was banned from the mess tent. As our Italian team member told him, 'You smell like you've been eating the dead cats!'

One of the climbers who dropped out had been planning to climb on supplementary oxygen, so all of a sudden there was a spare oxygen cylinder. Until that point, I hadn't even considered climbing on oxygen. It had always seemed like cheating to me, and I was sure I would be fit enough to summit without it. But that was before the sustained period of kicking my heels in base camp. I knew now we would only get one crack at the mountain, and in my head I *had* to succeed. I didn't want to have spent all that time bored out of my brain, and go home without a summit. Plus (I convinced myself) it would be preparation for climbing K2; I decided to look upon it as giving oxygen a trial run as part of my long-term training.

In truth, that was merely me struggling for justification. I wish now that I hadn't copped out and taken the 'Os'; it was a moment of weakness I'll always regret.

The following morning, I set off with Sammi and Dave to make our push for the summit. Having left my big boots up at Camp 1, I had to stomp through knee-deep snow all the way up to 6,400 metres in my trainers, which was a soggy and chilly experience. Once kitted up, we pushed on to Camp 2. Next we had a choice. We could either camp there and make a huge push for the summit, or trudge up the mindless snow headwall in front of us to Camp 3, a tiny flattish space on the northwest ridge face. At an altitude of 7,450 metres, this would leave us with far less of a push to reach the top. While we weighed up our options, which seemed to us the most important decision on earth, matters of far greater import were taking place below us.

Across the glacier from Cho Oyu base camp is the Nangpa La, a high pass on the ancient trade route between Tibet and Nepal. For days we had watched yak trains tramping across to take their wares to market. But on 30 September the line of people crossing the snow were not traders but seventy-five unarmed Tibetans who had each paid around five hundred pounds – equivalent to four years' earnings – to escape Chinese tyranny in their homeland. We had seen with our own eyes on the short journey up from Kathmandu how disenfranchised the Tibetans were in their own villages. What we didn't witness were the young Tibetans refused an education, and those publicly beaten, imprisoned or 'disappeared' because they were seen as a threat to the Chinese regime. All these young people wanted was a better life, and they were willing to risk their lives to find it. Most were pilgrims – monks and nuns seeking to join His Holiness the Dalai Lama in Dharamsala, India. They'd started their journey crammed into the back of a single truck that delivered them from their small towns to a point near the border. They had been told to bring only enough barley meal to last four days and one blanket between two, as they needed to move light and fast to keep ahead of Chinese border patrols. In fact the walk to Nangpa La pass took them ten days, on empty stomachs and very little sleep. Many were children, barely old enough to complete the walk.

When we returned, the two Steves told us how everyone in base camp had been shaken out of their tents by the sound of two loud, short, sharp cracks. As experienced police officers, they recognised the sound of gunfire and hurried out on to the moraine along with some of the other climbers. They saw a line of stick figures moving across the glacier on the other side of the valley. The refugees moved slowly, in single file, the deep snow and altitude preventing them from progressing any faster. The snowfield is a huge white blanket to cross, with no cover, nowhere to hide. Running up behind them were Chinese soldiers, and they were armed. What followed was captured on camera by Romanian journalist Sergio Mattei, and is available to view on the Internet. You can clearly see one of the soldiers run to a vantage point, raise his AK47 to his shoulder, take careful aim, then fire. At the front of the line, one of the pilgrims falls into the snow. You can hear one of Sergio's comrades gasping, 'They're shooting them like dogs.' Then there is staccato automatic gunfire, strafing over the escapees. Another gunshot. The stick figure at the back of the line stops and stiffens, as if someone has called her name. Her body then spasms, and she falls gently into the snow, curled into a ball as if clutching her stomach. The Mattei film shows two others shot, one of them at close range. They fall into the snow as the Chinese soldiers close in on them, firing repeatedly into the line of fleeing refugees. You see one making for the safety of the ridgeline at the top of the pass, shot from behind by a soldier. The wounded figure falls into the snow, but then gets up, clearly having been shot in the leg, and stumbles on, trying desperately to escape. They are then are shot again.

Horror and disbelief spread through base camp like a sickness. The fact that it all took place on the other side of the valley made it seem distant and disconnected from those witnessing it, yet it was unmistakably real – and the drama was about to come right into the climbers' own backyard.

Some of the climbers filmed soldiers pouring out of base camp, seemingly excited, shouldering their rifles as they ran. A Tibetan refugee was seen taking refuge inside the toilet tent by one of the climber, who described how the man clasped the bag of used toilet paper in terror, trying to hide himself 'behind a bag of still-warm shit'.

Steve told me that the Chinese soldiers had paraded their captives into base camp, lined them up with their hands handcuffed behind their heads, and battered them with their rifle butts. Steve said this was even worse than witnessing the shootings, partly because it was happening right in front of them rather than on the other side of the valley, but also because he had children the same age as some of the refugees being abused in front of them – and he was powerless stop it. He might be a policeman and trained to deal with violence, but in occupied Tibet thousands of miles from home, faced with a bunch of teenage soldiers stampeding around with Kalashnikovs they were obviously only too happy to use, what could Steve do? What could any of them do? The Chinese could have executed every last one of the refugees as they knelt there in the snow, and there would have been absolutely nothing anyone could do to prevent it. Steve said that the two soldiers who'd fired the shots were honoured by senior officers in a ceremony filmed by a Chinese television crew. The same Chinese soldiers we'd shared snowballs and tea with were being publicly commended for shooting unarmed nuns and children in the back.

Experienced mountain guide Luis Benitez reported that seven people were shot and shoved into a crevasse, but to this day there is only one confirmed fatality: Kelsang Namtso, a seventeen-year-old Tibetan nun, shot in the back and killed. Steve told me that three Chinese soldiers approached and repeatedly kicked her body before taking her bag, but then she was left out on the glacier until two thirty in the afternoon of the following day. Thirty-two others were injured and captured by the Chinese. Some are still unaccounted for, and rumoured to be serving hard labour. Seventeen remain missing. The refugees included seven children ranging from seven to twelve years old, as well as seven teenagers. One of these, Jamyeng Samten, was fourteen when he was captured. He was taken to a Chinese prison, where he was tortured, stabbed repeatedly with an electric cattle prod and beaten, before being sentenced to hard labour. When he was finally released, he ran again, and this time escaped over the border to India where he resides today.

Guide Luis Benitez chose not to retreat from base camp but to head up the mountain to Camp 2 and make an attempt on the summit. This may seem peculiar, but there was no precedent for how anyone should act in this situation. When he returned to base camp some days later, he found that no one had reported the incident to the outside world. Benitez was horrified at what he considered the 'atrocity of silence', the fact that every expedition there at base camp had at least one sat phone, yet no one had contacted a journalist or newspaper on the outside to let them know what had happened. Benitez got on to the satellite phone to report the incident to adventure website Explorer's Web. This landed him in extreme hot water with the high-end mountaineering companies, who considered this foolhardy at best.

Everyone who was there during that period describes base camp as being impossibly tense, exposed, vulnerable, uncertain what was going to happen next. It highlighted what a weird place these base camps are. Approximately six hundred people live there for several months at a time, and it feels like a small town. However, unlike most human settlements, there is no law, no police force, no government, no mayor. It's just a loose assembly of expeditions, each made up of highly independent, individualistic people with big egos and their own goals. In such a situation, there is no objective protocol on how to act. There is no one to take charge or 'sort things out'; you're suddenly alone in a crowd with too many leaders and no group cohesion.

Thankfully the horror didn't reach the international press until after we had left Tibet. I'm pretty sure we would all have been detained in China for an extended stay if we hadn't already been across the border in Nepal. China initially responded with a news report claiming their soldiers had been fired upon and were acting in self-defence. The Mattei video clearly shows this was not the case. They then posted a press release saying the incident had been an example of 'normal border management'. From the Tibetan perspective, the twenty-eight-year-old who had hidden in a base-camp toilet managed to escape, crawling on his stomach across the border by night between the guards who had shot dead his friends. When he reached Dharamsala, he was given an audience with His Holiness the Dalai Lama, as are all refugees who escape Tibet to freedom. When he told his story, the holy man replied, 'Do not be afraid, this has happened many times before, but we never had witnesses. Speak out to the world.'

Two years later, Steve Lawes returned to Kathmandu to attempt Everest. While he was there, he went to the refuge where many of the escapees were still living. This excerpt is from his diary:

> 10-year-old children showed me pictures showing them in prison with soldiers around them. They showed me pictures of a body being poked with a cattle prod, complete with sparks shooting from the prod into the body.
>
> They told me that Kelsang's body was thrown on to the floor and soldiers used the cattle prod to make the dead body jerk and jump about. I was in tears at this. Young children do not make up things like that. I can still see those images 7 years later.
>
> During my interview I was asked point blank 'Did you witness a murder?'
>
> I replied 'Yes. In the UK if you shoot and kill someone who is running away from you and posing no threat whatsoever then that is murder. So yes I witnessed murder.'

Had we heard the news up there on the mountain, Dave, Sammi and I would have been in the same predicament as the climbers at base camp. I'm not proud to say this, but I'm pretty sure we'd have pressed on with our push for the summit. However much the news would have shocked and horrified us, there was nothing we could do to influence the Chinese army.

*

In the end we decided to push on to the higher camp, taking only one sleeping bag between us to save on weight. As night fell, we spooned together, cuddling unashamedly for warmth. We wiled away the hours with me telling wildlife stories, tall tales set in places that seemed a very long way from our tiny tent – a mere pimple on Cho's vast shoulder. Every few minutes, one of us would sit up to check the stove, which was boiling snow for water. Here in this exposed place, even getting drinking water was a chore that involved gathering a panful of soft snow (taking care to go some distance from the tents and check that the snow wasn't yellow), then placing a pot with a little water in it over the fire so that the heat is transmitted through the snow more efficiently, otherwise the pot will burn before the snow melts. It's vital to keep the stove out of the wind, but at the same time you need to make sure it has ventilation, or you could all be suffocated by carbon monoxide. At altitude, water boils at a lower temperature, so you need to boil it longer to kill off pathogens or cook food; this doesn't apply when melting snow for drinking water, as you can generally count on it being pure and uncontaminated up so high. The stoves often struggle in thin air, sputtering, losing power and frequently going out altogether, hence the vigil throughout our resting hours until 1 a.m. when we stepped out into the cold.

Before setting off we each chewed a cereal bar and drank a litre of water, which was to be the last food or drink that would pass our lips for ten hard hours. Even in our insulated water bottles, the fluid we'd spent long hours melting froze solid within minutes. The final task was the awkward and annoying one of probing beneath thick layers of down and fleece to locate a tiny chill-wilted penis, then trying to pee away from a fierce wind without soaking our precious clothing or the tents of comrades. It goes without saying that you didn't want to expose any tender flesh for a nanosecond longer than necessary. Once we'd completed our ablutions, we pulled harnesses over our down suits, clipped on our crampons, and grabbed our ice axes. Dave and I turned on our oxygen cylinders and put the plastic masks over our mouths. There was no immediate sensation, other than it being slightly harder to breathe, and a bit more cumbersome and claustrophobic. I persevered, knowing the steady stream of oxygen would prevent altitude sickness, stop me losing deoxygenated brain cells and aid my circulation, thus making frostbite less likely. The effect was the same as if I'd been 1,000 metres closer to sea level, and I felt the benefit as the hours wore on.

Imagine going out on the coldest winter day ever and doing hill sprints till you collapse – at high altitude; that's how your lungs feel after every single step. You cough up blood from sinuses, your throat and lungs are rasped raw by cold, dry, thin air, and the cold makes your fingers and toes feel like they're being stabbed with ice picks. It was also surprisingly steep snowpack, with two vertical icy rock bands which would have been a doddle at the local crag, but in down suits, huge mitts like the comedy hands spectators wear to baseball games, crampons and pack, the climbs seemed pretty fiddly.

Way above us, we could see the bouncing lights of another party, jinking side to side as they progressed upwards. In the darkness it was hard to get any sense of time or place, so I had to rely on the altimeter on my wrist. Every few minutes I'd roll my sleeve back, watching the hours tick by, and the metres tick upwards. The magical milestone approached with sickening slowness, but eventually the dial clicked from 7,999 to 8,000 metres. We were in the Death Zone. I had become one of the select band of mountaineers who had entered that hallowed world that had once been thought beyond the reach of mortal man.

Soon the sky began to lighten, deep, deep blue washing the heavens; then the peaks began to glow white, as if lit from within. And every single one of them seemed to be below us. The rocky peak that had towered over us at base camp was now a tiny toadstool way below us. Every fibre of my brain was screaming at me to stop, to soak in this extraordinary spectacle unfolding as the light grew and changed, but there were still many hours left in the day, so we slogged on, staring at the snow in front of our feet.

We were going strong, and finally strode on to the summit plateau, the eerie white light giving a ghostly life to the peaks around us. As we stepped on to the level ground, the sun rose behind Everest to our east and a gorgeous orange-pink light ignited the most dramatic 360-degree view I've ever seen. Five of the world's fourteen 8,000-metre peaks were there, crocodile-backed glaciers lumbering down into the valleys and out to the vast brown of the Tibetan plateau.

It sounds obvious, but from the top of a mountain, you can see further. For a man of my height standing at sea level on a clear day, the horizon is three miles away. Here on the summit of Cho Oyu, it is 230 miles away. On a cloudless and piercingly clear day like this, you can survey an area the size of Sweden. No photo or video panorama could capture the wonder of that vista. Even memory couldn't hope to record a microscopic fragment of the spectacle. It would have been breathtaking had there been breath in our bodies. This was why I'd come here, why I'd endured sickness and boredom. For that moment I felt like a god, surveying the rest of the cowed and credulous world from my throne in the heavens. I was standing higher than anyone else on Earth, driven there by the power of my own legs and lungs, revelling in a glory that only a few thousand humans will ever witness. Yet at the same time as you rejoice in your achievement, it is impossible not to be struck by how tiny and insignificant you are; a mere speck of dust in an infinity of time and space that is oblivious to you and your little life.

Both Dave and Sammi would go on to greater achievements on Everest and K2, but this was the first 8,000er for all of us. For one perfect moment we stood together on the summit hugging with glee, enjoying our triumph, but up here, out of the lee of Cho herself, the winds were excruciating, and with minus 40 degrees on the thermometer, five minutes at the top was all we could manage. That was long enough for me to take a piece of card from the pocket of my down jacket. It was photo of my mum, dad and sister that I'd carried with me all the way from the UK, along with a roll of prayer flags. The same ferocious wind that was about to drive us from this exalted place would soon bleach the prayers and their faces, but in doing so would carry their dreams out over the Himalaya, to circle the world for all eternity.

The mountaineer's worst fear is giving everything for a summit, then having to come down with the tanks on empty – the descent being far more dangerous. However, after five boring, frustrating weeks, I couldn't wait to get down off that mountain and the hell out of Tibet. Sammi, who had not used supplementary oxygen, made it to Camp 3 and then collapsed in a dead sleep. My cylinder had clearly done its job, though, as I still had plenty left in my muscles. In fact I was feeling stronger and stronger with every downward step. I kept on going and reached Camp 2 in an insane two hours (though much of that was done on my arse-sledge). Dave arrived shortly after and settled down to eat the food we'd cached. In no mood to hang around, I carried on going. It was a hideous slog to Camp 1, and the moment I got there I fell asleep on my pack out in the snow. After about half an hour I roused myself, packed up all my gear, put my trainers on and set off again. Sixteen hours after stepping out into the night to begin our summit, I stumbled back into base camp to greet my bewildered Sherpas and colleagues. I had only drunk a litre of fluid and had no food since starting. It was over, and I could take my wasted, thin, hairy stinking carcass home . . .

After waiting four days for the yaks to arrive.

THE ROOF OF THE WORLD

For some strange reason the summit of Cho Oyu left me feeling empty inside, with none of the sense of accomplishment I'd had on much smaller peaks. Part of it was undoubtedly the horrific drama that took place while we were in thin air. Real human tragedy on that scale puts into perspective the essentially selfish and egocentric First-World activity of climbing mountains. But there were personal reasons too. I was disappointed in myself for taking the supplementary oxygen. There is no doubt I could have made it without. Because of the oxygen it had seemed too easy. I'd taken six weeks out of my life for a major challenge, and had pretty much run up and down the thing. We value most what we have worked for; things that come too easy have transitory pleasure.

Despite the exultation of standing up there on the roof of the world, extreme altitude mountaineering will never be the love of my life. For me climbing is about solitude and exploration, reaching a summit or clinching a difficult pitch with a few good buddies on hand to rip on you for how badly you're climbing. That season around three hundred people set out to climb Cho Oyu, and I reckon about fifty made it. Everest was the goal of some five hundred climbers, trying from north and south, and about 50 per cent made it. Fair enough, this is far fewer than wander up Snowdon on a sunny Saturday, but these expeditions are meant to be special. And as far as the climbing goes, there are sections of vertical snow and ice, but all have fixed ropes and so pose little real difficulty to the experienced climber. The real challenge is altitude – not being able to breathe properly and getting endlessly sick – and knowing that if you get the wrong sock combination or your boots let in a bit of damp, all your toes will turn into dried prunes and fall off. How is that fun?

That being the case, how do I feel about Everest? The highest mountain in the world is the first that anybody ever hears about, and any mountaineer who claims they have never coveted its summit is a liar. I have many friends who have given inordinate sums of money, and in some case their digits, in the hope of ascending the highest peak on Earth so the last thing I want is to denigrate their achievements. While it is no longer the epic trial that Mallory and Irvine undertook in the early 1900s, with months of hard travel even to reach the peak and then requiring superlative route-finding and technical climbing skills in order to survive on it, even today there is no such thing as an easy 8,000er; to reach the summit is a phenomenal physical feat in anyone's book.

But a word of warning to any high-achieving athletes who might think, 'OK, so I've done a marathon, an ironman, swum the Channel . . . Everest is next.' This is folly in the extreme. Mountaineering is not like other endurance activities. I sincerely believe that you need to earn the right to attempt a peak like Everest, doing your time learning the art of mountaineering. My performance on Cho Oyu proved this elegantly. I had a decade of experience and many expeditions under my belt, yet even so I made many misjudgements that could have killed me. If you run out of puff on an ironman race, the St John ambulance first-aiders wrap you in a foil blanket and you sheepishly limp home. Get knackered on a big open-water swim and the support boat picks you up and give you a mug of hot chocolate. On Everest, if you don't cut the mustard above 8,000 metres, you will most likely die. Any fellow climbers who come to your aid will at very least forfeit the summit they have given many months and tens of thousands of dollars for; at worst their sacrifice could cost them digits or death. Corpses have been abandoned for years high on Everest, because getting them down is nigh on impossible. Adventure athletes who take on Everest as their first-ever big mountain are totally reliant on the knowledge and experience of their guides; they may be naive enough to believe otherwise, but the fact is they are incapable of making informed decisions themselves.

Over recent years there have been several high-profile incidents that illustrate the travesty Everest has become. In 2012 a weather window complication almost identical to the one we faced on Cho Oyu hit Everest. At peak season, with hundreds of climbers massing to attempt the summit, several days of snow kept everyone confined to base camp. There then followed three days of good weather, offering a narrow window for the ascent – and everyone at base camp immediately made a push for the summit. Photos hit the international press of a queue of climbers, over a hundred strong, on the upper slopes of the mountain. It looked like a London underground station escalator in the rush hour, only these weren't City commuters but mountaineers stranded for hours in freezing temperatures while climbers ahead of them battled with bottlenecks such as the Hilary Step. Many suffered frostbite and others came close to death, all because of overcrowding – in the Himalayas, where every other peak for a thousand miles would have been empty. This is not what mountaineering is supposed to be about.

In his wonderful book *Mountains of the Mind*, Robert Macfarlane tells how the Romantic poets Keats and Shelley were drawn to ascend mountains by an aesthetic ideal, a desire to 'escape the atomised, socially dissolute city. You could be lonely in a city crowd, but you could find solitude on a mountaintop'. One has to wonder what those poets would have made of a hundred-strong queue on the world's highest peak.

The following year there was a high-altitude contretemps involving Swiss wunderkind Ueli Steck, Simone Moro and Jonathan Griffith. The three were climbing on the Lhotse face of Everest above some Nepalese Sherpas who were fixing ropes for the commercial clients below. According to the Sherpas, Steck's party kicked snow and ice down on them – a claim Steck strongly denies. When the European climbers returned to their tents in Camp 2, the normally affable and reserved Sherpas amassed in force – it's said a hundred were involved – and rocks and punches were thrown. According to some reports the Sherpas would have killed them if other Western-ers, including climber Melissa Arnot, hadn't intervened. Reports of the incident have been cloudy at best, but in a subsequent interview Steck was quoted as saying, 'we pay a lot of money to be there, so why should I not be allowed to climb? And vice versa. The Sherpas are also allowed to climb. Can you say that people should wait until the Sherpas fix the ropes? Of course, and that could be a rule. People speak of an unwritten rule that you have to wait for the Sherpas who are up there, but if you don't use their ropes, what's the point? If there's good weather? I spoke today about it with Elizabeth Hawley [the then eighty-nine-year-old chronicler of Himalayan mountain-eering]. She said, you know, guys, you shamed that lead Sherpa, and in Asian culture this is the worst thing that can happen.'

In other words, the Europeans might have insulted the pride of the Nepalese by climbing above them and disregarding the unwrit-ten rule that they have precedence on the mountain. Traditionally the Sherpas, though far more capable climbers than most Western-ers, were extraordinarily humble and remained in the background while their clients claimed the plaudits for conquering summits. Nowadays there is a new breed of Sherpas; no longer glorified por-ters, they are fully qualified mountain guides – proud, fearsomely strong with goals of their own. Moreover the livelihood of entire villages depends on the income these Sherpas command during the ascent season. The 2013 brawl made the entire Western climbing community intensely uncomfortable, as most climbers idealise the quiet, reserved Sherpas who risk their lives so rich clients can real-ise their dreams. It didn't fit with our rose-tinted image of how they should act.

But by far the worst chapter in the tumultuous recent history of Everest came in 2014. On 18 April an iceblock weighing an esti-mated 64,000 tons collapsed into a passage known as the Khumbu Icefall, and killed sixteen Sherpas in one single, brutal cavalcade of ice and rock. The Sherpas were fixing ropes and carrying gear for their Western clients who would follow. Damian Benegas and Rob Casserley, who were with me on Cho Oyu, were on Everest at the time and joined the rescue effort, tending to the injured and recovering the bodies of those who died. The awful tragedy of what happened there threw the whole business of Everest – and it is a business – into sharp perspective. In their local villages, mourning families performed pujas (blessing ceremonies) while their government originally offered insulting payouts of $400 per man lost – subsequently increased in response to community anger. Meanwhile in base camp the concern was whether clients should continue up the mountain or not. Most seem to have opted for a cautious approach, withdrawing on the assumption that climbing on the mountain would cease for the year. However there were others who felt they'd committed too much to walk away from their summit ambitions.

Thirty-nine-year-old Louisiana adventurer Joby Ogwyn was due to complete the first wingsuit flight off Everest's summit, filmed live by the Discovery Channel, which had invested millions in the event. Ogwyn later described how he, his climbing partner and a cameraman also travelled to the icefall – to bring supplies to survivors and help with the search for the bodies – before having to decide what to do about their own climb up the mountain. He said that some Sherpas were still up for the trip and indeed, days after the disaster, Ogwyn posted on his Facebook site: 'Today is a brighter day. We are staying on the mountain to honor our friends and complete our project.' But others were angry that if the project went ahead it would be desecrating the memory of the Sherpas who had fallen. Eventually the whole Sherpa community decided not to climb and the Discovery Channel pulled the plug on the wingsuit jump. Rumours circulated that some Sherpas had threatened a repeat of the violence that Ueli Steck had faced the previous year, and with some threatening to go to Kathmandu and burn down the offices or homes of any operators who stayed and climbed. Yet, apparently, there was still determination in some quarters to continue up the mountain regardless. One American climber was said to have declared on social media: 'I refuse to give in to the Everest mafia [i.e. Sherpas]'. Another, whilst respectfully acknowledging the community's grieving, noted on the *National Geographic*'s website: 'Sherpas are not dragooned on to Everest . . . They know the risks.' Another climber, apparently unable to refund the not inconsiderable cost of his aborted trip, was reported to have declared in frustration: 'We have been screwed by the Sherpas. We are the hand that feeds the whole business, so without us, no operators. Without operators, no jobs for the Sherpas or their workers. But then we're told, "Go home and come back next year."'

I wasn't there, I wasn't under the same moral and financial pressure – and reports from the mountains are not always the most reliable – so perhaps I have no right to comment on any of this. Nonetheless, I can't help but cringe at such behaviour. It's only a mountain, it's only a climb, it will still be there tomorrow. With hindsight, surely the only decent thing to do was to give whatever help you could, pay your respects, erect prayer flags to the fallen and then go home to raise money for the victims' families. But that wasn't going to happen because Everest is not like other mountains. People go there under corporate pressure, some with First-World millions behind them, governed by forces that have no business in the big hills. Too many seem to have no understanding of the unspoken and unwritten climbers' code, and what I believe mountaineering is all about. Some commentators make a distinction between mountaineers and summiteers. While the former may be in it for the experience, the latter are not about the journey, but the outcome. Rather than their relationship with the mountain, it's all about 'conquering' a certain peak. This has led to the explosion of commercially guided expeditions, where huge sums of money are paid (£70,000 fairly standard for Everest) to get people to the top of a mountain. They stay in plush catered camps, often with wifi, Flatscreen TV and hot showers. The mountain will be strung in fixed ropes, and they carry little or nothing themselves up the peak, instead relying on strong Sherpas to carry their stuff, and sometimes themselves to the top. This is the very antithesis of the self-sufficiency that climbers laud in a mountaineering accomplishment. It has also been suggested that summiteers become so focused on their personal goals, that standard morality goes out of the window. It's now a commonplace occurrence for people to have oxygen cylinders and gear stolen from high camps on Everest. Undeniably more repugnant for me, though, would be the situation in 2006 that followed 34-year-old British climber David Sharp collapsing under a rock overhang about 300m below the summit of Everest. One witness stated that at least forty climbers continued up past him to the summit, none of them stopping to attempt a substantive rescue. Of course, those climbers might have been unable to change events if they had. As a Japanese mountaineer who climbed over three struggling climbers leaving them to die was reported to have claimed, 'we were too tired to help, above 8000m is not a place people can afford morality.'

Again, since I wasn't there and I wasn't under the same pressure, I realise I cannot pass judgment, but this sums up so much of why Everest no longer appeals to me. The allure of the world's highest mountain will always draw me in, but there is too much ego there. I see too many people hell-bent on proving themselves against the mountain, oblivious to the code, honour and loyalty that is dear to me in mountaineering. I may have another 8,000-metre mountain in me at some stage, but these expeditions are long, arduous and expensive, they need to be special, to be about purity and joy. I don't go to the mountains, to my place of solitude and contemplation, to get involved in politics, posturing and intrigue. I go to the mountains to escape all that bullshit! I'm not going to give up months of my life to be surrounded by hundreds of other people, many of whom haven't earned the right to be there and cannot take care of themselves or others.

Perhaps I have become a part of the problem. It won't have escaped the sharp-eyed reader of these pages that the Nepalese Sherpas who cooked our base-camp food and helped with all our carrying on Cho Oyu merit barely a mention in my story of the climb. I couldn't name any of them now. They kept to their cooking tent, and though I was friendly with all of them, none became real friends. I used their help and their broad shoulders, but for me the climb was all about me and my Western friends. If I go back, I will make a conscious effort to change that dynamic, but for that Cho Oyu climb, I was one more Westerner turning up and using the local people as hired help to get me where I wanted to go. It's easy for us to say that climbing is part of the Sherpa culture and that they know what they are getting themselves into, but actually I think that's far from true. Intriguingly, the Sherpa people who inhabit the Khumbu region that includes Everest and Cho Oyu have words in their language for flanks and sides of a mountain, and many for high passes, but they have no word for 'summit'. As I was to find on later expeditions in Bhutan, for the Nepali and Tibetan peoples mountaintops have traditionally been considered the homes of gods, and therefore sacred. In Bhutan, it is forbidden to climb to the summits of mountains. For the peoples of the Himalayas, climbing is a comparatively recent innovation, and many still consider it to be blasphemous and sinful, daring to challenge the will of their normally peaceful gods. Sherpas have become the world's finest mountaineers out of economic necessity, because they need to feed their families. Like I said, I'm just another part of the problem.

I stress again that I have weighed in with an opinion on events that I personally didn't witness – something that invariably makes me shudder when others do it. The events on Cho Oyu gave me a taste of quite how distorting the base-camp rumour mill can be. It's hard enough to assess events of this nature while you're there, let alone when you weren't even in the country at the time. These tragedies of the high mountains come under the media spotlight and get tossed around the world and discussed by po-faced, self-appointed 'experts' in bars and on chat shows. Couch potatoes will express outrage at Simon Yates for cutting Joe Simpson's rope, or at the antics of Alex Lowe or Scott Fischer, in the same way as they might shout their criticism of a football game. What do they know about life in thin air in the 'Death Zone'? I don't want ignorant fools judging how I behave in the mountains. That is between me, my ropemates and the high, hard rock.

THE LOST WORLD

'All the most exciting charts and maps have places on them
that are marked "Unexplored".'

Arthur Ransome, *Swallows and Amazons*

Imagine going to the top floor of the Empire State Building, throw-
ing open a window and stepping out on to the ledge, the world of
cars, cabbies and chaos far below. You slide yourself over the shelf,
feet finding space, then scrabble blindly on the featureless stone wall
for purchase. Your fingers, clinging to the ledge, are the only thing
between you and the void. It's the kind of vertiginous nightmare that
has people gibbering in the night, but it's a pretty accurate description
of where I find myself after four days' climbing, eating, sleeping and
sweating on a vertical sandstone cliff face in Venezuela's Gran Sabana.
A day's climbing above us lies the promise of a forested plateau hold-
ing untold natural treasures. Below, the steep skirts of the mountain
drop a thousand metres to savannah that stretches away to Brazil
and Guyana; we are as high above the plains as a glider would soar.
Jewelled hummingbirds hover inches from our faces, investigating
these strange visitors into their world, and swifts wheel through the

air hawking for insects about our ears. It is an exquisite panorama, and all the more incredible because I am the first human to have set eyes on it.

Expedition Borneo had gone down incredibly well both with the British and worldwide viewing public, nominated for a slew of awards including an Emmy. Not surprisingly then, the hunt was soon on to try to find another expedition that would match the integrity and honesty of the Borneo project; featuring authentic, old-fashioned exploration, discovering forgotten parts of the planet, finding species that were new to science, and trying to afford a degree of protection for wild parts of the planet that were under siege. Our next target was the Guiana Shield.

A mountain range that lies along the borders of three countries, Guyana, Venezuela and Brazil, the Guiana Shield is constructed of the oldest rock on the planet, the remnants of an ancient Pre-cambrian seabed. Over millennia, weak bedding planes have been eroded, leaving towering sandstone edifices known as tepuis that rise above the jungles like craggy fortresses. The first explorers to make their way there in the late nineteenth century looked upon the unscalable might of the tepuis and fantasised about what might be found on their summits. Their anecdotes inspired Arthur Conan Doyle to write *The Lost World*, a novel in which the pith-helmeted hero Professor Challenger climbed the face of Mount Roraima to discover that its plateau was home to dinosaurs including stegosaurs and soaring pterodactyls, and a bunch of savages who predictably set about barbecuing his team. More recently, the gorgeous Pixar film *Up* was set on the tepuis. To the viewer it probably seems that the animation is pure fantasy. Having been there, I can tell you that even Pixar could not capture the magic of the place. Today Roraima has a tourist path to the top, and the Angel Falls area of Auyan-tepui is swept daily by tourist fly-bys. Yet even now, many of the tepuis remain unclimbed, and there are forested areas of the Gran Sabana that are still to be documented.

It was 2007, and I was still an integral part of the expedition team, as involved in the research and development of the programmes as the stuff in front of the camera. In my first exploratory trip, I travelled solo into some of the illegal wild west gold mining towns of Guyana, filming Brazilians who were blasting away pristine rainforest streams with huge hoses, poisoning the clear waters with toxic mercury in order to separate gold from the silt. I stayed on my own in frightening frontier towns, without the benefit of a local contact or common language; on one occasion I spent the night huddled in a makeshift bed on top of sacks of concrete in the backroom of a general store and liquor shop, listening to a brawl taking place on the other side of the flimsy planks. Local people were kept cowed and intoxicated by powerful cartels, and disputes between the miners were settled with shotguns and pistols. It was an intimidating, brutal place, testament to my fond belief that humans are far more scary than animals and wild places could ever be.

The crew spent six months trawling the Guiana Shield in search of areas where we would stand a good chance of finding new species, and one location kept cropping up again and again: the tepuis. Mount Roraima was home to several endemic species, including a black prehistoric-looking frog that crawls instead of hopping; when threatened, it rolls and bounces away until it tumbles into a puddle or bromeliad.

On my first flight over the region I sat spellbound like a child on their first drive round a safari park, nose pressed against the glass of my light aircraft, seeing a million lifetimes' worth of adventure melting away into the mist beneath me. From that moment on it was only a matter of finding the right peak, the right goal for our mission. Roraima itself was too well known. We needed a peak that had never been climbed if we were to be true to the spirit of exploration. We needed vertical rock walls separating the table top from the jungle below, in order to have any chance of finding truly endemic life on top. Lastly, we needed a peak that could be accessed and climbed inside a month, for that was the maximum our budget and timescale would afford us.

The last part would probably be the toughest to get right, but we were aided by the quality of the team. My research yielded two names, Ivan Calderon and John Arran, two of the finest rock jocks in the world, and the most respected and experienced climbers of the tepuis. John had led the hardest climb in Britain a few years previously (E10, for you rock nerds out there) and gained a name for himself by soloing (that's climbing without a rope) one hundred extreme-grade rock climbs in the Peak District . . . in a day! He also led the first freeclimb of the 1,000-metre face of the Angel Falls. Despite his achievements, John is a quiet and humble man, who gives the impression he's no big deal – something I find deeply impressive. Being well acquainted with the area, he'd suggested several peaks in the region of Yunek village, and I had the privilege of recceing those peaks by air. As my tiny Cessna came out of the clouds, it was engulfed by immense table-top peaks, waterfalls tumbling in diamond and chiffon trails from their summits, smoky clouds drifting over the verdant forests that covered each plateau. The plane was reduced to the significance of a gnat among these gargantuan sandstone monoliths. It didn't seem at all far-fetched that their summits might be home to forgotten worlds. To the south of the village was our prime objective: Upuigma, also known as El Castillo – the castle. As soon as I saw the rain-laden clouds skulking about its vertical walls, I knew this had to be our mountain. You can see all of Upuigma from the ground. Its (apparently) flat summit is no more than two square kilometres and its perfect box shape is visible from every angle. No one would ever think that there might be an easier route up it somewhere and we were cheating. Even to a non-mountaineer, Upuigma looks impossible.

Having made our selection, Steve and I spent a few days carrying out a recce of the area around Upuigma on foot, walking in as close as possible to its dominating walls, assessing our approach, sweet-talking the folk in Yunek village and trying to get them onside. And all the while our excitement was building. There are certain wild places where you can't help but sense a metaphysical spirituality that compares to the Nature Shock Darwin described himself being overpowered by. Situations where you find yourself being distracted by an electric-blue butterfly, then as it alights you become fixated on the luscious bloom it has landed on. Then as it takes off, you are smitten by the wonder of the gnarled ancient tree the bloom is attached to, the canopy beyond, the peaks that frame them. Then suddenly it is all too much, and you feel you'll burst with the wonder of it all. The Gran Sabana is one of those places. The mountains bristle with an electric charge that is otherworldly. Sometimes the light penetrates a tissue of clouds, painting the rockfaces in burnished bronze and ivory. Perhaps it's something about their great age, a sense that there are titanic and primeval forces at work there that dwarf not just you, but your entire species.

In addition to myself, John and Ivan, the party would include Steve, and behind the camera, Keith Partridge, who seems to have shot every important mountain film of the last decade, including *Touching the Void*. KP has a squaddy's haircut, hands like spades, and looks as if he should be ordering raw recruits to do press-ups. He's as tough as rhino jerky, but with a soft centre. Like Steve he's loyal, honest and caring, and after a few weeks in his company you'd trust him with your life. Tim Fogg had more than proved himself in Borneo, if for no other reason than that the tougher and edgier things got, the calmer and more considered he became. At fifty-four he was fitter than me, and is still my first-choice expedition companion.

Much as I drew comfort from being in such exalted company, I knew I'd have to raise my game if I was to live up to their standards. We each had a job to do: John and Ivan to get us to the top, Tim to keep us safe, Steve and KP to make the film. My job concerned the part of the expedition we couldn't predict. Having summited, we needed to find something interesting on top or we wouldn't have a documentary. When Steve and I had our clincher meeting with the big boss at the BBC, he said to us with a straight face and no sense of irony: 'You'll just have to stay on top until you find a new species.' Our American co-producer piled on even more pressure, repeatedly asking what we were going to find on top. Our inevitable response was, 'We don't know – no one's ever been there, that's the point!' We were left in little doubt that unless we found some actual dinosaurs, they would be disappointed.

As for the climbing, I think Keith summed it up best on day three when he was enthusing about the team: 'This is one of the strongest teams ever assembled; we've got Tim – the best ropes specialist around, Ivan – one of the best climbers in the Americas, John – one of the best climbers in the world . . .' And then he made eye contact with me and paused for a few seconds, trying desperately to come up with something, anything. 'And Steve . . . Steve's . . . er, pretty solid.' I felt like a Sunday league pub footballer who's found himself in a cup final at Wembley. With the pressure being so intense, I had taken my training to another level in the run-up to the expedition. I'd pushed my climbing grades to their limit, been working on diet and resistance training and finally managed the training Holy Grail of one-arm chin-ups – generally getting into the climbing shape of my life. If I wasn't ready now, I never would be.

*

Our plane landed at the tiny village of Yunek, two days' walk from Upuigma. The Pemon people who live in Yunek have to be among the luckiest folk on Earth. As we touched down on their football field and promptly blew over their goalposts with our backdraught, we found ourselves in the prettiest village I have ever seen. The thatched roofs on their round mud huts were framed on all sides by a backdrop of some of the most exquisite of all the tepuis. I stood for a moment gazing at the turrets of Acopán-tepui, which resembled a magnificent castle from a children's story, its rockfaces higher than the Petronas Towers (the world's tallest building). To the north, the Chimantá Massif, which was truly, well, massive. You could fit the whole of Detroit on its summit. And then, directly south was our mountain, Upuigma.

This is one of the most mysterious, impressive landscapes imaginable, and for many reasons the most exciting for modern-day biologists. The walls of the tepuis range from a few hundred to over a thousand metres tall, are vertical or overhanging for their entirety, and very few have easy routes up them. Whereas on your average alpine slope the plants and animals change gradually as you ascend through various altitude and climate zones, on the tepuis the plants and animals simply cannot travel between the base and summits of the peaks. The tops of the tepuis resemble islands with the blank sandstone walls acting like oceans. With the exclusion of things that can fly or be borne on the wind, anything that lives on the tops of the tepuis has evolved in isolation. As many as two-thirds of the 1,500 or so orchid species are only found in this region. Some of the mountain tops have more frog species than are found in the whole of Europe, and a third of those are only known from one mountain top.

And it's not merely that the walls create a barrier to movement. On the tops of the tepuis at perhaps 3,000 metres of altitude you find a weird world. Wet, cold at nights; scorched by UV in the day.

Yet if you threw a stone from the top it might fall a vertical mile to the savannah below. Here it is scorched, dry and home to entirely different fauna and flora. Most life borne to the summits would perish, but occasionally something would survive, thrive and then adapt, to eventually become a new, highly specialised species. Biologists have found that almost every species they've discovered on certain summits is endemic – that is, found there and nowhere else on Earth. This fact is what made our trip so exciting. Upuigma had never been climbed. A Venezuelan, Captain Cordoza, made an attempt in the 1940s, but after a month he had to give up – and he hadn't even got as far as the rockface.

We spent the night at Yunek in a thatched-roof hut, hosted by its current inhabitants – the world's largest community of cockroaches. And they were very happy to see us. I opened my rucksack later that evening and about a hundred shiny black roaches the size of my little finger screamed, 'Quick, boys, leggit!' and scrambled to the four winds. This scene was reproduced two weeks later in the lobby of the uber-posh Hotel Intercontinental, and I had to rush around like a madman, stamping scattering roaches into the marbled floors. I also managed to release a fair few of them at Heathrow baggage reclaim. A few managed to lay low until I got around to unpacking at home – where they made friends with the Madagascan cockroaches I had unwittingly invited back to my place the previous year.

My love of weird animals has not always been as much of a benefit to my life as it is today. I'll never forget the look of horror on the face of one particular date when she realised she'd be having a cuppa in a lounge filled with giant millipedes, cockroaches and scorpions. She never returned my calls, and we didn't manage a second date. And one of my housemates was forced by his girlfriend to find new lodgings after she found out that Bob, the eight-foot snake I'd told her was 'at the vet's', had actually been on the loose around the house for nearly a month. Back then I could come home and be cheered in by the calls of the geckos who hide behind my paintings, and the chirps of the escaped crickets I used to feed to my tarantulas (until my decorator put them on the windowsill one summer weekend, and they literally cooked).

By lamplight our Peruvian cook told us something of the mythology of the tepuis. As a child, she had been taught of the malevolent spirits that reside inside them, and had learned only to glimpse their reflections in puddles. One peak you shouldn't even speak of the name, as this would lead to downpour. While she was telling the story, Ivan cajoled her to speak its name. She was wowed by his film-star looks and shyly whispered what it was called. Literally two minutes later, thunder cracked the heavens and a torrential rainstorm erupted from the skies. Ivan looked genuinely spooked by the whole thing!

The rainstorms cheered the local frogs, and gave us all a taster of what was in store over the coming weeks. The rain smashed into the thatched roof of our hut with such force that even the cockroaches were cowering. Within minutes, rivulets of brown water were flooding between our packs and camp beds, carrying away flip-flops and reading material. As if this was a biblical flood, and our temporary home was the Ark, creatures began emerging: flying termite alates, scorpions, lizards and a small snake that slithered out of the woodwork. Back home in England it would have been classified a freak cloudburst and considered worthy of a mention on the evening news; out here it was a mere shower. We spent a sombre evening, sitting in the dark munching tinned tuna and pasta, swiping away persistent roaches, and imagining how it would be to be caught on one of Upuigma's vertical rock walls in one of these downpours. On such whims of nature life and death can hang, and it was a quiet team that bedded down to a chirruping frog chorus that night.

The next morning we woke to find that the crickets and roaches had managed to nibble right through the vacuum-packed bags that held our dehydrated food. Chucking away the tainted bags wasn't an option, because I'd counted precisely how many we would need for our expedition and we couldn't afford to lose any. Those that weren't too badly compromised we fixed up with gaffer tape in case we got desperate later.

Our walk to the base of the mountain took us across savannah that had been artificially burnt clear of forest by the Pemon. Usually such burning is carried out by farmers so that their livestock can graze the fresh green shoots that come up in place of the forest, but the Pemon have no livestock. They told us that they burn the forest purely in order to make it easier to walk to neighbouring villages. It's a terrible tragedy that countless miles of forest in the Gran Sabana National Park have been razed in this manner. By the end of the day, after having trudged through several Vietnamesque fresh burns, we looked like Welsh coal miners, smeared black with ash.

It wasn't all devastation though. As we crossed the tannin-stained rivers flowing down from Upuigma, we discovered that the riverbanks were ablaze with flowers such as the 'lady of the night', so called because it resembles a pair of red-hot lips. The stems of this plant are – not surprisingly – said to hold a powerful aphrodisiac. There were also beautiful purple and white orchids, pollinated by moths, flies and giant wasps. Wading through the fast-flowing waters with tens of thousands of pounds' worth of filming equipment on our backs turned out to be a nerve-racking experience – one slight slip could have had serious consequences for the expedition and our attempts to film it. We had been counting on paying the villagers of Yunek to act as porters for us, helping to share the load. Unfortunately it seemed that money didn't have much use for them as they rarely traded with the outside world. Instead, we had to arrange for an outboard motor to be flown out to them, which they could use to drive the village's only wooden boat. Even this wasn't enough to secure the help of sufficient porters to shift our gear, so every member of the team ended up carrying as much as we could get on our backs. Everything that wasn't essential we left behind, hoping that it could be brought in later by helicopter provided we managed to find and clear a landing site.

It was about twenty miles to reach base camp, assembled on the plains at the base of the skirts of Upuigma, with palm trees swaying gently, frogs chirping and burping about us, clouds playing around the summit of our peak and a bed pitched in soggy charcoal. One particular frog caught my attention; with dark cinnamon-coloured tiger stripes along its flanks and thighs, it's known as the convict tree-frog. I pitched my tent on the grimy ash-tainted ground, looking on with envy as Tim pitched a far more comfortable-looking hammock up nearby. We all drifted off to sleep, but then around midnight, there was a reprise of the previous evening's deluge. It swamped us, threatening to wash my tent away. Rivers of fresh water hammered at the tent walls – again, a stark reminder of how grim it would be if we encountered conditions like this on the rock. Suddenly, my tent door was wrenched open, but it wasn't the wind, it was Tim. Absolutely sodden, bedraggled, and looking very sorry for himself, he pushed his way inside. Storm winds had blown away the tarp over the top of his hammock, which had collapsed. His sleeping bag had turned into a big sponge and with nothing to sleep on or under he was shivering like a penitent puppy. My tent was cosy for one man, cramped with two, and with only one sleeping bag and mat between us, there would be no sleep that night. We huddled together for damp warmth, not for the first time freezing in the tropics, knowing that in the morning, the team would not be sympathetic.

During the slog up to the base of the rock conditions we alternated between shivering in infernal downpours as we dragged ourselves up steep mud slopes, to searing in heat on scrubby boulder-fields. As we walked we studied the hulking rock above us, noting the way it seemed to continually change in character, and we argued constantly about the best route to the summit. When you're the first to make an ascent, picking the best route up can mean the difference between triumph and ignominious failure. Having never climbed tepuis sandstone before, I personally had little idea what to expect once we got hundreds of metres above ground level. Every so often I would point and say, 'What about that crack? That looks reasonable to get a hand or fist into.' And John would reply, 'That's an optical illusion. I reckon that crack is five or six metres wide, and full of green goo.' After a while I took the hint and decided to leave it to the professionals. It seemed their main landmark was colour. Dark orange rock would be sublime, clean, ancient sandstone. At very least vertical, usually overhanging, but blissful for climbing. White patches would likely be less steep, and contain more brittle, loose rock so should be avoided. Black was permanently wet, grassy and lethal, and green was covered in vegetation and just as bad.

John and Ivan chatted constantly about the route, their conversations going something like, 'I reckon we should take the dihedral to the right of the chimney with the vegetation to the left – the pro's a bit ropey though.'

'What about the layback with the scoop and the overhanging roof leading to the sketchy rib? That'd go at about E7.'

'No, the crack with the tree-covered terrace right above those roofs – I reckon that's no more than 11A, we might even be able to pull through the overhang, that's going to be the crux.'

At this point, producer Steve, the only non-climber on the team, would chip in, 'Would you mind speaking English, you bunch of nerds!'

Occasionally our forest path would be crossed by a tumbling tea-brown stream, its tannic waters as sweet as Evian. Ivan would stride through like something out of a shampoo advert, his flowing black locks tied back with a bright scarf, mahogany carved mid-riff and rippling biceps with prominent veins and climbing scars. He put on a show that would make Michelangelo's David green with envy.

As we washed off the sweat and sun-block (for which we paid later in fried skin) a sapphire-throated hummingbird flashed about us, its wings purring, investigating these strange sunburnt invaders into its usually quiet world. After a few minutes he disappeared, only to turn up again later, as if to check we weren't some weird hallucination.

Our high camp within twenty minutes of the wall gazed out over hundreds of square miles of savannah all the way to Brazil and Guyana, with Angasima-tepuis to the east looking like it belonged in a cowboy film set in Monument Valley, except sticking up out of dark green jungle instead of desert. We pitched our tents in the scrubby vegetation on a bunch of flat rocks covered with fossilised ripples like those you see in shallow sands at the seaside. We were a thousand miles from the ocean, but these rocks had been formed when they were laid down on a vast but shallow estuarine seabed 1.8 billion years ago. There were no fossils in them, because they were formed before there was multicellular life on Earth. Looking at those flickers of deep, deep time sent a shiver up my spine. We were inconsequential in the lifetime of this ancient landscape, and the mountain was oblivious to whether we lived or died on its faces.

Moving about anywhere on the boulder-field of the upper slopes was treacherous. When it was wet, the rock was as slippery as if it were covered in motor oil, and even really large boulders would come unseated underfoot and start rolling down the steep hillsides. It also broke and fell apart easily, which didn't bode well for the actual climb. The last thing I wanted to do was dislodge a huge boulder and brain my colleagues.

We set up a camp that would be in place for the remainder of our time on the mountain, far enough back from the cliff that rockfall would not be an issue, while doing our best to make it as comfortable as possible for those who would be staying here. With a campsite made up of tumbled, greasy boulders, this was a forlorn hope. Tarpaulins were stretched out in an effort to bridge gaps, and we set our sleeping mats down on the flattest surfaces we could find. We were in for yet another sleepless night. The next morning we stretched aching muscles, unfurled curled spines, hurriedly ate a breakfast of porridge oats and honey, then started hacking our way through the dense moss-soaked foliage, and up to the face of Upuigma. The morning was dry, but even so a curtain of water poured off the summit, and from out of fissures in the rocks above, forming a neat waterfall that entirely encircled the peak. We walked through this sodden curtain to access the rock, but because of the overhang, water fell way beyond the base of the rock and into the trees. We started our climb behind a thin, broad waterfall.

During my aerial reconnaissance of the peak some months before, I'd filmed with a small handicam, assessing every possible line up the blank buttresses of Upuigma. John and I had then studied those images and photos in his home in Sheffield in the UK, and chosen this section of wall as our best objective. Now that we were closer to the rock, John and Ivan sat for many hours studying it through binoculars. They'd identified a fault line that should give them a shot at the summit, but we had no doubt there would be some nasty surprises along the way.

Ivan led the first pitch, and seemed to me to be making a right epic of it – which showed that everything on the mountain was a trick of the light, playing with your mind and eyes. The rockfaces that, from a distance, had looked no more than 100 metres high were more like 500, and the wall above me, which had appeared vertical, was actually overhanging, with few good handholds and little in the way of protection. As a fervent believer in the purity of free climbing, John had wanted the whole route to go 'free', with no aid climbing whatsoever. This goal went out the window within metres of the ground. Ivan pulled on his gear, using any method possible to get up a section of rock that was clearly incredibly physical, and with some very sketchy moves.

Seconding up after Ivan was without doubt the hardest single pitch I've ever climbed. Even to get on to the rock I had to clamber along a grimy ledge, with chunks of bush giving way beneath my feet and beachball-sized rocks bouncing down towards my belayer. I used a leaning palm tree to get myself on to the wall, trying to wipe all the slime off my shoes to give myself traction. Had I not been fresh and in the best climbing shape I'd ever been in, it would have been beyond me, with tiny fiddly holds and nothing for the feet whatsoever. Twenty metres up, I felt my finger strength failing, and lunged blindly for a hold above. Nine out of ten times there would have been nothing, and I would have fallen. For the first time Upuigma smiled on me, as my whole hand closed around a satisfying jawbone of stone. It held, and I hauled myself upwards, heart pumping, sweat soaking my jungle clothes. As anyone who's ever done traditional rock climbing will know, the gulf between the person who leads and the person who seconds the climb is cavernous. In short, if the second slips off, the rope from above will catch them, and they will rarely fall more than a few feet. The leader on the other hand could take a 'whipper' fall, so they are completely dependent on the placement of their protection. Had Ivan suffered a bad fall here, we were so far from help that the consequences would have been unthinkable.

Many people describe those who do so-called extreme sports as 'adrenalin junkies', or suggest they have a death wish. For people like John and Ivan the opposite is true. John solo climbs routes that I will never in my life be able to climb even with ropes, but it is so within his capability that it is no more challenging to him than it is for me to climb a ladder. Far from 'dicing with death', John is in control up there – and that's where the thrill lies. Knowing that you've developed your skills and accumulated sufficient experience to eliminate the danger. Once upon a time, all human beings had to rely on their own experience and abilities to survive. Nowadays we live such sanitised, safe, nannied-to-death lives that to be put back in the driving seat over our own survival is all too rare.

That said, there are occasions when I find myself totally out of my depth and have to acknowledge that my skill is no match for what's in front of me. The top of that first pitch was one of those occasions. Looking at what was immediately above my head, I felt my stomach pitch; there was no chance at all I would ever get up it. Never. A herd of rabid Rottweilers could have been below and I'd still not have made it. Even Ivan shrugged and said, 'Zees ees no for me, notheeng for holds, no protection – eez a John peetch for sure.' (Excuse my attempt at his accent – put it down to jealousy over him upstaging me with his rippling physique.) John duly took the lead and glided up the rock with effortless grace. We watched awestruck as he climbed, in places moving four or five metres above his last piece of protection on impossibly hard rock. A fall from this height would have been fatal, but then this was John climbing, and a fall was never going to happen.

John is just the latest in a long line of daredevil pioneers drawn by the uncharted wonders of the Guiana Shield. The great pioneer of the Gran Sabana was a 1920s American bush pilot with a name worthy of a film-star: Jimmy Angel. Angel cut his teeth flying with Charles Lindbergh's flying circus, before being coaxed into flying into southern Venezuela by an Alaskan prospector in a bar in Panama. The wild-eyed prospector told Jimmy tales of mountains caked in gold, and offered unimaginable riches for anyone skilled or crazy enough to find it. Angel was to spend thirty-five years of his life on a daredevil mission to find the promised treasure. It seems insane now, looking at the horrendous terrain on top of these mountains, that anyone could think of landing a plane up here. Nowadays even the finest pilots struggle to land a helicopter on the summits, yet Jimmy managed it, not once but time and again. There were to be no riches, though. The prospector from Alaska fell sick and died, leaving Jimmy in unimaginable isolation on top of one of the Venezuelan tepuis, surrounded by streambeds run through with gold ore. Though Angel managed to escape with his life, he could not find his way back to that mountain of gold.

Perhaps Jimmy's closest call was crash-landing his plane on the summit of Acopán-tepui. Even today there is only one way up this immense peak with its overhanging rock walls near a thousand metres in height! It took him several desperate weeks to find his way back to civilisation, and nearly claimed his life. It did ensure his legacy in the process – he was the first man to spot the tumultuous waterfall tumbling a vertical kilometre from the summit to the forest below, one of the world's natural wonders. The Angel Falls were later verified as easily the highest waterfall on the planet, and Jimmy Angel's ashes were scattered there after yet another plane crash ended his life many years later. Angel embodies the spirit of adventure in the Gran Sabana, and his legacy and that of his successors is littered all over the plains in the form of plane skeletons, a grim reminder of what a landscape like this can do to aspiring explorers.

By the end of the day we had ascended a respectable 100 metres. Progress was very slow, as Tim rigged alternate ropes for Keith to film from, and Ivan and John sought a route up a totally blank green wall, then out through some vast roofs that hung out over our heads like the vaulted ceilings of an elemental cathedral. Over the savannah far below, rainstorms moved like whimsical ghosts in a celestial holding pattern one behind the other, the billowing curtain of their storm-head chasing up the slopes towards us. It was a remarkable sight. Each isolated storm moved across the otherwise sunny savannah, then minutes before it hit, the calm skies whipped into strong wind, and we were engulfed in clouds. Luckily the rock was so overhanging that we never got wet! It was a grandstand view at a game of the weather gods. I spent most of the day sitting back in my harness with thousands of swifts circling and chirruping loudly in the blue skies above, looking on in awe as two of the most extraordinary athletes I have ever seen danced up what looked like impossible terrain, only their grunts and puffs giving any clue as to their level of exertion.

Towards the end of the day, as the skies darkened, we took stock of our situation. To haul up our gear and set everything in place would take perhaps three hours. We were no more than 100 metres from the ground, and had ample rope to descend and leave fixed ropes in place. We decided to descend and sleep at camp, and to climb back up the ropes the following day. After slogging over the boulder field, we returned back to our measly camp in the dark, soaked, starving, sweat-drenched. There was precious little respite to be had in amongst our sorry collection of tarpaulins, and little in the way of sleep. The one small solace was that the porters had picked up on my geeky obsession for crawly things and one of them brought me a scorpion he'd found amongst the cooking pots. I put it in my shoe for safekeeping to film later, and didn't remember it again until I was about to put my toes in my shoes the next morning!

To save our precious dehydrated food for the climb, we again cooked up a simple soggy stew of rice and tinned tuna. Sitting around the spitting Primus stove, faces blackened and sheened with old sweat, the team ravenously spooned down their cat-food dinner, picking pieces of leaf and dirt out with grubby chafed fingertips.

Though it at least meant some hot food, coming down was actually a bad call. The following morning it took four hours for all five of us to get up to the face and then ascend – climbing the ropes – back to the high point of day one. Only one of us could ascend on the ropes at any one time, it was twice the height of the Statue of Liberty, and then we had to haul all the gear up, so it was nearly noon before we even started to cover new ground. All the way I was suffering from almighty butterflies because the next pitch was to be my first lead of the trip. Normally the lead is shared between climbers, allowing the leader to recover before taking on the next hard pitch. There was no real need for me to take a lead here – John and Ivan had it covered – but my pride was on the line. This was my expedition, I had planned it, pushed it when it seemed to be a fool enterprise, and it would be for me the peak of my achievements. There was no way I wanted to be dragged up it like a tourist by the better climbers; I needed to earn my place in this company.

The pitch began with a grotty chimney whose floor dropped out into space, filled with swift shit and cockroaches. The climbing suited me fine; it wasn't fiddly or technical, and there were fat muddy ledges running inside that enabled me to bridge the gap with one foot on either side. I swelled with huge pride when John, clearly impressed, commented, 'Steve really likes to get stuck in'. The climbing inside the chimney was unpleasant, slippery, physical and grimy. Outside the chimney, the sense of exposure made the climbing incredibly demanding mentally. The moment I stepped out of the security of the chimney and back on to the rockface, I experienced that dizzying pitch in my stomach as I looked down and realised the drop went on for an eternity, hundreds of metres down to the jagged rocks below. I might as well have been perched on the ledge of a plane, about to do a parachute jump. It made me want to scuttle back into the safety of the grotty chimney again! The climbing wasn't made any easier by the fact that every few yards some very surprised swifts would rocket out of their nests, wings buffeting the walls and then my face, before they thundered through my hair and out into the big blue. Unfortunately, the chimney was very difficult to get out of, and at the end of the pitch I stopped to relieve myself into the crack, not realising that John was below me, finding out for real what it felt like to be pissed on from a great height . . .

As soon as I'd finished setting up and equalising the belay, I gave John the signal to come up and join me. Before he reached me I had a divine experience. A tiny hummingbird, bright yellow with red cap, green breast and white eye patches, buzzed about the rockface, then perched on a branch close enough that I could have reached out and taken him into my palm. He eyed me up for a while then disappeared. Minutes later he flew back, hovered at my feet, levitated up to my face and hummed about a foot away from my eyes, moving from one side to the other as if to get a good perspective of this strange intruder, then buzzed away again. Minutes later, he reappeared as if to say, 'No, really, let me get this straight!' and then hung, defying gravity, in front of my face, looking me straight in the eye. I got on the radio in my usual over-the-top enthusiasm and the other guys responded with total disbelief. However over the following days they all came face to face with the inquisitive birds, and we even managed to film one of them whirring inquisitively around Tim's ears. This is quite an achievement – when I tried to film hummingbirds in Costa Rica, I spent an entire day kneeling in front of some Heliconia flowers where hummers were feeding, in a tropical downpour with hungry leeches scooting up my trouser legs, and still never got as close as we were on Upuigma. It may have been that the bright colours of our helmets were exciting their innate desire to seek out colourful pollen and nectar-bearing flowers, but to us it seemed that they were inspecting us, trying to figure out what we were.

Day two was a big climbing day that didn't get us very far. The route above was elusive and our direction changed with every single pitch, dog-legging backwards and forwards across the face. In order to film, we had to send Tim ahead to fix ropes for the camera, which was time consuming, and then for every metre we climbed we had to haul over a hundred kilos of gear up behind us. This endless effort slowed us down so drastically that it was nearly 6 p.m. before we stopped climbing and started to think about sleeping. Darkness fell half an hour later. We ate a dinner of cereal bars and handfuls of raisins hanging in our harnesses, shivering in the cold in our sweaty climbing smalls while Tim and John fretted with the portaledges below us.

A portaledge is a sheet of canvas strung tight over a rectangle of metal poles and hung from a vertical or overhanging rockface by a spider's web of straps. You sleep on the ledge still wearing your harness, as the thing tips and sways alarmingly every time you move. Ivan preferred to sleep swinging in space in a hammock with a single piece of gear attached at either end. Creating our swinging campsite in the dark was a nightmare of tangled ropes and twisted equipment, but in typical British fashion we laughed and joked away as we shivered in the icy cold. Tim told us about his years working on the British Antarctic survey, and John and Keith swapped stories about the legendary climbing figures they had either filmed with, competed against or partnered over the years. As so often when you are in the company of such characters, moments that could be hell on earth feel almost like a Sunday afternoon down the local pub. Their ease was infectious, and I settled into fixing us up some freeze-dried food on a ledge as broad as a greeting card, while my teeth chattered and we all chuckled away at silly stories. John picked the short straw, having to share a bed with me – in his words, 'built more like an all-in wrestler than a rock climber' – which meant the poor guy ended up sleeping on a piece of canvas the size of a mantelpiece.

I didn't expect to get a second of sleep crammed into my ledge with John, but funnily enough it was all rather wonderful, rocking gently with hundreds of metres of open air beneath my back. It seemed that one minute I was squeezing myself in and whingeing about the lack of space, and the next I was peering out at a sunrise of quite startling colours staining the skies beyond my swaying bed. I can honestly say I've never seen anything so divine in my life. You could see all the way to Brazil and Guyana, and the view was punctuated by the aeronautics of the thousands of swifts hawking for insects about the cliffs. As they swooped in unison past us, the wind through their wings made a sound like a power kite or a huge samurai sword being swiped through the air in a Bruce Lee movie. As I started to rouse myself and get up out of my sleeping bag, Tim got up out of his ledge to relieve himself. Unfortunately, in doing so he managed to stand on the edge of the portaledge and Keith's weight on the other side totally unbalanced the whole platform. It flipped, inverting completely, tipping Keith out of his comfortable sleeping position and dropping him into the abyss. The first we were aware of this was a strangled yelp from Keith and Tim's frantic efforts to haul Keith back in. He'd been sleeping in his harness and the safety ropes had caught him, but even so, to be woken from peaceful slumber to find yourself bouncing above infinity is a shock to the system guaranteed to bring you round quicker than an ice-cold shower.

We lay wrapped up in the warmth of our sleeping bags while we chewed on a breakfast of cereal bars and handfuls of boiled sweets, putting off until the last minute the moment we'd have to put on our grubby clothes and cling to the harsh rock with our blistered fingers. John took the first pitch while I belayed from below on the ledge, but unbelievably he seemed to be struggling. This felt bizarre, as the pitch didn't look that hard; indeed it had been a toss-up whether John or I would lead it, and I'd been quite keen. There was a fair bit of struggling before John called down his explanation: 'You're going to have to be really careful here, Steve, there's a big loose rock. Whatever you do, don't touch it.' Knowing John, I should have realised immediately what an understatement this was. Pushing up twenty feet above the belay, I reached out in search of hand holds to my right. There was a sickening, nails-down-blackboard scraping noise, and it seemed as though the whole cliff face moved. Not a word of a lie, the loose rock was the size of a wardrobe, and every hold I needed for my right hand and foot was on it, with Ivan directly below. Using the boulder, the pitch would have been a piece of cake; without it, it was almost impossible. If I put any weight on the boulder the whole thing would come off the rockface, and a few tonnes of stone would plummet on to my friends below. As the prospect of being responsible for the deaths of people I cared about etched itself into my mind, I tensed up. In my panic, I committed the cardinal sin of holding on too hard, so my fingers and forearms were burning with lactic acid, veins popping, muscles pumping with exertion. Every new hand and foothold felt like climbing on broken glass, with even the slightest nudge causing the leviathan rock to graunch sideways, sending a trickle of rock dust down on to Ivan below. On Keith's footage it's difficult to see me in person, but the audio from my radio mic is clear, practically in tears, ordering myself to get it together. It took me fifteen minutes to climb past the boulder, but it felt as if it had taken hours. I'd sweated so much and was so flooded with adrenalin that I could barely talk when I reached the belay. Shivering as if I'd just drunk fifty strong espressos, I grabbed John in a big bear hug. While he said something calm about it being a 'nice bit of climbing', my bottom lip wobbled uncontrollably.

John's response exemplifies my biggest challenge in making adventure films: stiff-upper-lip British adventurers see it as a sign of weakness to show any emotion or fear. No matter how hardcore the situation, they face it with the same matter-of-fact attitude. We had almost died, yet John's response was 'Bit loose that boulder, wasn't it?' delivered as if he'd found an overripe avocado in his packed lunch. It's something we struggle with in expedition television, but also probably explains how I've managed to make a living at this: I have no problem letting everyone know when I'm frightened!

Fear has its home in the amygdala, an area of the brain above the spinal cord. It's key to the functions of emotion and memory. This triggers the release of endorphins, noradrenalin and dopamine, neurotransmitters that are the lifeblood of the fight-or-flight response. The adrenal glands start to secrete adrenalin, the heart rate and breathing increase, the digestive system is shut off, blood supply to the brain and skeletal muscle increases while the supply to other non-essential parts of the body slows. The bladder relaxes, and in extreme cases this may result in wetting yourself. (The need to do a nervous wee is well known, but has much more dramatic effects in the animal kingdom. Birds of prey squirt out their bowel contents before taking flight to hunt, thus 'lightening the load'; snakes and other reptiles evacuate their bowels spectacularly when stressed, not only making themselves lighter, but also covering themselves in foul-smelling goo, which makes them less appetising to predators.) Your limbs can also become jittery, poised for explosive action. Sadly many of these responses are exactly the opposite of the calmness you need when you're in trouble on a climb. There is nothing worse than a case of 'Disco leg' when nerves set in on a tough rock route; vibrating Elvis hips destroy your stability and force you to hang on harder, thus using up valuable energy. However, the response has evolved for a reason. Provided you can keep it under control, fight-or-flight will hand you the physical tools to do stuff you could never manage normally. The second wave of chemicals secreted are the endorphins. These include natural opiates, which may be many times more potent than morphine, allowing you to battle pain more effectively (whether that be through injury or through physical exertion) as well as giving a sense of well-being. And then finally, dopamine, the happy hormone, is released. This appears to be some kind of reward for dealing successfully with a stressful or dangerous situation. Clearly all of these chemicals have the potential to be addictive, but it is possible that, from a Pavlovian response, we can also become addicted to the activities that we associate with these chemicals, such as exercise, orgasm and fear.

Behavioural geneticists have identified certain 'warrior genes' that seem to occur in extreme athletes. They're also sometimes referred to as psychopath genes. People who have these genes are often dopamine-dependent and more likely to be sensation-seeking. They may also struggle to create an enzyme which regulates serotonin, a chemical in the brain that calms people down. It's the brain's handbrake, and a deficiency can make it difficult for an individual to control aggressive impulses or anger. It's a controversial field of study; for a start, people are more than a sum of their genes. These findings have been arrived at by tracking tendencies and statistical potentials across huge study groups. It can therefore be difficult to determine the relative importance of nature versus nurture. And despite the extremely negative connotations of the term 'psychopathic', in scientific terminology the word describes a spectrum of behaviours including, at the milder end, socially acceptable tendencies such as thrill-seeking or hedonism. Some of the most accomplished figures in our society would be classified as socially functioning psychopaths. Business leaders exhibit four times the level of psychopathic tendencies as the rest of the population; when it's hiring and firing time they won't stop to take into account the personal tragedies of those under them, they make big impulsive decisions without fear of retribution, their focus on the balance sheet rather than the cost in human terms. And these tendencies are not confined to big business. My girlfriend is an

Olympic athlete, and reports that some professional athletes betray traits that verge on socio- or psychopathic: tremendous drive, single-mindedness, the capacity to withstand and even enjoy pain. Many athletes are also morally flexible, able to justify any actions that result in personal accomplishment, those who have embarked on outrageous doping programmes being a classic example. It's an intriguing area of study, and without doubt goes some way to explaining the psychology of some ultra-driven athletic adventures and explorers. There is no doubt though that my colleagues are far more sane and balanced, and driven by purer, more altruistic goals. Folks like John and Ivan are always the first to shun food if there's not enough to go around, the first to volunteer for a dangerous lead when everyone's scared. They'll always haul the biggest load, carry the heaviest backpack, take the most miserable sleeping spot. They are good people, through and through.

As the day wore on we were starting to gain altitude, climbing exhilaratingly well and fast. The one factor that was going to limit us was having to stop early to put up the ledges again. But the route had another surprise in store. 'Steve, we're not going to have to bother with the ledges tonight, there's a cave up here we can probably kip in.' Again the fabulous John understatement. From the ground, I had taken it to be a hairline fracture in the face, but the cave turned out to about ten feet wide. Inside, it was practically a canyon, with huge chockstones wedged higher up in the cleft, a dry leaf floor and an empty dark chasm at the back, which caveman Tim was dying to get into and explore . . . until John took a poo into it, and we discovered it had a howling updraught, which managed to fill the air with a nasty smell for the rest of the evening.

We sat around wide-eyed and chatty, drier and warmer than we'd been in over a week. We took a precious sip each from Tim's hip flask of Irish whiskey, and swapped tall tales from our many adventures. Foreboding and fear began to give way to excited optimism, all of us starting to believe we might actually make it to the top. There were mercifully few biting bugs, and there was just enough room for everyone to lie flat out on their soft dry-leaf bed, for the best night's sleep I can remember.

We woke to brilliant beams of sunlight cutting into our troglodyte paradise, swallows and swifts flitting out from their roosts above to begin a day's hunting on the wing. Finding the way out of our cavern and back on to the vertical rock was the first challenge of the day, and it was my turn to take the lead. The next pitch was one of the most satisfying leads I've ever done: a new line, never climbed before, right at the limit of my abilities in the E for 'extreme' grades, yet somehow coming together, with each delicate finger- and foot-hold following on from the next like notes in a perfect operatic aria. More than ever before, the climbing made sense for me; it had the feel of a dance rather than an athletic endeavour. It may not have seemed this way to the watchers below, gazing on as this overheavy, muscle-bound meathead huffed his way up the vertical wall, but I felt liberated, confident, challenged yet free.

Just as the route was starting to thin out, the handholds disappearing and threatening to leave me stranded, I looked across and saw that the opposite wall of the cave was now within reach. I bridged out, near doing the splits, transferring the weight from my burning hands to the sticky soles of my climbing shoes. Then I lunged up to the top of one of the high chockstones, lodged in the gap in the cave many millennia ago. Pulling myself up on top of it, I made an intriguing discovery, a miniature ossuary clearly decades old. Every square inch was covered with tiny bones. It could well have been the detritus from an ancient bird of prey eyrie, scattered prey remnants from several generations of feasting on the animals of the high mountain. Most of the bones were parrot and swift skulls and skeletal bones, from the birds that were roosting above, but there were far smaller bird skeletons, as well as the skull and remains of a rodent. That might not sound very exciting, but there were not supposed to be any mammals up there – if we could find even one, it would without doubt be new to science. With my heart thumping from excitement and effort, I pushed on out of the crack, and emerged to find another surprise wonder: what we would later christen 'the hanging gardens'. It was a broad, vegetated ledge about the size of a squash court, hung with diminutive Bonzai tree shrubs, delicate orchids, small palms and ferns like a Chelsea flower show rock garden in the clouds. The bushes were bustling with dozens of noisy green parakeets that chirped and squeaked as they flew around me. I also found   and filmed in glorious macro close-up – a bizarre winged insect I'd never seen before. It turned out to be the winged adult of an ancient group known as the embiids or webspinners, but way larger than anything my entomologist colleagues had ever seen. Two different species of hummingbird buzzed in to check out the alien invader, red blooms and white orchids hung from vines and tangled vegetation along its walls. It was like a miniature Garden of Eden, dropping away to views of the Gran Sabana that were some of the most overwhelming on Earth. And I was the first human being to see it. I wanted to stay there for hours, letting the place saturate my memory so it would never fade. It was as intoxicating as champagne, a moment in time mine and mine alone that no one would ever really be able to share.

After fixing a ropes system to bring up my colleagues, I returned down to the cave, to find everyone eyes bright with excitement. They apologised for having dismissed my enthusiasm two days earlier, as the hummingbirds had been busily hovering about them, studying them as they belayed me. While huge soggy chunks of vegetation plummeting at our heads had been an unfortunate unpleasantness on the vertical climb, here in the cave the dead leaves were dry and desiccated, tissue-paper thin. Leaves we inadvertently kicked up were borne on the updraught that continually coursed up the face, and spun magically about us ever upwards, helicoptering and dancing like thousands of butterflies in the afternoon sun. When a group of battle-hardened climbers stand transfixed in awe at the sight of dancing, levitating leaves, you know you're in a very special place.

After four days hanging in space, the top seemed to be within our grasp. We were higher than the Eiffel Tower or the Empire State Building, and our entire route had been on vertical or overhanging rock. Once out of the hanging gardens, the rock suddenly gave us a pleasant surprise. Though this was the steepest, most overhanging section of rock we had yet been on, it was also of the finest quality. On rock the colour of ginger snaps, our feet latched on to blank overhangs held by nothing but the sticky abrasion of the surface itself. Every fingerhold we reached for was sharp and positive. This is the reason people want to climb tepuis. We followed perfect cracklines into which camming protection slipped perfectly and gripped with satisfying reliabilty. Though extraordinarily hard, with exposure and height that made my head spin and my guts lurch into my throat, it was some of the most perfect climbing in the world.

The third pitch from the top turned out to be the best of all. John led the way, passing under a dramatic ceiling. There was nothing for the feet, just a grippy shelf underneath the roof for the hands; Keith had climbed ahead on the ropes to film me, and had a ringside seat as I seconded the pitch, trying to emulate John's elegant example, crabbing sideways, lunging for a fragile layback then splaying my legs to find a nubbin of a foothold half a walnut high. Dropping down again, then holding on with the fingers of one hand, forearms burning with lactic acid, to rip out the protection before moving on to the hardest moves – the crux of the section. The cam came out with a satisfying pop, but even so, my weight and inferior technique had already taken their toll. My whole body started to shake with an exaggerated shiver of strain, my feet started to slip from their braced position on the featureless slab, and I sprayed sweat and saliva with every angry puff.

'Got no footholds!' I hissed, rubber soles searching for traction. My arms were empty. Nothing. My fingers began to quiver and my legs started to wobble with fear. I reached up to take the one positive hold, the one I'd staked all my efforts on reaching. Nothing! It wasn't wide enough for me to get a decent hold on. It was the ledge or nothing. And then, inevitably, my fingers slipped from the rock, and I fell, disappearing back into space, my scream echoing around the amphitheatre of ancient sandstone . . .

Keith was perfectly placed to film me pitching off into space, yelping with genuine fright, falling completely out of shot . . . before bouncing like a bungy jumper a good fifteen feet below, with vertiginous empty space beneath me. It's one of the most tense moments of the documentary. When you're on the indoor climbing wall and come off, the fall is inevitably no more than a few easy feet. When you're adventure climbing and your belaying partner cannot see you, the rope is slack and traversing sideways, and inevitably will stretch as well.

Though the fall itself presented little real danger (due to the size of the overhang I merely swung in space, well clear of the rock), getting back on to the climb was pretty nerve-racking. I attached a couple of thin pieces of cord around my ropes and, using their grip, climbed my way back up the ropes. Every shunt upwards made the ropes saw backwards and forwards over a blade of rock above. I won't say it was razor sharp, because that would obviously be untrue, but it was probably as sharp as the blade on a butter knife. Anyone who's seen quite how little it takes to cut one of these ropes when it's taut will understand my nerves. It was a tense few minutes, watching the lines above me – which held my life – fray and fur up with the friction, and I was very glad to have my sweaty fingers back on the rock again!

John graded that pitch harder than anything I'd ever climbed before, and the next pitch was to be my hardest lead ever. My confidence was by now soaring, and bolstered even further by the fact that producer Steve had been picked up by a helicopter, and was hovering thirty metres away from me, filming on the high-definition camera. Eager to demonstrate my new-found confidence, I led out under the overhang, revelling in the drama of the moment and the fact that a helicopter was whirring mere metres behind me. I knew that there would be only a few more pitches left, and we would be on top.

John raced through the final pitches in the late afternoon as the light was fading. In John's words, those last fifty metres were the hardest on the whole route. The rock was vertical with no overhang, but covered in sodden moss and running with dirty black water. The only holds and places to protect yourself were the insubstantial shrubs poking through cracks in the rock. John has developed a special grade for this muck, and gave these two pitches the hardest level of severity – J for jungle 4. Then, suddenly, the jungle levelled out and Keith, John and I were on top. Hearts pounding away with excitement, we plunged into the forest with my machete leading the way, trying not to destroy plants that had possibly never been studied by science, every step imposing the first ever human footprint.

While Tim, Ivan and Fuco (one of Ivan's friends here to help with the hauling) prepared to spend their night on a ledge below us that was no more than a foot wide, with their feet dangling out into space, Keith, John and I hacked our way through the most magical moss forest in the world. Lurid lava-coloured mushrooms bloomed from the humus floor, confused hummingbirds buzzed like bees around our faces, the pineapple tops of gargantuan bromeliads and

Carboniferous ferns sprouted like something from a Hollywood dinosaur movie. The sights we saw during those first hours were unbelievable, even more so as we were unquestionably the first ever to see them.

We found a rock wall perhaps a hundred metres back from the top of our route, peppered with caves and other formations. John disappeared into a crevice, then called back with an excitement I'd never heard from him before: 'You've got to come through here, guys, this is AMAZING!' It was tricky to follow him, as the crevice was only just big enough to accommodate my shoulders, but it took us through a twisting sequence of caves before we leapt over a yawning gap, turned a corner, then popped out into a gallery of phenomenal beauty. We were on a ledge with a white sand floor, protected from the rain by a craggy overhang. The ledge extended into a rock lip hanging out at the level of the treetops. It was as if the gods had built us the perfect balcony from which to survey our new Lost World. There are simply no words to describe the excitement and wonder we felt. As the sunset bled to twinkling starlight, we lit a fire, sat back in bubbling ecstasy, oblivious to the hunger in our bellies. We felt like cavemen. It was the most perfect moment of my life. The only thing that marred it was the knowledge of how our friends must have been suffering on the ledge below. Setting up our sleeping bags in the soft sand, we laid our heads down, exhaustion finally taking hold.

My dreams of tigerskin-clad Amazonians clubbing woolly mammoths for tea were broken by the birdcalls of a drowsy dawn. I looked up from my sleeping bag to see the camera in my face and Keith behind it wearing a big happy grin. Instantly, I remembered where we were and knew it was going to be a very good day.

We had woken inside a cloud. The dark stronghold walls loomed over our sandy beds, but were only occasionally visible, as the clouds steamed, billowed and seethed through their crags and crevices. The sandstone has been etched and carved through deep time into pillars, spindly statues and twisted columns. Through the ever-changing lens of the fog, it seemed that trolls, griffins and gargoyles were peering down at us through the smoke from a snoring dragon's snout. The smoky damp absorbed and deadened all sound. The odd piercing call from an unseen bird resounded in a muted echo, a unique and eerie soundscape. We could have been beamed down by Scotty to an alien planet. Then, as the sunlight burned away the cloud, we were afforded glimpses of the exquisite panorama that lay beyond. I have travelled the planet for a living for nearly two decades, been to over a hundred countries, and seen the seven natural wonders of the world. None of those equalled what we saw that morning – and we were the first human beings to see it. I had nothing but pity for poor Keith, who somehow had to capture what we saw on a meagre video camera that could never do it justice.

Our first task was to drop ropes down to the others so that they could join us. They were haggard and hungry, but overjoyed to finally be on top. Next, we hacked our way to a place that our aerial recces had identified as a good spot for a helicopter landing. Here, if all was safe and well, we would meet with Steve Greenwood, who would come in the chopper bearing extra supplies and the main filming cameras. The hack took longer and turned out to be harder and wetter than we'd bargained for. After two hours of thrashing we finally made it through, by which time my machete hand was shredded. Not that I was even aware of the discomfort at the time – there was too much going on around me. Halfway through our journey, we broke out of the forest and found ourselves on a broad sandy ledge overhung by another rock wall – the perfect place for a base camp. Traversing the length of the wall, I was struck by lines of footprints along the edge. The first tracks were bird prints, but then . . . surely not? Yes! The prints of a small rodent, running close to the wall in perfect symmetrical patterns. And that wasn't all. Running the full length of the wall were prints left by a rather larger mammal that had five toes with evident claws, which led me to surmise it could be some kind of opossum, a member of the weasel family, or a giant rat (they have some in the area the size of small dogs). The plot was certainly thickening!

The helicopter managed to place a skid on a large, flattish rock, and drop off a cargo net of kit. Steve came bearing not only the high-definition camera but a resupply of un-cockroached dehydrated food, and . . . a case of beer! This was his special surprise treat to me, as it was my birthday. As we'd been drinking murky puddle slime for the past few days, even a nice bottled water would have tasted pretty good. A warm can of local lager was like the elixir of the gods. Tired and dehydrated as we were, it went straight to our heads, and we sat around giggling, toasting our great fortune! It was without doubt the most memorable birthday of my life. Before us was a glorious canyon we christened 'Happy Valley'. To our backs the wall fell away to a vast view of the savannah. In front to either side was vertical black rock rising to the mountain's summits. The interior was more colourful than a village flower fete: a mess of boulders carpeted with bromeliads, moss and epiphytes. There were the pink and white blooms of red-lipped pitcher plants, which fire their pollen out in a spume in response to the low-pitched vibration of a pollinating insect's wings. There were bladderworts – carnivorous plants which thrive inside the water bowls of the bromeliads and feed on the insect larvae that also live there – and bright sundews, which close like sticky Venus flytraps around unsuspecting bugs. This is a bad place to be an insect – even the plants want to eat you! This is down to the fact that these summits are so-called 'rain deserts'. The huge amounts of rain wash away any soil, so the plants can't gain nutrients through their roots. Instead, they have to gain their nitrates and phosphates from the tissue of living things. There were also abundant orchids, some of which were unquestionably new to science. Orchids are a fascinating group of flowers, and very much drove the exploration of this area, and much of the tropical cloud-forest. In the nineteenth century, explorers called travellers slogged their way through these jungles on the hunt for the most dramatic blooms, which would then be shipped back to Europe for the delectation of royalty and the mega rich.

Movement around Happy Valley was extremely difficult. There was no soil between the rocks; the carpet of bromeliads seemed to be rooted in empty air. This meant there was no telling where solidness began and ended, and every so often you'd sink in up to your thigh, with your foot dangling in space. Nevertheless we had a thoroughly productive day, filming this prehistoric wonder from every angle before retreating to our new base camp. Our most exciting find of all was a tree frog we discovered hiding inside a bromeliad. As we continued on our way we found more of these frogs; some bromeliads contained as many as four or five. We had been told by the leading Venezuelan herpetologist that it was 'inconceivable there would be frogs on top of Upuigma' and that if we did find one, it would certainly be new to science and endemic to the peak. Birds can fly and seeds disperse on the wind, but how could a terrestrial creature climb well over a thousand feet of overhanging rock? In all probability this frog had evolved here in isolation. We set about taking a slew of photos to send to the experts on our return, but within a couple of hours it had reached the point where my constant cries of 'I've found another frog, guys!' were met with general boredom: 'Give us a shout when you've found a new species of elephant or something, will you?'

The next two days were alive with discovery. I set up a profusion of traps, hoping to catch creatures. We had brought along collapsible mammal box traps. The mammal, drawn inside by the tempting scent of peanut butter or banana-flavoured baby food, steps on a lever and the door shuts, leaving it boxed in but unharmed. I placed these around the sandy rock walls, where the plentiful small mammal trails told of exciting but unseen animals scampering around by night. I found a large green praying mantis, which flew away, and a small wriggling salamander that I dropped and lost before we could record it – devastating as there are only two species known from the area, and it would most certainly have been new. Despite these frustrations, I spent my days wet, muddy and as happy as a little boy, pulling apart the giant bromeliads for them to pour pints of brown water down my trousers.

One of the big successes was filming a beautiful triplet of falcons that were noisily active about the area of our camp. We had assumed it to be a common bat falcon, but through careful scrutiny of the *Complete Birds of Venezuela*, found that the bat falcon didn't occur above 1,400 metres and nested in open territory in trees. What did fit the bill was the orange-breasted falcon; a bird that had been seen as high as 2,200 metres (our altitude), and nested in rugged cliff faces, such as those found on these tepuis. The exciting thing was that this bird was impossibly rare. The book listed every single verified sighting in the last thirty years (about ten), the last of which was on nearby Roraima . . . in 1999. Perhaps the best news was that our birds here on Upuigma's summit were a breeding pair. One of the trio of birds was slightly duller in plumage than the others, and whenever he took off, the other two birds would noisily fly at him as he attempted to perch, refusing to allow him to land. Adult raptors often chivvy their progeny in this manner, forcing them to stay airborne and bolster their flying skills.

The biggest drama, though, was saved for our penultimate evening. One of my tools for catching insects was a portable UV light aimed at Tim's white-sheet sleeping bag. This form of moth trap, or 'bug sheet' as it is known, is one of the most reliable ways of attracting airborne insects. My favoured hypothesis for why they gather on the folds of the sheet goes like this: moths and other night flying insects navigate by keeping the moon at a constant angle from them. As the moon is so far away, the distance between them and the moon effectively never changes. In the natural world there are few other sources of bright light at night, and so the moths are confused by these strong closer sources of illumination. When they come upon an artificial light, they mistake it for the moon and try to keep flying at a constant angle from it. The artificial lights, though, are not an infinite distance away, so they end up getting steadily closer and closer, flying around it in ever-decreasing circles, until eventually they crash into it. The previous night our moth trap had been a dismal failure, but tonight was to be quite the opposite.

It was long after dark and the sheet had been in place for several hours while we huddled around the stove making our dehydrated meals. After we had finished, Steve wandered down to check the sheet and we heard him exclaim, 'Oh . . . that's extraordinary!' Keith grabbed the camera, and we raced down to join him. Steve was kneeling beside a white-collared swift, which was lying in the sand, clearly knocked senseless. As I picked up the bird, there was a loud THWACK! And another bird dropped into the dirt alongside us. As this was obviously something to do with the bug sheet we raced to turn the light off. It was *covered* with huge moths. One species had wings the size of my hand and was there in great numbers. Another tepuis specialist moth was coloured to blend in with the mineral strains on the sandstone walls of the tepuis. Despite being the size of a paperback novel, it was almost invisible. There was another loud thwack, and another swift fell to earth. It's difficult to know what was happening; perhaps this first glimpse of artificial light had intrigued them, and they had come to take a closer look. Or maybe their navigation systems had been thrown out by the light (some, but not all, swiftlets echo-locate like bats), or they had swooped down to feast on the unnatural aggregation of flying insects and in their frenzy had crashed into the walls. Whatever the reason, it was causing flying chaos amongst the birds, so we switched it off. As I gently coaxed the dazed bird in my hand, she struggled faintly and I opened my fingers. 'Please be all right little thing,' I whispered. She shook out her wings and took off.

But there was no time for thinking. A glossy black scorpion had also been attracted by our light, so I caught it, and started talking to camera about it. Tim was crouched by Keith's shoulder, trying to attract my attention. Knowing that he would never interrupt while we were filming unless it was something important, I stopped talking and looked up.

'Steve,' he said, 'look into that mammal trap – there's something inside it, but it hasn't set the trap off.'

I picked up the trap, slamming my butterfly net over the top as I did so, but in the chaos the tiny furry prize fell out. In panic, I scrambled around, but couldn't see it. I'd lost it. Disaster! Then I sensed scrabbling in the trap in my hand. The creature had fallen straight back into the trap! Gingerly I took it out. It was like a large dormouse, with huge ears and black eyes, capacious whiskers, and it snuffled in my hand apparently oblivious to having been caught. It's difficult to see how a mouse could have clambered up all that rock. But somehow it must have done. The only question is: when? If it had been within the last few centuries, then maybe this was essentially the same as the mice found hundreds of metres below on the savannah. If on the other hand it was any earlier, and this mouse's ancestors had been trapped up here, then they would almost certainly have evolved into a new species. To claim it as a new species, though, we would have had to euthanise it, and take the specimen back with us, and I wasn't willing to do that. Instead we took plenty of photos and video footage, and then released it back into the rock.

After all the excitement I didn't sleep a wink that night, and I wasn't the only one. Keith and John, who are not themselves obsessed with zoology, were jabbering about it round the campfire as if we'd been present at an event of historical significance. And that's how it felt.

After four nights on top, we all woke with the familiar excitement in our bellies, only for it to plummet when we realised that the time had come to leave our paradise and head back to civilisation. That morning, up before the dawn, we were all wandering round trying to take photos with our eyes and suck in every single element of the wonder around us. To memorise a place that we would surely never see again. Usually at the close of an expedition, no matter how wonderful it has been, some part of you is glad to be heading home. Some part of you is crying out to end the hardships and tuck into a decent meal. Not here. We simply were not ready to leave. It had all been too soon, there was too much left to explore, too much left to learn. I wanted to stand there on our ledge and just look. I knew the cameras would never be able to do it justice. The wonder of this place would be tarnished by time and the distorting lens of television. I had discovered this place. I was the first man to climb to its summit plateaus, the first to hold its precious and unique species, the first to sleep on its magical sandy balcony. It was mine, and I wasn't willing to give it up yet. But you can't bottle a place like Upuigma. You can't take a photo or film, or write words that will capture its essence. And that, I guess, is why I love the place so much.

As I write this, eight years later, only one other expedition has summited Upuigma. Most of its secret gardens and summit valleys remain unexplored. But then perhaps it should remain that way: a perfect Garden of Eden, preserved in my memories. Untainted by everything that has followed since.

THE FALL

'There is a saying in Tibetan: "Tragedy should be utilised as a source of strength." No matter what sort of difficulties, how painful experience is, if we lose our hope, that's our real disaster.' *Dalai Lama XIV*

I lie in the dust, my ropes arranged over me like tinsel on a tumbled Christmas tree, staring at the pulp that used to be my foot. It looks as though someone has hit the heel with an axe, and my heel bone is clearly visible through the neatly divided sludgy yellow fat pad, which is supposed to cushion every footfall. My mind battles between the overpowering need to look at it, to stare, and the sickening horror at seeing a piece of me so mangled. It doesn't seem real. It doesn't look like a real foot anymore; certainly not one of mine. And can I really have just fallen all that way, and still be breathing? I battle to hold panic at bay, while my climbing partner busies himself flushing the wound with water, washing flecks of dirt and brown leaves out of the gash. I focus on his level-headed actions, impressed by how together he is, despite the jitters he cannot hide. The cleaning has the unfortunate side-effect of better exposing the ivory-white glint of bone through the gore. I have fallen at least thirty feet, three or four storeys and on to hard hard rock. Later we'll learn that I've broken my back in two places, but for now it's the shattered foot that focuses our attention. It's a classic distraction injury. That and how we're going to get me out of here without a helicopter.

I've detailed the events of my fall in my earlier book, *Looking For Adventure*, but wrote those words as someone who was absolutely certain they would make a full recovery. The last seven years have unfortunately not borne that out. So much so, that I define everything in my life as either before the fall or after it. It changed everything. Admittedly, I am lucky to be here at all, but what has happened since no one could have predicted. Before covering those events, I'd best give a quick recap of the awful mistake that got me here in the first place.

It happened not long after I'd returned from the triumph on Upuigma. This was one of the busiest years of my career, which saw me working on nine different television series and bouncing from one expedition to another, with barely a day back in the country to draw breath or see old pals. When I did finally get a weekend in the UK in early June, Tarx and I packed our ropes and hopped in the car bound for the nearest real rock to us in the Wye Valley. It's an area with some simply stunning climbing, but on a sunny Saturday the crags can get busy. We thought we were being extremely canny heading to a less well known climbing spot, with a bit of walk in to the face, which was enshrouded in trees, and known for having loose and chossy rock. All things that were well worth putting up with to have the place to ourselves. Every single one of those factors was to prove important as events unfolded.

We started off sharing leads, climbing hard, pushing ourselves to the limit, as we knew we would only have two days' climbing together that entire summer, and wanted to make the most of it.

All the routes were new to us, and with parts of the rockface like overgrown shrubberies and some of the rock crumbling or coming away to the touch, it gave us a spicy morning. We'd been doing pretty well, though, until a short but heavy burst of rain sent us scurrying for the safety of the trees. Sitting under the shade of a hefty beech tree, we munched on cereal bars and chatted, killing time till we could get stuck in again. The rains didn't last long, so we ditched our anoraks and started paying out the line, ready to get under way. On a nice exposed sunny rockface, half an hour ought to have been enough for the rock to dry out. If it had been dry, my future would be very different. If I'd waited another half an hour. If I'd taken on something easier and less threatening, instead of taking on the hardest climb I'd done since Upuigma. If I'd heeded the guidebook's advice . . . So many ifs. Instead, rather than letting common sense delay me, I set off up a route that would have been right at the limit of my abilities on a good day. And the minute I got on it, I realised all was not well. The climb followed an obvious crackline in which all the gear would have to be placed. There was a substantial flake of rock inside the crack, against which everything would have to brace. And it was loose. It shifted around, graunching unpleasantly every time I touched it. Any cams or nuts that were slipped in alongside it would be useless. To begin with, I simply climbed past the problem, choosing not to put any protection in at all. But then I was quite high, and started to get a bit nervous, so I put in a couple of nuts, more for peace of mind than anything else.

By this stage I was nearly ten metres off the ground and the climb was proving to be more of a challenge than I had expected. The inside of the crack was green and slimy, partially from the rain, and partially from not having been climbed for a while. The slime meant that there was no traction for my fingertips, feet, or gear. I was starting to get pumped with the effort, my fingers tiring, fore-arms bulging and veins popping with the effort. This was when I committed my cardinal error. I should have turned back. I should have down-climbed while my fingertips still had some strength left in them. But I was confident. I had just been away with John Arran, and seen how much faith he placed in his gear. How he could have happily hung a truck on a single nut, and would sleep at night suspended by a single well-placed cam. These things were bombproof! So I slipped a cam into the crack, yelled down at Tarx to 'Take', and sat back on my rope to have a rest.

'You'd better be really sure of that cam,' Tarx yelled up to me. I looked down at the rope beneath me. Every single bit of gear had lifted out of place, and was now hanging on the line, like windblown socks on a washing line. The breath caught in my throat as the awful potential hit me. My whole life was hanging on that one single cam. Ever so gently, I eased myself back towards the rock, trying not to do anything that might unseat the cam, perhaps making it 'walk' towards me. I needn't have bothered. There was no gentle slip, or easing out of position. It popped from the crack with a gunshot 'crack', pinging back towards me. The next two things that happened were straight out of Hollywood cliché. The first is that I seemed to hang for a second in mid-air, legs bicycling over a vast gaping chasm, before finally falling. The next is that, as I fell, it seemed to take an eternity; time slowed down and I can honestly recall every leaf on every tree as they flashed past me. I fancy I saw Tarx's face below me contorted in horror, I thought of the expedition I was supposed to be leaving on the following week and how this might scupper that, I saw the rock below and knew it was going to really hurt. Memories and thoughts rushed through my mind.

Scientists have studied near-death experiences and found this phenomenon to be a constant throughout social groups and societies around the world. One hypothesis is that your brain slows your perception and plays back your life experiences, searching for a relevant past situation that might provide a solution to your predicament. It's also true that, once the traumatic event is done, as a result of the disproportionate effect those few seconds have had on your life, your subconscious expands it in memory, giving it greater credence and impact than it actually had at the time.

Whatever the reason, the fall seemed to take hours. When I did hit the rock below, the deceleration was not so much like making a landing, it was like being hit by a truck. It was as if the rock had raced up to hit me, rather than me collapsing down on to it. Almost all the initial force was delivered through my left foot, which took the lion's share of the punishment. I then spiralled off backwards, and tumbled several metres further down to land flat on my back.

Several years ago, for a programme about venoms, I spent some time with a Brazilian tribe called the Sateré Mawé. These wonderful people had an initiation ceremony where their young boys would go through a trial by bullet ant. Bullet ants are officially the world's most painful stinging insect. The venom has evolved solely for causing pain in large vertebrates, and is so potent that even one sting is said to feel like being shot, delivering a white-hot pain that sears through your whole body. The Sateré Mawé put on gloves that have hundreds of bullet ants woven into them, and dance with them on for about fifteen minutes, being stung countless times. For three hours after I wore the gloves, there was nothing in my world apart from pain. I was passing in and out of consciousness, weeping like a newly bereaved widow, powerless and emasculated by the force of pain.

This was worse.

It was now that Tarx showed his true colours. Like so many of the people I really value, faced with a crisis he became utterly calm and methodical, dealing with the situation as if he were a professional paramedic. He stabilised my position, went through some simple checks to assess whether my cervical spine (i.e. neck) was broken, then set to work on what was clearly the main area of damage: my foot. Tarx eased off my left climbing shoe, doing his best to calm my screaming, which he later said reminded him of his wife when his son was being born. I could see instantly from the look on his face that all was not well. Through his calm, his complexion had gone grey. Grabbing the first-aid kit and water from his rucksack, (bravo, I never bring a first-aid kit for a day at the crag!) he flushed the wound out, and bound it as well as he could with bandage, attempting to stem the flow of blood, and to hide what was a thoroughly gruesome mess. My ankle was dislocated, and pointing off at a strange angle. Much more horrific, though, was the fact that the impact had driven my sharp heel bone down through the fat pad of my heel, cleaving it as neatly as if it had been struck by a hatchet. Beyond the skin was yellow fat, then peeking out from the blood was the bone itself. We stared in sick fascination.

Our next problem was getting help. Tarx pulled out his mobile phone and held it up to the sky. No service. He yelled and yelled for help, hoping someone might be wandering nearby and would come to our aid. Nothing. So we were on our own. The next call would be whether he would leave me where I was and go and make a phone call or bring the cavalry. Here, my bravado took over. No, I was going to make it back to the road under my own steam. Tarx sprinted ahead off down the path with both our rucksacks, returning to half carry me down the trail towards safety. The steep forest track had taken twenty minutes on the way up. It took more than double that on the way down. Several times I overbalanced and my foot grazed the ground. I dropped to the floor as if I had been shot, in the most fantastic amount of pain I have ever experienced, leaving behind a vibrant red splash on the pebbles.

It was a good two hours before we got to hospital, and I was finally placed on significant pain relief. It didn't help me much, knowing that the accident was 100 per cent my fault, caused by my impatience, my attempting to climb beyond my means, and my simple lack of ability. The ten days in hospital that followed was hell, but also incredibly uplifting. Visits, flowers and a vote of confidence poured in from an array of television dignitaries in, and from my close colleagues. Obviously I was determined to get back up and running within weeks, and the first thing that had to be addressed was my back. I was released from hospital wearing a heavy body brace that made me look like a storm trooper, and strict instructions to wear it for four months. That wouldn't do at all. So I took myself to see spinal specialist Ian Harding. He looked through my X-rays, took a deep breath and sat me down for an adult chat.

'OK,' he said, 'you've been incredibly lucky. I had three guys in yesterday, all of them fell off ladders and things, none of them as half as far as you, and none of them will ever walk again. A fall of that distance on to rock, I think it's testament to your physical conditioning that you'd ever walk again, let alone be walking now.'

This was obviously good to hear, but it didn't help me with my burning problem. 'The hospital doctors say I need to wear this back brace for four months,' I said, testing the water. 'Do you think I need to have it on that long?'

Ian held the X-rays up to the light again, and paused.

'The breaks don't penetrate through your vertebrae. They're stable, reasonably structurally sound . . .'

I nodded enthusiastically, this sounded positive.

'However, you still have a broken back. If you put it under stress, these fractures are weak, and will break, and you won't walk again.'

I frowned. That didn't sound so good.

'On the flip side,' he continued, 'you have phenomenal core musculature.' I tried not to look too proud of myself. 'But if you wear that brace for four months, all of that will go. And you'll probably have back problems for the rest of your life.'

'I promise, I'll be careful,' I enthusiastically responded.

'Right, well, I have your promise on record.' He half smiled. 'I don't think your definition of "careful" is the same as most people's, but as long as you promise not to be doing handstands or throwing somersaults . . . you can take that brace off now. Burn the thing, for all I care.'

Ian's words were the shining light in some pretty glum times. Unbelievably I did follow his advice to the letter. The back healed 100% within a few months, and I have not yet seen any lasting effects from it. How I wish I'd gone and found such similar advice for my foot. Sadly, the doctors had given me a good prognosis for that, telling me the breaks and dislocation would heal up with two months. That sounded pretty good to me, so I'd seen no need to challenge it. After leaving hospital, my determination was to be back filming within six weeks, and I managed it. But it was with a grimace on my face and in agonising pain that I wasn't willing to admit to. I got through it by telling myself that I wouldn't have to endure it for very long. Turned out I was wrong. After six months hobbling round, with my ankle steadfastly refusing to heal, I decided to go and see a specialist. In a ludicrously opulent office lined with green leather and walnut, the specialist twisted and turned the offending joint. I did my best to grin through the pain. 'Nothing wrong with that,' he declared. 'You'll be back playing rugger in no time, old boy.' Then he grimaced, perhaps realising he wasn't stinging me for anything like enough cash. 'Still,' he said, 'best to do another X-ray, to be on the safe side.' Private health care being rather different to our National Health Service, I was back in his office clutching the X-rays in about half an hour (though £800 poorer). He pulled the films from their envelope with a look on his face that suggested this would be nothing more than a bit of box-ticking before a trip to the bank. Then his face scrunched up into a frown. 'Ah,' he said. My stomach dropped into my boots. He stared intently at the X-rays, twisting and turning them around. 'I'm terribly sorry,' he said, 'this doesn't look good at all. Good job we got that X-ray after all.' I smiled and nodded with a positivity I didn't feel. 'Thing is, the duffers who set your ankle . . . well, they put it back in the wrong place. They might as well have put it on back to front.' He showed me where my ankle joint ought to be. 'Should be a space here, see, so the whole kit and caboodle can move about. But there isn't. Nothing but bone grinding on bone. I'm terribly sorry, old chap, but you'll need to have this fused.'

Fused? That didn't sound good at all. The bones of my ankle and leg joined together? Surely that would mean I wouldn't be able to run any more? 'Well, that's not strictly speaking true,' he pondered, 'some people get back to relatively active lives after that operation.'

I'd heard all I needed to hear. I took the X-rays, thanked him warmly, and headed off in search of a second opinion.

Six surgeons later, I'd heard the same thing repeated enough that it was starting to get worrying. However, it was also round this time that I heard of yet another surgeon who was doing ground-breaking surgery for people who were 'beyond hope'. I mentioned this to the surgeon I'd most trusted, who had already done three operations on my ankle to trim away excess bone spurs and keep it moving as well as possible. His face darkened. 'It would be unprofessional of me to advise you against this . . .' everything about his face and demeanour told me he was dying to do just that, 'but whatever you do, this ankle is going to come to a fusion. You can try this new surgery, but the results are poor, and it's going to put you through hell. I mean, I understand why you would want to at least try, and like I say, I can't advise you against it . . .'

Holy God, how I wish I had listened to him.

The new wave surgery involved having a fixator cage drilled into the bones of my leg, and multiple wires drilled through my foot and ankle. For four months, I would have to crank the contraption apart like some medieval torture device, trying to open up the gap in the ankle and set it back in the right place. The problems started right from day one. With a total of ten pins and struts drilled through my flesh and bones, I returned home to my parent's house, on a diet of maximum-dose Tramadol (a hefty opiate painkiller). This horrible chemical left me feeling constantly sick, but it didn't block the pain; the agony I endured was simply indescribable. As we wound the struts open to leverage the joint, I would smash my head against the wall to take my mind off the agony. I didn't sleep a wink the first four days, just lay in my bed drenched in sweat, screaming as if I was going through childbirth. It was clear that something was wrong, and my dose of tramadol was doubled. No improvement, save that now I was tripping my tits off, seeing goblins stalking around my bedroom, and as sick as a dog. After six days without sleep, my sister insisted I try acupuncture. Within seconds of the first needle going in, I was out cold on the bench and snoring like a freight train. Sadly, the relief only lasted an hour or so. Finally, my agent Jo called in a favour from an old doctor friend. Serge was a pain specialist, and booked up for months in advance. However, he waited in his surgery until I could get in and see him. He checked the wounds on my grotesque-looking foot and asked what I was taking for pain relief. I told him. 'Wow,' he said, 'that's a very high dose.' And then he looked down at his notes. 'And what else?' he asked.

'Errrr . . . nothing else,' I replied. He looked up. 'What?' He drew in a breath. 'My dear boy, around fifteen per cent of the population lack the receptor that Tramadol works on. I have no doubt that you are one of these people. For the last eight days you have been en-during this –' he gestured down to my leg – 'with no pain relief at all.' With that he scrabbled around in his drawers, and took out all he had to hand: some ibuprofen. I took two, and about ten minutes later fell asleep in his office chair.

I'd love to report that this was the end of it, but sadly it was only the beginning. Not wanting to waste the four months when I obviously couldn't be filming, I decided to go on the road, doing a live talks tour round the UK. We went to twenty-odd venues, some of them seating as many as 2,500 people, and I would do talks about my adventures and wildlife, sitting on stage wearing a pillow case over what friends were now calling my budgie cage. My beloved mum and dad came with me, helping me in and out of hotels, and keeping all the wound sites clean, which was itself quite a full-on job. And for good reason. Three times in the four months the wounds got infected, and after some hours it would feel as if each one of the wires was superheated white-hot. Then a fever would set in, and we'd dash to a different hospital for IV antibiotics and morphine. The worst of these trips was when I was really pretty ill, in terrible pain, and placed on the geriatric ward in between two poor old souls who were dying very noisily on either side of me (and yes, I am fully aware of how callous this sounds). Halfway through the night, I crawled out of bed and dragged myself along the floor and out into the corridor to try to get away from the awful noise. And then one of the kitchen porters recognised me from the television. For the next few hours, I had what felt like a constant stream of nurses and doctors coming to have their photo taken with me. At some point in the morning a senior member of staff saw what was happening and raised merry hell. From then on in it seemed like, if someone wanted a photo, they'd close the curtains round my bed, and pose for a selfie thumbs up next to me, too weak and hurting to tell them to go and get stuffed. Mid-morning I discharged myself and got a taxi back to Mum and Dad's house.

Those were the lowest days. I'd been determined to be one of the few people that end up being able to walk on their fixator frame, but instead was on crutches for six months. Determined to be independent, I left Mum and Dad's and tried to go home and fend for myself. The day I went home it snowed, and the underside of my crutches got iced over. When I placed them down on the wooden floor as I went through the front door for the first time, the crutches skidded away, and my foot hit the ground hard. And then I went down as if I'd been shot. There was no way I'd call my parents to let them know I'd 'had a fall', that I couldn't make do on my own after all. I'd always gloried in my physicality and fitness, but my body had let me down. I lay there in my doorway for what seemed like an eternity before I was able to get myself up and crawl inside.

THE LAND OF THE THUNDER DRAGON

'Indicating his twisted legs without a trace of self-pity or bitterness, as if they belonged to all of us, he casts his arms wide to the sky and the snow mountains, the high sun and dancing sheep, and cries, "Of course I am happy here! It's wonderful! *Especially* when I have no choice!"

In its wholehearted acceptance of *what is* . . . I feel as if he had struck me in the chest. Butter tea and wind pictures, the Crystal Mountain, and blue sheep dancing on the snow – it's quite enough!

Have you seen the snow leopard?

No! Isn't that wonderful?'

Peter Matthiessen, *The Snow Leopard*

I sit motionless in the dark, snow freckling my cheeks, back pressed against cold stone. Fighting to stop my teeth from chattering, and my eyes from closing I train my eyes off into the black. I know that a short crawl ahead of me lies the ravaged carcass of a mountain goat, torn in half by the mighty rare predator I'd come here to find. However, I can't see it, or anything, as I am keeping all my lights off so as not to give away my presence. The thick clouds mean I can't even perceive the difference between the vast Himalayan summits around me and the black of the night sky. Nocturnal mammals have subtly different eyes to us humans. Their retinas contain more of the light-perceiving structures known as rods, and fewer colour-perceiving cones. Added to that they have the benefit of the Tapetum lucidum or 'bright tapestry', a layer of cells that reflect light back through the retina. Their vision may be practically monochrome, but in darkness that renders us totally blind, they see as well as if it was dusky twilight. Knowing this, I've tucked myself into a small alcove in a sofa-sized boulder, hiding myself from whatever is lurking out there. This seemed like a good idea in the sunshine of late afternoon, standing alongside the ravaged carcass with my crew around me. They'd looked at me as if I was insane when I suggested this solo midnight vigil, but buoyed by bravado I'd gone through with what was indeed a lunatic plan. Now, sitting here in the pitch-black, knowing that superior eyes could be watching me, the folly seems almost laughable.

What was that? A noise off behind my right shoulder. The trickle of a tiny pebble dislodged, bouncing click click click down the steep rocky hillside. I stiffen, trying not to make a sound as I turn on the video camera in my lap without the rustling of Gore-Tex. The next sound is the most terrifying I have ever heard; a guttural big-cat snarl like a panther caught in Tarzan's pit trap, no more than a few metres behind me. It's followed by a scrabbling, and a small landslide of pebbles bounces down around my ears. Then silence. Somewhere off in the darkness is a big cat that could tear a mountain goat in half, and I am here, alone, and suddenly feeling a very long way from home.

When the frame came off my ankle, the following months should have been a steady improvement to total health. After two months more extreme pain, it was clear this was not going to happen. I totally refused to accept, or admit to anyone that my ankle was refusing to work. Instead, I continued to battle away at my schedule of expeditions, television programmes and writing, despite being in a non-stop state of rehab. I was on painkillers and anti-inflammatories for six years without a break. The operations were starting to tot up, and being in chronic pain all the time was creasing my face with lines. People who knew me well fretted that I looked tired all the time, my patience and politeness were being eroded, and I'm sure I was nothing like as much fun to work with as I had always prided myself on being. But I didn't want to admit my weakness, my fallibility. Least of all to myself. When the next *Lost Land* expedition came up, I should have declared on my health forms that I struggled to walk a hundred metres without pain, but that might have meant them taking someone else. Someone younger, fitter. Someone who might go on to supersede me and destroy all that hard work and sacrifice that had got me where I was. Under 'existing conditions', 'ailments', and 'regular medication', I simply put a black cross. No one was taking my place on this expedition.

The Himalayan Kingdom of Bhutan is a real-life Shangri-La. 'The Land of the Thunder Dragon' seems to have steadfastly refused to be tempted into the excesses and extravagances of the modern world; it treasures what is important, and that's what makes it special. It's one of my very favourite places in the world, and in 2010 one of my greatest privileges was to spend five weeks on expedition here with the BBC, making their *Lost Land of the Tiger* series. The series had a simple aim. In the wild, tigers face a battle for survival in which the odds are stacked against them. At the turn of the last century there were more than a hundred thousand in India alone. Today, their numbers have dropped below three thousand worldwide, spread out over a massive range. Those that survive are generally in tiny reserves that are little more than safari parks. Unfortunately, tigers require vast home ranges that intersect with other tigers. They'll patrol these territories – which can be the size of a small country – throughout the year, only occasionally coming into contact with other animals to mate. This means that the current situation simply cannot work. Tigers will be forced to remain in artificially restricted home ranges, and mate within a confined and limited group. The result will be a depletion of variety in the gene pool, and an accumulation of genetic defects. The alternative is that tigers continue to wander, in keeping with their natural drive, but that takes them through some of the mostly densely populated places on the planet. Inevitably, tigers come into conflict with livestock and with humans, and occasionally people get killed. It's obviously pretty tricky to convince a poor Indian farmer that the big cat that has killed his valuable cattle and terrorised his family is actually of considerable significance to international conservation and shouldn't be trapped or shot.

A bold solution has been posited by conservation organisation Panthera, who are championing the idea of 'tiger corridors'. These vast (though often narrow) channels of wild land cross international borders, and link up the existing known populations of tigers. The majority of tigers live in India, and viable tiger corridors would mean displacing millions of people. In the south of the Himalayas, however, Panthera identified a chain of tiger habitat stretching from Nepal in the west to Burma in the east where the land is wild and sparsely populated due to being so geologically rugged, and could theoretically be joined up with relative ease. The biggest challenge was that much of that territory was over 4,000 metres in altitude, and tigers were not thought to occur that high. The other intriguing part of the puzzle was a small country, right slap bang in the middle, whose tiger populations were little known: Bhutan.

The aim of our expedition was to visit several wild areas of Bhutan and find out if tigers were present. Then to attempt to get an idea of how many might be living in the country, and assess if it could be the key to the grand tiger corridor scheme. To these ends, we'd hooked up with Dr Alan Rabinowitz of Panthera, who was very much the driving force behind the whole project. Alan is the most inspirational human being I've ever met. Diagnosed with terminal leukaemia some years back, he has refused to be cowed by the disease, and his occasional frailty, and has redoubled his efforts to save the tigers he loves so much. Due to other commitments, Alan arrived at base camp a week after the rest of us. We'd all been doing our jobs, putting out camera traps, tracking, filming all the wildlife around camp, but it seemed somehow as if all we were doing was making a television programme. There was a lot of grumbling about the fact that no one on the expedition was going to see a tiger, that we were going to spend all this time filming lumps of shit . . . which probably wasn't even tiger shit.

Then Alan turned up. He stepped out of the RIB from the white-water river that raged past our tents, strode straight into base camp and spread out a range of maps and photos on the base camp tables. Every cameraman and soundman was poised, hovering around waiting for him to speak. They were not disappointed. Alan talked with intense passion and focus for over an hour, first of all about the wonder and importance of big cats, then of the joy he has taken in tracking and fieldwork – of how a simple track or scat could be its own reward, more important than gold dust. He used the maps to demonstrate why the area was so genuinely vital, then showing us horrific photos of tigers being skinned alive and of vast hauls of tiger body parts. He made us all believe that the work we were doing here was the crux of the survival of this iconic species. In sixteen years of wildlife telly, I've never seen anything like it. Hardened wildlife filmmakers and biologists stood transfixed, hanging on his every word, some brimming up with indignant tears. And then the second he had finished speaking, everyone was spurred into action. We all had a purpose, we were all important, we could actually *do* something practical to make a difference. We were empowered, and had a focus and a job to do.

This special hour, more than anything else in my career, has shown me how conservation *has* to work. If you tell people only how terrible ecological degradation is, you horrify but intimidate. You leave them feeling helpless and dwarfed by the scale of the problem. We don't like to feel that way, so we tut, shake our heads and change the channel. However, tell people they can make a difference, give them the tools and direction, and they are empowered, charged. People in that frame of mind can move mountains. I learned more from Alan about how to get things done than I had in the whole of my career up to that point.

For my part, it gave me renewed impetus to ignore my failing body and hit the trails along with everyone else. I upped the dosage of my drugs, used my snake stick as a walking aid, and got stuck into long, long days of yomping through the forests.

Over the weeks that followed, camera traps kept a beady eye on the surrounding forests, while I trekked the trails around the base camp in lowland Bhutan on the hunt for signs of tiger activity. Normally my chances would have been slim, but our hit rate was much improved by the presence of Bruiser. Bruiser was a somewhat portly chocolate Labrador with a very special talent. He was very, very fond of a particular tennis ball. Purely for the chance to play around with his special ball for a few minutes, Bruiser would wander the trails all day long, his nose close to the ground, on the hunt for the tell-tale scent of cat scat. He couldn't differentiate between the different species of cats – that would have to be down to our own detective work – but he could locate weeks-old flecks of poo that we would never have seen in a million years.

It took a fair amount to convince my cameraman and soundman that this was a worthy subject for a documentary. We would hit the trails for as much as twelve hours a day. Every hour or so Bruiser would start snuffling his nose around something and we'd go in for a closer look. Most of the time the scat would be leopard or one of the species of small jungle cat. We did have one minor triumph, finding scat on a tree spanning a small river. Using a bit of elementary detective work, I analysed the crime scene and decided it was from a rare clouded leopard, so we put a camera trap in place. The very next night, a lactating female clouded leopard was filmed returning to the exact same spot. I can't tell you how chuffed I was. Over the last decade I've developed a real passion for tracking animals, and in some cases, finding and deciphering the tracks of animals has become more satisfying than seeing the animals themselves. Occasions like this, though, when your detective work can be vindicated, are moments of true smugness. It's like watching a Poirot movie, and working out whodunit.

This trip to Bhutan, tracking animals that I knew I would never see, was a terrific learning experience. Tracking is a monumental part of any naturalist's job, but here I learned to read the stories left behind in the sand with far greater depth than I ever had before. In the past I'd have contented myself with working out what animal had made a particular track; now I set out to determine the animal's sex, whether it was adult or juvenile, and generally tried to get into the animal's head by assessing its gait, depth of tread, etc, to work out what the animal was doing at the time. I've had the privilege of filming wildlife for a living for sixteen years now, and have filmed tigers close up on several occasions. In India, our jeep was charged by a territorial young male, who got to within leaping distance of us, nearly giving my cameraman a coronary. Here in Bhutan we were certain we would not have an experience like this, but every time I found even an old degraded print a thrill coursed through me like little lightning. It was the thrill of discovery.

The lowland forest was packed with glorious endemic wildlife. Golden langur monkeys are one of the most beautiful of all monkeys; the face is black, with dramatic Emperor Ming the Merciless eyebrows that give them a condescending air. The fur is a creamy golden colour, and the tasselled tail hangs down like a pendulous bell pull. They would sit almost silently in the high treetops, gazing down cautiously at us as we watched them chewing leaves, fruit and flowers. As our boats cruised down the torrential river alongside camp, we'd stumble upon wild water buffalo with huge curved horns that seemed so heavy they could barely raise their heads. Tracking in the valley south of camp, I found a dead straight line dragged through the sand: the marks made by a big snake travelling over long distances using the energy-efficient 'inchworm' technique rather than normal serpentine slithering. After following the trail for more than a mile, we lost it, but soon after managed to find and catch a three-metre-long Burmese python, coiled in amongst the vegetation. It was covered in engorged ticks, so before returning it to the scrub, I picked them all off, giving the snake a little respite from the parasites.

I was also lucky enough to be on the team which performed the first running of the Drangme Chu, the extraordinary whitewater river which flowed from the east of the country and down out of the foothills until it ended up at our base camp. We were nearly a week thundering down rapids that our team were the first to run, in one of the most enjoyable expeditions I've ever been lucky enough to be on. Our tiger evidence was sparse: a few highly degraded prints that were probably from tiger, and eyewitness accounts from lower down the river where the banks started to be inhabited. The best bit of evidence was the sad story that a year before a local man had found a dead tiger cub near his house. He still had the pelt, so this at least provided a suggestion that tigers were using the Drangme Chu as a natural corridor across that part of the country.

Towards the end of our stay at base camp, the results began to trickle in. Bruiser had found, and I had identified (Alan concurred) several different scats packed with hair from Sambar deer that were definitely from Bengal tiger. We also had a selection of footprints, and camera-trap images, which Alan analysed to reveal at least three individual tigers wandering the trails near our camp. It was a tremendous success, the first time Bhutan's tigers would ever make an appearance on television screens, and be made known to the outside world. This was just the start, though, we'd all secretly been expecting this result from the base-camp forests.

Tigers need several things in order to survive. They need large amounts of wild land. They need large prey: whereas a leopard may make do with the occasional peacock or rabbit, tigers need to bring down at least one large animal a week. They need water, both to bathe and cool themselves, but also to slow down prey. Charging prey animals into water is a well-known strategy for tigers. And finally, tigers need cover. They are ambush predators, and will generally approach to within less than ten metres of their target before launching an attack. If you remove any one of these factors, it is highly unlikely that you'll find tigers. Here at base camp, all of these could be found in abundance. What was much more intriguing and important in our search for a Bhutanese tiger corridor was the land to the north of the country.

The Himalayan highlands were not known to be home to any tigers, and no tigers had ever been recorded at high altitudes. So it seemed like a hiding to nothing to be heading up there in search of tigers. But there was very good reason for our efforts. To the south of the Himalayas, the Indo-Gangetic plain soars into the foothills then the major mountains themselves. From the Hindu Kush in the west, it spans Afghanistan, Pakistan, Nepal, India, Burma and on into China. The area at around 4,000 metres in altitude is extremely sparsely populated by human beings, very wild, and has national borders that blend seamlessly together. If it was proven that tigers were living and moving in this area, it would open up a natural

1,500-mile tiger corridor that would take only a fraction of the effort to protect.

Cameraman Gordon Buchanan and his team had been tramping to far corners of Bhutan over the course of several months, placing camera traps on high mountain ridgelines, game trails and other locations where it seemed likely a large cat could be travelling. One area that had been beyond their work was into the mountains on the border with Tibet: and specifically the massif of Ganchey Ta, also known as Tiger Mountain. With trusted soundman Nick Allinson and director Sanna Handslip I was to wander up into the high mountains to see if we could find any proof.

This was to be my first venture into 'real' Bhutan. Our light aircraft dropped us on a small field, the only flat section of a rugged mountainous landscape. The field was on a high point that doubled as the locals' football pitch. We were instantly greeted by a gaggle of inquisitive youngsters, all dressed in local garb known as 'gho'. These costumes were introduced in the seventeenth century, yet almost everyone in Bhutan wears them daily. And this isn't a tool to appeal to the whimsy of tourists. I've never been to a country where the national dress is more omnipresent. Almost everyone I saw was clad as they would have been for hundreds of years. This appears to be a manifestation of the tremendous pride the Bhutanese take in their heritage and culture, determined to preserve it against the onslaught of the outside world.

Perched on the side of the hill we'd landed on was a white plaster monastery with red-slated roof, and dozens of boys clad in red Buddhist robes poured out of the big carved wooden doors to greet us. Those who couldn't descend stuck their heads from high arched windows decorated with intricately carved wooden shutters and balconies. Below and to the south a forested valley dropped away, trees infused with tissue shards of cloud. Above and to the north, huge snow-crusted mountains gleamed with the ferocity of burning magnesium, reflected flaming sunlight. Long, tall banner-like prayer flags stood on the high ridgelines, vibrating with the cool breeze. Red-billed Himalayan chough called and whirled above us, and a cuckoo perched in the top of a nearby conifer and sounded its familiar voice. It was like being inside an Oriental silkscreen painting.

The next morning, we met up with the convoy of donkeys that would take our filming equipment up through the forested trails and into the high Himalaya. I didn't want to admit to anyone the amount of pain I was in with my ankle, or how difficult walking actually was, so I took everything heavy out of my backpack and stowed it on the donkeys. In order to keep up the façade, I plumped up my sleeping bag, and a pillow inside my pack, so that it still looked full and heavy. I shovelled down the painkillers, found two hefty walking sticks, and walked ahead of the others, using them to take the weight off my crushed foot. The rocky path led upwards through both broadleaf and conifer forests, drowning under a blanket of green moss. The carpeted cavern resounded to the muf-fled calls of trogon and wren-babbler, very occasionally a flash of colour would reveal the birds themselves as they flitted between downy boughs. The gold medal for wildlife spotting would have been the hanging bell-pull tail and russet flanks of the red panda, which does reside here, but in very tiny numbers. Unlike the giant panda, bamboo makes up only a small part of their diet. Instead they largely feed on eggs, birds, insects and small mammals. They are not that closely related to the giant panda but form a family all of their own, with their closest relatives being the mustelids: wea-sels such as otters, badgers and wolverines.

Several times along the way, my heart jumped as I encountered fresh cat scat, and then superb footprints. When you study a cat or dog track, you have to take care not to be sucked in by the toe marks, which can splay and spread and give you a false impression.

Instead you focus on the interdigital pad between them, which maintains its shape and size no matter what the substrate was. Since the start of the expedition, I'd had marks on my thumbs and fingers in indelible marker to show the pad sizes and scat diameters of tiger and tigress, and the leopards that live alongside them. On close inspection all these marks on the trails turned out to be leopard. Unlike tigers, the resourceful and adaptable leopard *Panthera pardus* can survive with little cover and much smaller prey, and is known to occur in altitudes of up to 4,800 metres, where it gives way to its more specialised cousin the snow leopard.

Our first night under canvas was an utter horror show, which reminded me of quite how much I value my own expedition planning and equipment. We had pulled up to spend the night at a sort of porter's way station. It was a dark barn-like building lit with paraffin lamps, where the donkeys could chow down on hay, and our porters could curl up under blankets. Nick and I sat giggling away with them till the early hours, drinking the local beer. This is called Druk 11000 and comes in litre bottles. It tastes and smells like goat urine when warm, but is quite drinkable after being chilled in a Himalayan stream for a few hours. It's a little like a game of Russian roulette, though. The makers claim it has an alcohol content of 'maximum 8 per cent', boasting: 'Its aroma, flavour and taste has mesmerised, enthralled and fascinated the beer consumers throughout the country, with a smooth and relaxing effect.' What they don't mention is that half the bottles in any one batch lull you into a false sense of security, being weaker than a can of Budweiser, before you suddenly get hit by one lethal secret bottle than could floor a rhino. Druk had been our undoing many times already on this expedition, but neither of us had learned our lesson. Instead, at about 1 a.m, we staggered out to a flattish bit of ground alongside the barn to put up our tents . . . just as it started to rain. It was then we discovered that half the poles, pegs and material for our tents was missing. And then the rain started to come down in biblical sheets, as Nick and I stomped about in the mud, cursing the heavens, our judgement, and most of all Druk 11000.

The storm continued through the night, much of which was spent trying to stop everything we owned being swept away or soaked. The following morning, we emerged bleary-eyed from our caved-in excuse for a pair of tents, neither of us having slept a wink, yet still with outrageous hangovers. Not for the first or last time in my life, I vowed never, ever to drink again.

Once we got to around 4,000 metres above sea level the scenery changed. First to stunning rhododendron forests, in bloom of reds, pinks and purples. As a kid, we had shedloads of these huge bushes growing in the woods around our house, and we hated them, because our goats used to eat them and get poisoned. Here, where they originate, with the soaring mountains behind them, they were beyond stunning. They were offset by the sight of festoons of Himalayan monal, one of the most gaudy birds you'll ever see. They're a kind of pheasant, but the males look as though they've been clad in metallic Christmas wrapping paper, with electric blue, bottle green and a spray of feathers atop the crown. The female is the typical dowdy brown, and here they were bunched in groups known as coveys, which chattered fussily as they hurried for the rhododendrons, panicked dumpy dowagers making for cover.

Our first destination was the tenth-highest town in the world, the Laya village, which is only accessible by a three-day walk. The people who live here have one of the most fascinating traditional lifestyles of any you'll see around the world, and though a trickle of Western visitors pass through, their lives have changed little in thousands of years. The houses are made of stacked rocks, clad in white plaster, and with wooden doorframes and borders decorated with paintings of flowers, and in many places with paintings of tigers. There were also disconcertingly manifold images of huge erect penises, a symbol of fertility and rebirth which is splashed all over Bhutanese buildings. The locals wore long, straight, straggly black hair under odd little hats woven out of wicker, and formed into the shape of a small upturned funnel, with an additional spike on the top. As we approached, we greeted the people with the local phrase, 'Gazampo la', which elicited the same response. That was generally where the chat ended though, as it was the only Laya word we learned. Thankfully we were accompanied by a Laya-speaking guide who could translate for us.

The people of Laya are self-sufficient, getting everything they need from the fields of crops around the village. The only way they have of making money is through the trade of an extraordinary item. We wandered up into the surrounding mountains with one of the Laya men, and he showed us how to collect a small innocuous spiky fungus that poked up through the soil. This is cordyceps, a bizarre fungus which infects and inhabits the living bodies of insects. The spores are ingested by bugs, then start to grow, until finally they burst out like some kind of body-snatching alien. It's something I've encountered in many places around the world, mostly in the tropics, where you'll happen upon the sinister sight of a moth, ant or cricket that lies in perfect repose, but with the often dramatic toadstool-fruiting cordyceps sprouting from its body. Here the cordyceps infect caterpillars, erupting from their heads in a curling, twirling spike. What's perhaps even odder is that they are much prized in Chinese traditional medicine, and worth their weight in gold. Literally. We were given a dose of the panacea in some neat alcohol that could have stripped paint, and it certainly didn't do much for me. Although it did make a mess of my vow not to drink again.

The Laya told stories of having seen tigers and their prints around the village, both recently and historically, but this was obviously far from scientific proof. Instead we decided to carry on up towards Tiger Mountain to see if we could find any evidence for

Top Ivan sitting on our ledge waiting for sunlight to burn the fog away

Above Upuigma

Descending Kaieteur Falls in Guyana

Top The Laya village in Bht

Above Laya villagers, with one of their curious h

Above left Lizzie crossing the Weasel river, Mount Thor behind

Left Mount Asgard on Baffin Island

Above Pushing on as the light fades on Asgard

Ploughing up through Arctic glaciers towards Asgard base camp

e left Dinner, a single flapjack
twenty hours' climbing!

Trying to lap drips from the
face well after midnight

Auyuittuq National Park

ourselves. As we continued upwards, the clouds cleared, revealing the real giants of Bhutan. Gangkhar Puensum, the world's highest unclimbed peak at 7,570 metres, is here on the border with Tibet. Summiting high peaks is banned in Bhutan, as it is seen as disrespectful to the sacred place these pinnacles are seen to be. The idea of 7,000-metre peaks that have yet to be climbed set the adventure glands salivating, but I struggled on below, battling against horrible pain even to travel up the mountain paths. Looking up at the virgin snow slopes, mentally picking my line up them, I had cause not for the first time to wonder if I would ever climb into the mountains again.

Nearing the alpine meadow where we hoped to pitch our tents, I stopped to point out circling vultures above us. There were perhaps six huge Himalayan griffon vultures, plus a bearded vulture, with its characteristic wedge-shaped tail. I talked to camera about how it was unlikely to be riding a thermal this late in the day, and that their presence was more than likely due to a carcass on the slopes. I even teased the possibility that it could be the remains of a predator's kill. Perhaps even the kill of a big cat. Turned out that my hyperbolic detective work was spot on.

The high-altitude meadow was not completely uninhabited. At the lower end of it was a yak herder who had about thirty yaks tethered around his wooden shack, where he was living with his wife and two delightful snotty-nosed little girls. Director Sanna decided to do a quick interview with him, asking if he'd ever seen tigers in the area, obviously expecting to get some predictably dull answer. Instead, his very first response was, 'Yes, I see big cats around here all the time.' I didn't get too excited about this. One thing I've seen over and again when asking local people if they've seen a certain animal recently, is that you can rarely count on their reports being accurate. The following is a conversation I have had literally a thousand times in the course of my job:

Me: 'So have you seen any snakes around here?'

Local person: 'Yes! There are thousands of snakes here, we see them all the time!'

Me: 'Really?'(excited) 'When was the last time you saw one?'

Local person: 'Well, not me, but my next-door neighbour's cousin saw one just last spring. Or it could have been the year before.'

Me: 'You don't say.'

The handsome yak herder was clad in a grey-and-black goh, his no-nonsense face was stained nut-brown, eyes thin against the ferocious high-altitude sun. He looked trustworthy, but I posed my next question ready to be disappointed.

'Really?' I asked. 'When did you see one last?'

'I see them almost every day on these hillsides,' he replied. 'They killed one of my yaks last night.'

I stopped dead, looking at my translator to confirm that I'd heard right. He nodded.

'Would you show us where?' I asked.

The yak herder nodded, and pointed off up the slopes.

It was then that Nick and I had the only quarrel we've had in eight years working together. Essentially I'd been lecturing everyone on the team about acclimatisation and the need to make a gradual ascent up the mountain. We'd already done our vertical ascent for the day, and I'd been telling everyone that they should listen to my vast experience and make sure they rested as soon as we reached the high meadow camp. However, now that this extraordinary story had come up, I wasn't even prepared to let them stop for a cup of tea. They were supposed to slog on up an extra hundred vertical metres to the kill site. Nick accused me of putting the story before their health. My worry was that dark clouds were approaching over the mountains, and the air temperature was falling. It looked like snow, which would cover all traces of the kill on the mountain.

But Nick is a professional and he slogged up the steep slopes alongside me, muttering darkly that if they all crashed with altitude sickness it would be my fault. I had my heart in my mouth, praying that this wouldn't turn out to be a wild goose chase, and even more so that I didn't wake the next morning to a comatose crew with murder on their minds. As soon as we reached the kill site, it was evident the first part of the gamble had paid off. The yak herder had removed the carcass, but the murder scene remained: black blood-stains, clumps of dark hair and other signs of a gargantuan struggle. All of a sudden I was transformed into Sherlock, seeing the battle through the clues that had been left behind. I saw the cautious, slow footprints of the predator approaching the yak as it browsed, head down, on a flat section of grass. The cat had put a low rise between herself and the yak, skirted around and approached from above it, moving on her belly. Finally, she had sprung from no more than two metres away. The fight had been surprisingly brief, considering the size differential between predator and prey. The yak could have been ten times her size.

I knew all this because her footprints were crystal clear. The interdigital pad at the back was clearly too small to be a tigress. These were the pugmarks of something even more precious: the snow leopard.

These mystical endangered cats are as rare as hen's teeth. There could be six thousand in the wild, there could be two thousand, we know so little about them it's impossible to tell. They inhabit the wildest parts of mountain ranges and do all they can to avoid people, although occasionally, as here, they take livestock. Yaks are usually too large a prey animal for snow leopards, which seldom weigh more than 50 kilos, but there was no doubt whatsoever that this was our culprit.

There are few animals that are known to be as hard to capture on film as the snow leopard. It is the Holy Grail of wildlife filmmaking. Camera legend Doug Allen spent eleven weeks in the mountains of

Ladakh, and saw a snow leopard once. He got ten minutes of film, and it remains the finest footage that has ever been shot of them. And here I was, in a remote Bhutanese valley . . . with no camera traps, no long lens, no thermal-imaging camera, absolutely nothing to help us find and film an animal that was most definitely here . . . and hungry.

I went to sleep that night in my tent with my mind whirring. All I could think of was the excitement of seeing my first snow leopard; an animal I hadn't even dared to believe I would ever see. I had my trusty Swarovski binoculars with me (they don't just make odd crystal figurines, but arguably the best bins in the world), which cost more than my car, so even though we wouldn't be able to film it, I at least would stand a chance of seeing one with my own eyes. In my half-dreams, outrageous technical plans of rigging Heath Robinson camera traps using climbing rope tripwires, were interspersed with odd dreams of coming nose to nose with a slinky snow leopard, and becoming best of pals, springing about the mountains together. I was shaken from these strange images at around 1 a.m. by furious barking. The dogs down at the yak herders' cottages were going bananas, barking with an intensity that could only mean one thing. Hurriedly I pulled on my down jacket and stepped out into the snowstorm, which had hit right on cue. Heart thumping into my ears, I tramped over the crunchy fresh snow towards the sound of the barking. The dogs never stopped with their uproar; something had got them thoroughly spooked or angry. And then I stopped dead. A fresh cat track is unmistakable, and new snow is the finest medium on Earth for it to be left in. You can tell them apart from dogs instantly. The cat has a much more rounded profile than the elongate print of dogs, but even more telling, dog prints in a good substrate always show the evidence of claws at the end of each toe. Cats (other than cheetahs) have retractile claws which can be drawn back into sheaths when not in use, and those claws only register when they are exposed; for example when they are leaping in for a kill.

Before me in the snow was a line of sharp pugmarks, and they were without question from our female snow leopard. I had a small handycam with me, which had a nightshot function that allows you to film in infrared, as long as the subject is close. As I traced the prints through the snow, I told the story of what I was seeing. The prints were evenly spaced, and with uniform depth. Despite the dogs being tethered only a few hundred metres away, she was walking, calmly, almost arrogantly through the meadow, making no attempt to hide her presence. And then I stopped dead.

She'd stepped down into a muddy part of track, which was damp enough to have prevented any snow settling there. Her tracks here were deep. And they were still filling with water. Seeping fluid was still trickling into the prints, and I could see the tiny dissolved particles of dirt in the water swirling around in the pugmark. She had stepped here perhaps only a minute beforehand. The awful possibility came clattering in. A snow leopard does most of its hunting by night. They have the preponderance of light-gathering rod cells in their retinas, plus the *Tapetum lucidum*; a mirror-like layer of cells that reflects light back through the retina one more time. It meant her monochrome night vision would be exceptional. Even on an overcast night like this, she would see fine. Human beings don't have a Tapetum, and have advanced colour vision and depth perception, but far lower concentrations of rod cells in the retina. My vision was limited to the tiny white beam from my headtorch. There was a lurch in my stomach. She could be watching me right now!

Suddenly my bravery evaporated. Snow leopards are not known to attack humans, and I've spent half my life trying to convince people that wild animals mean us as humans no harm, but there in the darkness on my own, all that reasoning went out of the window.

Besides, my fevered mind reasoned, if she could kill a yak ten times her body weight, she wouldn't think twice about me. I turned tail, and started to trot back up towards where I thought the tents were. But something was wrong. I was seeing the same shapes in the darkness over and over again. In my fixation with the prints, plus the falling snow and darkness, I'd lost my bearings. I tried to calm my rising panic. Where the hell was I?

I have no idea how long I stumbled around in the blackness, but it seemed like an eternity. Finally my torch caught a glint of something. It was the flash of eyes. A reflection from mirror-like eyes momentarily dazzled by my torchlight. My heart stopped. I forgot to breathe. Two eyes came into focus. It was her! Then another two eyes . . . that can't be right. Two snow leopards?! Oh for crying out loud! Under the meagre torchlight the form behind the reflections came into focus. It was two yaks, staring dopily back at me. I had managed to mistake a 300-kilo hairy cow for one of the world's sleekest predators. I laughed out loud at my own stupidity, the tension released for a few seconds. Minutes later, my torchlight caught the edge of our toilet tent. I stumbled back into camp and collapsed on to my bed. If I'd had a bottle of Druk 11000 it would have lasted mere seconds.

The drama, though, was only beginning. The following morning I sheepishly retold the story to the rest of the crew. They laughed at me remorselessly for my stupidity; I'm pretty sure none of them believed my estimate of how close she'd been. 'The darkness plays tricks on you, doesn't it?' Sanna said with a smile. 'It's like being a kid again and suddenly seeing ghosts and monsters everywhere!'

We were due to head all the way to Tiger Mountain to shoot some final pieces to camera about the expedition and how important it had all been, but I couldn't resist scampering down to the yak herder's shack before we left, just to check if there were any more tracks around. What I found had me sprinting back up to the camp to get Sanna and Nick, cheeks bright red, puffing with the altitude.

'Guys, guys! You're not going to believe this, there's been another kill! Last night!'

Sanna and Nick looked incredulous, but when I've got a hold of an idea, you'd be better off trying to convince a Rottweiler to let go of a Pomeranian.

What we found on the slopes no more than a hundred metres above our tents blew my mind. The previous night's victim was not another of the yaks, but a bharal, or Himalayan blue sheep. This magnificent mountain goat bore huge curved horns, and lay pristine on the grass, eyes wide open in shock. The front half of the body was utterly perfect, untouched. The back half was simply missing. It was as if it had been neatly chainsawed in half by a charlatan magician. Even more dramatic, though, were the signs around the kill site. Here were the familiar pugmarks from our female snow leopard. But about them were prints that were greater in size. They were the size of my hand, and from a second animal. A male snow leopard.

With the exception of temporary coalitions of cheetahs, and prides of lions, big cats are solitary animals. They only come together at one stage of their lives. To make a family. Somewhere on this particular mountain, a pair of snow leopards had come together to mate, breed and raise cubs. Later, there might be a den somewhere on the rocky talus above us, full of tiny mewing kittens. I could not even begin to contain my excitement. Despite the fact that we were here to make a series about tigers, Sanna didn't try to dissuade me. There was no doubt in my mind that the cats would be back to feast on the remains of the blue sheep that very evening. If we had had even one camera trap, the decision would have been obvious; place them round the carcass, sit back and wait for the technology to do the work. Come back the next morning and revel in the glory of our images. But we didn't have any camera traps.

So how on Earth could we make the most of this once in a million lifetimes opportunity?

For the remainder of the day we wandered around the alpine meadows, catching charming film of male marmots wrestling with each other over their burrow systems, and getting more beautiful vistas of this dazzling part of the world, but I was hugely distracted. Every spare second, my binoculars were stuck to my face, trained on the high rocks above us, praying for a glimpse of the treasured beast strolling or stretching outside its den.

Late afternoon, we gathered in our mess tent to have a discussion about what we should do to capitalise on the extraordinary chance, lying so tantalisingly close by. My plan was ludicrous, but the only thing I could think of. I would take the handycam with its paltry night-vision function, and sit up in the darkness alongside the carcass to try to film anything that came in to feed on it. Nick has filmed wildlife by my side on every continent, and provided the voice of reason:

'It'll smell or see you from a mile away, and it'll bugger off. You'll never see it.'

Sanna was more prosaic. 'I can't in good faith as your director let you do something that potentially dangerous. If you insist on going, I can't stop you, but I'm strongly advising against it.'

'It's not dangerous,' Nick scoffed. 'It's a snow leopard, man – he's not going to see it! It's a waste of time, you sitting up there on the mountainside, while we sit in here knocking back the Druks.' He mimed popping the top off a bottle, glugging the bottle down, then wiping his face with his sleeve.

'Maybe we ought to come with you?' said Sanna.

'Forget it,' I replied. 'There is a microscopic chance with one of me. Zero with two or three of us. They can see in the dark, they'll probably smell me anyway. Two of us have no chance.'

As darkness fell, it began to snow again. Hard. Over the top of my thick down jacket and handycam, I borrowed Nick's waterproof poncho to cover myself like a mini tent. There was a car-sized boulder about five metres from the carcass, so I sat with my back pressed up against it, hoping the cat wouldn't be able to approach me from behind. I couldn't make out the carcass in the dark, or anything really. With the nightshot feature engaged, you could kind of make out the blue sheep's body, lying there with its dull dead eyes. The insane idea was that, if I heard snuffling around the carcass, I'd flash on my torch, which would help out the infrared feature on my handycam, and should give me some footage as the snow leopard scarpered off into the distance. Yeah, right.

I sat there in the total darkness for about three hours. The heavy snow muffled every sound, but with my eyesight obscured, I could only focus entirely on my hearing. The tiniest of sounds had my breathing rate increasing, and me shifting ever so slowly towards the origin of the noise, desperately trying to perceive what it could be. I hardly dared move a muscle, even breathing was kept to a shallow rise and fall, in order to keep my profile as invisible as possible against the rock. There was little wind to carry my scent around on the hillside, but I was sure the snow leopard would see me from a distance away and hightail it off into the hills.

At about 10 p.m. there was a sound to my right. Behind me, the slope steepened, and there was a game trail leading in, running parallel to the slope itself. I had an utter certainty that something was approaching. Infinitesimally slowly, doing my best not to breathe, I lifted up my handycam, and clicked the power button from off to on. The viewing screen was not out, but the tiny viewfinder became activated. For a millisecond, it washed me in a faint green light, illuminating me against the boulder. The response was a sound I will remember till my dying day. It was the furious piercing snarl of a panther in a pitfall trap from a Tarzan movie. The high-pitched bawl of a caged big cat, and it was mere metres from my shoulder.

I nearly screamed. There was a furious scrabbling sound, a bunch of small stones bounced down over me and into my lap, and then there was silence again.

And I was left, sitting alone in the dark, in front of a dead sheep, and knowing that at least one furious predator was out there in the dark with me.

So I did what any self-respecting nature hero would do in that situation. I shat myself. The first lesson you learn when working with any wild predator is that you never run. Prey runs. Turn tail and sprint, and even Usain Bolt would not outpace the most slovenly of predators. Plus your act of running, instantly awakens the predatory instinct to chase, to run down and to kill anything that runs away from you. Wildlife pro 1.01. You never, ever, ever run.

I ran.

Ran down the steep snowy slope, gibbering to myself under my breath in utter terror. I fell and slipped down on my backside, but didn't care. All I wanted was to get out of the darkness, out of the world where I was prey and totally outgunned by the animals around me. Where I was as good as a blind man. All I could see around me were glimmering eyes off in the night, watching me, waiting to pounce. I was totally and utterly terrified.

I stumbled into the mess tent to find Nick charging batteries and cleaning his sound kit.

'All right, my darling?' he greeted me. 'Surprised you lasted this long, to be honest. I had the book on you giving up after an hour.'

'It was there, Nicky boy!' I gasped. 'It came up behind me!'

'No . . . way.' Nick stared at me in disbelief. 'You saw it?!'

'Well, no, not exactly,' I stammered. 'I heard it, though. It was as close as you are to me now.'

He looked at me, gobsmacked. 'Did you get a shot?'

I felt that sick feeling in my stomach. Over the years working in wildlife films, I've had such quality people working with me that I could count on the fingers of one hand the occasions when we've failed to get the shot. But I knew this was one of them.

'Let's have a look,' I said, and pulled out the handycam, but I already knew there was nothing on it. I felt numb. I'd sat out there in the darkness, and had probably got closer to a wild snow leopard than anyone ever had, and yet I had absolutely nothing to show for it. There is a saying in television that if you didn't get the shot, it didn't happen. Here that was certainly the case.

The next morning we went back up on to the slopes, and back to my boulder. The sheep carcass had remained untouched, neither of the cats had come back to feed further. What was far more interesting to me, was the story that had been left behind on the ground. The prints of the snow leopard came in clearly along the trail above. It was the male this time, bigger, heavier, with a longer stride length. To begin with he walked relatively easily and in a relaxed manner, but as he approached, the footsteps were closer together, splayed and shallow as he crept in towards the carcass. The prints came to within three metres of where I had been sitting. I could sense his hesitation as I illuminated myself with the camera, and then, clear as day, the retractile claws came out from their sheaths, engaging like a runner's spikes as he sprinted off up the hillside, scraping through the tough earth like steak knives. Over the years I've been lucky enough to freedive alongside sperm whales and Great white sharks, to film lion kills and hold new species in my hands, to have a baby mountain gorilla take me by the hand in the Bwindi impenetrable forest . . . and yet this near miss remains one of my most treasured wildlife encounters. The storyteller in me knows that it was an opportunity missed, but the naturalist in me remains entranced by having shared the mountain darkness with one of the world's most precious and evasive jewels.

In the end we returned to the capital of Thimpu empty-handed. We had tall tales and gossip, but nothing that amounted to scientific proof. The rest of the team, though, had been rather more productive. Gordon had retrieved his camera traps from the high mountain passes, and watched the footage there in the field. I love replaying his reactions. They're so visceral, so real. In his camera trap images, tigers are clearly seen wandering the ridges at 4,100 metres above sea level. It was unequivocally the highest tigers had ever been filmed, and a convincing piece of evidence that Alan's idea of a high-altitude tiger corridor could have credence and could work.

Lost Land of the Tiger was made in association with Bhutanese scientists and people. We were there under invitation from the Bhutanese royal family, and the results were personally presented to the prime minister, whose reactions were extremely considered and positive. The programmes went worldwide, sending a message to over a hundred countries that if we do not act on tiger conservation *now*, and in dramatic, tangible and daring ways, then we will lose these iconic animals from the wild for ever. It felt like a triumph.

ROAD TO RECOVERY

'The test of success is not what you do when you are on top. Success is how high you bounce when you hit bottom.'

George S. Patton

Dawn lights up the frozen fall, making the icicles sparkle from within with pinky glow. Finger shadows grow and seethe amongst the white and blue ice as the sun peeks out from behind conifers and cliff faces. We teeter 100 metres above the valley floor, ice-axe tips testing slots and pockets in the freeze, seeking purchase you could suspend your bodyweight from. If the ice doesn't yield, you twist your torso away from the ice, swinging the axe inwards, at the last second flicking your wrist to embed the pick. In frightened moments, there's a tendency to lose your precision, to hammer away at the ice as if trying to batter in a six-inch nail. This wastes energy and showers you and your climbing partner in tumbling shards of ice. Far better to suck in, steady yourself, and aim like a sniper, reading the ice, finding your placement with care.

'Crack Baby', as this frozen waterfall is named, is the toughest ice climb I've ever pitched myself at, yet we steadily ascend as the thin

sun turns faint drips to incessant localised rain. It's a ludicrous enter-prise. A few months ago this was a waterfall, and it will be again in a few months' time. I am climbing on water, nothing more. Lost in the moment, tap-tapping to test the integrity of the ice, breathing, shifting my weight, I feel the clarity and purity all climbers covet. There is nothing in my world, nothing except my axes and the ice.

After limping my way up into the high mountains in Bhutan with a fake empty backpack, I then struggled through the entire third series of *Deadly 60* on even more dramatic amounts of ever-stronger painkillers. Wherever we travelled, from the swamps of Venezuela to the Abyssinian mountains, the crew had to drag along an exercise bike so that I could get the ankle moving before the day began. On one night walk in Brazil, we spent four hours yomping through the rainforest in the dark, me using two sticks to limp along. When I saw a spider or snake, I'd drop the sticks, we'd start the cameras rolling, I'd catch it, talk about it, release it, cut cameras then pick up my sticks and limp on. Around one in the morning a local land-owner mistook us for poachers and unloaded his shotguns at us. As I cowered in the dirt, shouting out to him not to kill us, barely able to crawl away, it seemed life had reached its most ludicrous.

But then when the series was done, I had to face the inevitable. The barbaric fixator cage operation had achieved nothing. I would have to have a fusion. It had taken six years, twelve operations, and a non-stop diet of drugs you're not supposed to take for more than six weeks. However, there was no ignoring the obvious now. It would have to be done.

The fusion is a fairly standard operation, often carried out to ease the crippling pain of arthritis. The cartilage of the ankle is removed, then the bones are bolted together. Pretty quickly they grow into one continuous bone, stronger than before, but you have no joint, and all movement has to come from the bones of the foot. After the ankle was fused, I had to learn to walk, and go through extended rehab, for the twelfth time in six years. Despite the joint being fixed in place, I found there was still significant movement from the bones of the foot. As with everything in my life, I had to make it a challenge in order to tackle it. I set myself goals and targets. The surgeon said I'd be out of plaster four months after the op. I made sure I was out in six weeks. He said I'd be walking well after another few months. I did it in a fortnight. He also said that I would never run well again. That wasn't good enough. Six months after I'd had the fusion, I got on a treadmill, and ran a couple of kilometres at a slight jog. A month later, and I went for a proper run, outside, my first in over six years. At the end, I was in considerable pain, but the tears were for a profoundly different reason. These days I don't run much for pleasure or for training. It's too awkward, and I suffer afterwards. However, if I have to run, whether for a bus, or to escape a charging rhino, then I can. As the months become years, little accomplishments start to accumulate. Inevitably, climbing was one of the first things to return. Admittedly it was mostly on indoor climbing walls, and I carried with me a new fear of falling that meant my grades were far from world-beating. But the fusion didn't physically hold me back. If anything, it had suddenly become my strongest joint. Mostly because I didn't have a joint anymore. I struggled to go up on my tiptoes, which made it harder to extend out to distant holds, but the lack of flexibility didn't pose any problems. Throughout my operations and rehabs, I'd always been back in the gym the very next day, which meant I still had enough upper-body strength to lug my weight skywards. Eventually other pursuits followed, until I was once more thinking nothing of a hundred-mile bike ride, of kayaking for twenty-four hours non-stop, or tackling a frozen waterfall the height of a skyscraper. I would never be the annoyingly irrepressible dynamo I was before, but there was a growing sense that I was on the way back. And the person I needed to prove it to more than anyone else was me. It was time for the next big challenge.

Each year I made several trips to the mountains, battling to regain that forgotten confidence. Now more financially secure than at any other time in life, I would go with a guide so I wouldn't have to lead. As my guide was Mike 'Twid' Turner, former Piolet D'Or (golden ice axe) winner, this certainly did not mean easy warm-ups to get my mojo back. Twid wanted me to rehabilitate myself through being taken to the edge again and again. He dragged me up some of the mightiest ice climbs in the Alps, teetering leviathan icicles that were at times a challenge even for his formidable skills. I also managed a few classic mountaineering trips with some of my old climbing coterie. Slowly, ever so cautiously, I started to take the lead, becoming more and more comfortable climbing above my gear and setting off into uncertain terrain, ice axes and crampon points sharpened and ready. Now that I was able to walk well, I could train properly. The steel was back in my arms, and I was starting to believe in myself again.

Unfortunately, adventure climbing has little to do with how many chin-ups you can do, or how far you can cycle. In sport climbing, where you are supported by bolts that are drilled in to rockfaces, you are to all intents and purposes safe. In traditional climbing – the style that so nearly claimed my life – you climb not only to the limits of your physical ability, but your nerve. And my nerve was shot. All of a sudden I was thinking far too often about what would happen if I were to fall, and the fear was paralysing. Perhaps the most dramatic example of this was when climbing in the Avon Gorge outside Bristol with my friend Andy Torbet. Andy is a formidable outdoorsman. Formerly a paratrooper and captain in the army he decided that this was not dangerous enough, so moved to Maritime counter terrorism, and underwater bomb disposal. When he left the army, he switched to expeditions and adventures, and now makes his living in much the same way as me; trying to get television companies to pay for his expeditions. Andy and I make good climbing partners, as we both have similar experience, climb at the same speed and to the same grades. Not essential, but it certainly helps. Conventionally, on a multi-pitch climb, this would mean one of us taking the dangerous lead, pushing ahead up the rock while the other belays from below. Then the second follows up, taking out the gear, reaches the leader at the belay point, then swaps over, taking the lead on themselves. You share the danger, share the stress, and thus share the experience. Our climb that day in the Avon Gorge was not hard. Graded VS, or Very Severe, it was about the level that we would normally warm up on, though multi-pitch – with about a hundred metres of climbing. I took on the first lead, and found it a breeze, Andy climbed pitch two, and then it was my turn to lead again. We were looking down to the Portway below, cars thundering past, oblivious to the two specks fastened to the cliff face above. I stepped away from the belay point and out on to the rock, moving out on what was obviously the route upwards. The climbing was easy, but there was nowhere to place any protective gear, and after only a few moves I found myself teetering on a tiny foothold. The next, obvious move, was perhaps a metre and a half above me. It was not hard, but would mean stepping up even further, perhaps three metres above my last piece of protection. It was easy. I could do it in my sleep. I wasn't going to fall. But if I did. If I did. . .

I crabbed around the rock to the right, looking for a crack to put some gear into. Nothing. I crabbed back again. I tiptoed up towards the left to find a better handhold. No luck. My palms started to sweat. My leg started to wobble. I looked down to Andy, no more than a kayak paddle's length away from me. He had a quizzical look on his face that clearly said, 'Seriously? Stop mucking about, Backshall, it's a piece of piss.'

But I couldn't do it. I could feel the panic rising in my chest and throat. My heart rate starting to thump. I had been committing the cardinal sin, holding on too hard, and so my fingers were starting to lose power, and my forearms to pump with blood. My thighs and calves were starting to vibrate in 'disco leg', wobbling without control. I was running out of gas, I was going to come off. Being terrified of falling was going to make me fall. The curse of easy climbing is that falls can be a much more unpleasant proposition. On vertical or overhanging routes, you'll fall into air, and if all goes well the rope will catch you and you'll swing harmlessly in space. On easy non-vertical routes you're more likely to have rock beneath you. From the slack in the rope system, and the parabolic swing I would take, I estimated my drop would be substantial, and on to jagged chunks of boulder. My world was spinning. It had become a whirling disco ball, with me tiptoeing on top, about to slide off into the abyss. There was nothing for it. I stepped back across, down-climbing towards where Andy stood belaying me.

Andy and I tend to communicate in a series of ever-escalating insults. A normal conversation will pick on every perceived weakness of the other, in a remorseless bout of taunting that would leave any outsider open-mouthed, and convinced that we genuinely hate each other. But this was no time for bravado. I grabbed him in a bear hug, which he somewhat bewilderedly reciprocated. He could see that, despite the lack of genuine challenge in what I'd been attempting, I'd been through something significant. Without a word, we flaked the ropes out and he took over the lead. My little tantrum had cost us so much time that darkness fell before we had the chance to finish the route. We climbed the last pitch using the lights from our mobile phones to illuminate where we should go. Clambering over the railings at the top of the gorge, I was a wreck. Psychologically, I was spent. We met up with some friends in a nearby pub shortly after. If I'd merely made a bit of a meal of a section of climb, Andy would have spent a good hour ripping the piss out of me. Tellingly, he didn't mention a word all evening, but I could tell he would think very carefully before he would consider having me on the end of his rope again.

For my part, I never wanted to climb ever again. Clearly my rehabilitation had to go much deeper than merely healing my flesh and bones.

THE LAND THAT
NEVER MELTS

'People ask me, "What is the use of climbing Mount Everest?" and my answer must at once be, "It is of no use." There is not the slightest prospect of any gain whatsoever. Oh, we may learn a little about the behaviour of the human body at high altitudes, and possibly medical men may turn our observation to some account for the purposes of aviation. But otherwise nothing will come of it. We shall not bring back a single bit of gold or silver, not a gem, nor any coal or iron . . . If you cannot understand that there is something in man which responds to the challenge of this mountain and goes out to meet it, that the struggle is the struggle of life itself upward and forever upward, then you won't see why we go. What we get from this adventure is just sheer joy. And joy is, after all, the end of life. We do not live to eat and make money. We eat and make money to be able to live. That is what life means and what life is for.'   *George Mallory*

It is midnight, and I am teetering a thousand metres above an Arctic glacier, curling my tongue into a straw to catch drips, licking the rockface in an effort to get some moisture into my hopelessly parched mouth. Our water ran out about eight hours ago. The sun was shining then, and we were climbing in just our thermal layers. That seems so long ago it's as if it happened to someone else. The midnight sun is now hiding behind daunting, imposing granite leviathans, icy katabatic winds coursing down from the Penny Ice Cap and over our exposed rock wall, and the temperature has plummeted so that even in my down jacket and balaclava a deep dead chill is taking hold of my bones. Above me, my climbing partner battles with the crux pitch, swearing with every vile word he can muster against the ever-steepening rock. The summit cannot be far . . . but then we've been saying that for hours. And even when – if, we top out, the descent will be a thousand metres of hell. 'Death on a stick' in climbing terms. I am out of my league, and have been since we started at 5 a.m. My nerves are frayed like an old moth-eaten cardie, fingertips mashed like tenderised pork medallions. Why am I putting myself through this? I wonder for the thousandth time that day. The rope tightens around my harness. It's my turn to climb. I take off my gloves, beat my hands to get some life into my fingertips, and swing out over the abyss, eyes fixed on the rock in front of me, determined not to look down, not watching the loose rock detached by my foot as it bounces once, then falls a thousand metres to the glacier far below.

Seven years after my accident on that rainy June day, and life was once again good. Rather than torturing myself by wanting to be back where I was, I had learned to compromise, to enjoy long days on easy routes in the mountains, enjoying it without having to challenge or scare myself. But then one day, I can't remember exactly when, I had a more serious pitch, and furrowed my brow in concentration, as I picked my way around the complicated conundrums of the problem. But then suddenly found myself at the top. No fear. No jelly trembles and wanting to be anywhere else on

Earth. I'd just got up it. Over following months this was repeated over and again. Granted I wouldn't be setting any records, but then I never did! Nothing could be clearer in my mind. Forget this easy armchair adventure nonsense; who was I kidding thinking I'd ever be satisfied with that? That was as good as giving up, and I wasn't ready to do that yet. I could take on an expedition again, and it could be something serious. The mountains were calling me once more.

The problem now was what to choose. Originally I had my heart set on attempting K2 with Samuli, but that would have taken three months, and that would bring me back too late to learn how to dance on national telly (how I wish I'd gone with my gut feeling and headed to K2; it was the best year for summits since records began, and Sammi crested the world's hardest and most challenging mountain in some style. How much greater an achievement than learning how to cha-cha-cha!). I got in contact with all of my climbing buddies – Tarx, Ro and Dave, John Arran, Nick – but they were all busy having babies and manning up to the responsibilities of the real world. I was at something of an impasse.

My saviour came in the form of a man described as one of the finest climbers on the planet. Leo Houlding is the closest thing the sport has to a rock star. In a genuine coup I had managed to get him the appear on the live version of my *Deadly* series some years back and we had sporadically stayed in touch. Leo himself is one of the most interesting characters in the adventure business. Originally having a reputation as being cocksure and crazy, he matured into one of the most opinionated and successful climbers ever. He also managed the neat trick of making a living out of climbing, while staying at the cutting edge of the sport for over two decades. I interviewed him for a radio programme on the psychology of adventure recently, and his take on why we climb is particularly enlightened. Leo points out that in the developing world, people don't climb or go on adventures. They are too busy making sure they have food to eat, and survive the genuine day-to-day dangers of their lives. Climbing is a First World practice, which began when we had enough leisure time, and when life became too safe for our capricious nature. 'Life is too easy, too safe,' Leo says, 'you want water you turn on the tap, you wear your helmet, wear your seatbelt, and probably the most dangerous thing we have to do is cross the road. We're not built that way, we're built for action.' Perhaps that's it, perhaps we're living out our physiological imperative, or maybe we're merely keeping sharp, making sure our bodies and brains are ready for when danger genuinely does challenge our survival.

Aristotelian philosophers have pointed our that in our cossetted world, there is no chance to develop valour and resolute commitment (because there are rarely instances in daily life where failure means death), humble self-awareness (because there is nothing that we cannot achieve) and proper respect for the natural world (because we increasingly dominate nature, and see it as a sum of resources put at our disposal). Climbing has the capacity to build all of these virtues, and therefore can benefit not only the individual, but the society they belong to.

Leo confessed to me that when he started freefall parachute jumping, he got a huge buzz, but after a thousand jumps; 'it was just plain boring'. Then he had to gravitate to BASE jumping to get the same adrenalin kick. He was then at the forefront of 'para-alpinism', speed climbing up rockfaces before leaping from the top, then going on to wingsuit flying, and finally escalating to proximity BASE jumping, where you try to fly as close to rock faces and the ground as possible. It took the loss of a dear friend, and the birth of his child for Leo to rationalize the risks he was taking, to step back and operate more within himself. I was surprised to hear Leo talk so frankly about this; I imagined he would have been extremely touchy about being labelled as an 'adrenalin junkie'. But Leo is remarkably self-aware. He realized that he needed the hit, and that in order to keep getting it, he would have to get more and more risky until fatal consequences were almost inevitable. His transition to epic big wall ascents, and monumental climbs in the Arctic and Antarctic were unbelievably an attempt to take more calculable and controllable risks. An insane idea to someone of my abilities, but natural to someone of his quality who can glide up a vertical face as if it's a stepladder. I envy Leo's talent, but not his addiction. If I were as hooked on adrenalin as Leo clearly is, with my much lower levels of physical ability, I would certainly have been killed many years ago.

It has been proposed that there are several types of risk takers, one of which is escapees, for whom climbing is a kind of displacement activity. Many of these may be running away from their past and present, will struggle in everyday life, and may be depressive or highly negative away from the big hills. I have known several of these, and they have a kind of foreboding intensity that hangs over them like a cloud. The other kind of risk taker is someone who is seeking self-awareness, self-worth or seeking to define themselves (though they may not know it). Leo would certainly fall into this category. Climbing is his philosophy, his meaning of life. The joy he gets from the hills is palpable, and impossible to fake. He takes deep aesthetic pleasure in its wonders, and it just makes him happy, and though my accomplishments are far less, that's exactly what it does for me.

In late 2013, Leo and I met to discuss the possibility of an expedition series heading back to Venezuela to climb another as yet unclimbed tepuis. The project didn't work out, but we'd chatted about my lack of plans for the summer, and Leo had promised to keep his ear to the ground. Some months later, out of the blue he got back in touch. Some friends of his would be spending the summer climbing in Baffin Island up in Arctic Canada. Leo was hoping to go. Would I join him?

Baffin Island. Every climber knows about the place and utters its name in hushed tones, much as an athlete might the Olympics. The first I remember seeing of it was a *National Geographic* front cover. It showed a blank wall of impossible magnitude, with three tents hanging off it under an overhang. It was an image of such visceral vertigo-inducing horror, such stupendous disbelief that any human being could do that, that I had photocopied it, and used it in every single television proposal I had written that involved climbing or adventure. In more recent years, I'd seen Leo's own preposterous film *The Asgard Project*, where he had skydived out of a plane on to a glacier before climbing Mount Asgard, simply the most vertical, impossible-looking mountain ever. I say preposterous, because the whole thing looked like a Bond movie, it was hard to believe it could be real.

Baffin Island. The Holy Grail of climbers. Potentially even more of a challenge to me than K2, as it involved thousands of metres of vertical rock (which as I have intimated, I am very much not built for).

There could be no doubt that it was totally out of my league. But nothing over the years has driven me more than terror and the knowledge that something is beyond me. I want to confront that fear and beat it, so it ceases to have power over me. There was of course the possibility that this time I had bitten off way more than I could chew. That this time I would fail, and fail in spectacular style.

The situation was complicated even more when Leo found himself another expedition for the summer and had to pull out. I was already in email contact with Jason 'Singer' Smith, who seemed to be the brains behind the project, but I couldn't turn up on my own and count on one of his team feeling like dragging me up something challenging. Nevertheless, a month after Leo had pulled out, I decided to go anyway. If nothing else, I'd haul loads up into Baffin with the team, enjoy being in the wilderness, have an adventure. That was when I got my second golden ticket, in the form of a call from yet another climbing legend. This time, it was Tim Emmett. Tim was Leo's long-term climbing partner and amigo, and they'd accomplished great things together. He is an ice climber of international renown, a base jumper and wingsuit flier, and a rock jock whose name and legend is known on every crag and climbing wall. Like Leo, Tim had been a guest on my live television show at my request, and we'd got on like a house on fire. He had a lust for life that was utterly infectious, like an irrepressible labradoodle puppy that wants to run around, climb up stuff, jump off it then do it again. Tim had not been able to go on Leo's Asgard project, and had always regretted it. He desperately wanted to do something big on Baffin, but couldn't afford the time or money to take a long period away from his wife and young son. We had a frank discussion. Despite being a world-class climber, Tim had no guiding qualifications, and we would have to go into the enterprise as climbing partners, not as guide/client. I couldn't pay him, but would need to find the money to cover his expenses, and as the flights alone would run into several thousand dollars, I couldn't afford it out of my own pocket. So I would have to come up with a sponsor and put in some serious training. I needed to be in the best climbing shape of my life, and I had only two months to do it.

As always, I threw myself into the training with gusto. Through rigorous dieting and long, slow bike and kayak trips, I lost five kilos of muscle bulk, mostly from my legs and humongous backside. Daily sessions on the fingerboard and at the indoor wall focused not only on increasing my grades but my endurance. I also got some much needed coaching on 'crack climbing', which was total anathema to me. On the kind of granite found on Baffin, the usual means of progressing is to follow an obvious crack line, jamming your fists, fingers and toes into a crack then camming them sideways to lock yourself in place. After my first session, it felt as if I'd been hitting the backs of my hands with a hammer, and I couldn't type or write properly for a week. There was a lot of work to be done.

Tim and I communicated regularly with Singer over email. He was a Baffin master, with dozens of ascents there over many trips. Though we wouldn't actually join his expedition, we'd aim to meet them at a high base camp to share stories and possibly Scotch whisky. We discussed many possible peaks and routes, but Tim had his heart set on Asgard. Asgard . . . the very thought of it made me want to puke. The twin peaks of the mountain were like two beer cans, spherical fortresses with flat tops and unbelievably sheer sides. To the back of the north tower was a route first climbed in 1972 by Doug Scott, which Leo had climbed and told Tim was the 'finest rock route in the world'. Doug had climbed it in forty pitches and one epic thirty-hour push. It was mostly in the low 'E' for Extreme grade, with some easier scrambling in the middle, and two crux pitches at the top – which were way out of my league. Tim reassured me that he would lead those, and that I could either second or 'jumar' up his ropes. We'd take lightweight bivvi bags in case we got caught out by a freak Arctic storm, but no stoves or food. Tim even suggested we do away with water bottles and take straws, to suck seeping water off the rocks as we went.

Finding a sponsor was the next challenge, but proved easier than expected, with Renault agreeing to pay all our costs, as long as we mentioned them in all of our social networking, and gave a talk for their staff at some point in the year. The expedition was on. All I had to face now was waking up in the middle of the night in a cold sweat, seeing miles of vertical granite below me, and knowing that I was going to fall.

Baffin Island lies in the Canadian Arctic and is the fifth largest island in the world, slightly larger than Spain. In all this vast landmass, approximately eleven thousand people, most of them Inuit, make a living – about the same as live in my small English home town. Baffin is something of a Shangri-La for lovers of mountains, with the largest vertical rock walls on Earth, and an infinite wilderness of bewildering majesty that you can be totally guaranteed you'll have to yourself. There's a reason for that. To fly in to the nearest Inuit community takes a full day from Montreal or Ottawa, and costs more than a flight from London to Sydney. Once you're there, it takes many days of hard, hard walking across tundra, glaciers and raging rivers before you even get to the peaks, and there are no Sherpas here; anything you need, you have to carry in yourself.

We flew in to Pangnirtung, located on the Cumberland Sound south-eastern Baffin. Some fifteen hundred Inuit people live here, and have been living here for around 3,500 years. The community had its heyday in the mid 1800s, when it was a centre for the whaling boom, with British and American ships having bases here to plunder the giant bowhead whales, probably the second heaviest animal that's ever lived after the blue whale, and rendered oil from the 'canaries of the sea', the smiley white beluga whale. By 1910, the majority of whales had been hunted out, and the foreign interests dwindled, but in 1921 they returned in the form of the Hudson Bay Company, which arrived here to catch wolves, wolverines, seals and other fur-rich animals. Most of the Inuit peoples maintained the same lifestyles they had done for the previous three thousand years, living in sealskin tents with whalebones for struts, catching fish with hooks carved from walrus ivory. The entire life of the Inuit revolved around the seasons of animal harvests, and the Inuit year was broken up into distinct periods when each could be exploited. The season of the running char would give way to the season of the nesting geese, the season of the skin tent, seal pups, denning polar bear, caribou hunts, berries and the season of the Arctic cotton grass. The exodus from the land and into Pang town and the resultant modern life only began in the 1960s, when an epidemic ran riot amongst the Inuits' dogs. Without the transport option offered by their huskies, the people sought out the larger settlement, and it has been so ever since. Now, despite its dramatic location, sitting in a bowl of steep-sided mountains with the glassy flat waters of Cumberland Bay in front of it, it feels like a world under siege. The buildings are all in a state of disrepair, with peeling paint, flapping forlorn shutters and torn plasterboard; the inevitable wear of a world eternally battered by Arctic winds. Folk sit outside the 'Pang Inuit Co-Op' smoking, wearing the uniform of hood over baseball cap, most men sporting spindly moustaches. The town is bound in by pack ice and snow for all but a couple of months of the year. Indeed, the bay had only recently thawed, and it transpired that several of our soon-to-be friends had had to trek for several days around the outside of the lake to get into the park, as no boat could take them to the trailhead.

Our home for the next month would be Auyuittuq National Park. Auyuittuq is an Inuktitut word meaning 'the land that never melts'. The park covers 12,000 square miles, which is larger than Belgium, but the only humans currently in the park were the party we were going out there to meet. Ten people in a wilderness of extraordinary beauty that you could lose yourself in for a lifetime. It was a tantalising prospect.

At the park's office we introduced ourselves to the park warden, Billy. He was an Inuit with nut-brown skin, an easy manner, and eyes like milky green glacier water. As he talked us through the protocols of the park, he put on a stern face as if about to give us an almighty bollocking, then a half-hidden smile would crack his cheeks and make his eyes sparkle.

Before you can be allowed into the park you must spend around three hours in the office, registering your route and intentions, as well as attending a mandatory lecture on how to avoid contact and conflict with polar bears. Tim and I were escorted into a room decked out with chairs and a projection screen, then Billy put an old VHS tape into the video recorder and pressed play. The video was clearly shot in the 1980s, judging by the excessively bright clothing and punch-permed mullet hairstyles (business at the front, party at the back) and was a collage of do's and don'ts for living in polar bear country. The number one concern is a bear's 'critical space'; the area around a bear into which you must never venture. Going into this space would be considered a threat and provoke an attack. Only problem is, for a well-fed bear in a good mood that space would extend a few metres, but for a bear guarding food or youngsters, one that's been fasting for days and is starving, or a male that's recently lost a battles with rivals, that critical space can extend for miles. And forget trying to escape their notice; polar bears have been seen walking 20 kilometres in a straight line towards food sources that they can only have detected by smell. From 20 kilometres away! That's like standing in Croydon and being able to smell someone's kebab on the other side of London! Bears do occasionally use the valley we were going to be travelling up as a method of moving across Baffin Island, and encountering them here would be a horror show. There are certainly no trees to climb to escape them! Most travellers in this part of the world carry a gun as a matter of course, but as we would be in a national park, this was illegal. So if we did encounter a bear, according to the video, our only option would be to bash our pots and pans – and hope the bear wasn't hungry. The video showed a man with a WWE wrestler's blonde hairdo standing on a snowy ridge in a bright purple all-in-one ski suit. Looking as if he'd escaped from an acid house party, he jumped up and down bashing his pots and pans together while a nearby polar bear eyed him up, sniffing the air, clearly making up its mind whether to eat him or not.

The fact that he and his fellow brave compatriots clearly did have massive shotguns *and* snowmobiles did nothing to inspire our confidence.

The final piece of advice was that, if a bear should follow through with an attack, we should fight back, punching the nose and eyes, screaming and yelling. This isn't as crazy as it may seem. The best way to respond to bear attacks depends on the species. With grizzly bears it's recommended that you should play dead (though it would take quite an extraordinary person to manage this), whereas with black and polar bears this would have no effect. Mock charges are rare – when they come at you, it's for real. You must never run because it triggers predatory instinct, and there is no point running anyhow as they could outpace an Olympic sprinter with ease. In fact over their native terrain they'd outpace a racehorse. All quite sobering when you're heading off into the wilderness with no protection whatsoever.

'Flash-bangs, guns and bear spray all work,' said Billy. 'But you can't have 'em. You're up there and we're down here. Something happens to you and all my staff are away whaling, you need to get yourself out of trouble. You're on your own.'

Well, that was a comforting thought.

Having spent the previous summer in Arctic Svalbard filming polar bears, witnessing their powers up close, I knew exactly what we were up against. One memorable encounter occurred when I was out in a kayak, a mile away from our main boat. I'd seen a bear swimming between the ice floes, and paddled out hoping to get a good shot on my small camera. The bear had been swimming in a dead straight line, with slow but steady doggy-paddle strokes. However, as soon as he got to within a hundred metres or so of me, his behaviour changed dramatically. Suddenly, from being in plain view, he started to swim in more erratic patterns, disappearing from view for minutes at a time. Eventually, my radio crackled into life, and the crew (who were watching from binoculars on the deck) got in touch.

'Steve, don't worry too much, but he's putting the icebergs in between him and you. It looks like he's stalking you.'

My blood ran cold (!). Suddenly I felt a long way away from anyone, very exposed and vulnerable, and not a little afraid. The bear took hold of a nearby floe in order to stand up high, and looked at me, sniffing the air. He then ducked underneath the 'berg and disappeared. For several minutes I sat in my kayak. The silence was deafening. Somewhere nearby the world's largest land carnivore was hunting me, and I couldn't see him. With a sudden splash, he surfaced – twenty metres away from me. His first few paddle strokes were almost nonchalant, then he took a big circle in order to swim at me from behind. The leisurely doggy paddle erupted into four or five strokes of genuine power and intent, driving him towards my kayak. I don't want to overstate it; knowing he was coming, I easily outpaced him, and as soon as he saw the chase was futile, he gave up and continued swimming. But there was no doubting his intent. He meant to eat me. What would we do in a barren environment like this: no trees to climb up, no weapons to protect ourselves, no kayaks to paddle away in . . .?

The day after the kayak incident we pulled up at a set of vertical rock sea cliffs teeming with millions of seabirds, gathered here to rear their chicks. The sky was so thick with guillemots that they seemed more like swarming insects than birds, and the noise was deafening. We were then astounded to see a polar bear swimming along the base of the bird cliff, looking rather out of place. It was then even more unusual to see him haul himself out of the sea on a slimy vertical chunk of rock, and begin to climb a cliff that us climbers would have found challenging. At one stage he came to a packed ice couloir and proceeded to use his mighty forepaw claws like ice axes and his back feet as crampons, hacking his way upwards, even doing the kind of bridging manoeuvre that a modern climber would do to proceed. We watched for an hour as he climbed upwards, obviously targeting the nests and chicks.

Which proved that if we did see a bear in the valley, we wouldn't even be able to climb the rock to get away from him!

As soon as our lecture ended, the park's office closed, which was annoying, as we still had six hours to wait till our boat left, and there were no restaurants or bars. Pang, like many Inuit communities, is completely 'dry'. The sun disappeared behind some ugly grey clouds, and it started to get piercingly cold. As we had nowhere to go, Tim and I decided to sort through our gear and pack, ready to start trekking out on the slatted walkway. Inevitably, this soon attracted the attention of the local twelve-year-olds, who'd turn up on tiny pink bicycles they'd clearly stolen from their baby sisters. They shared the hoody and baseball cap uniform of their older brothers, and before long they'd gathered sufficient confidence to start going through our gear and asking us to give them stuff.

It started off as a bit of a giggle. The kids were cheeky, bold and with big characters. They taught us some of the native language, telling us that 'icki' meant cold, and 'ocko' meant hot, before going on to try and teach us some more convoluted sayings. Tim and I grinned at each other with the knowledge of experience; more than likely the youngsters were trying to get us to learn phrases that would actually proclaim how tiny our penises were, in the hope we'd then announce it solemnly to an Inuit tribal chief.

It lost its appeal after an hour or so of having to take our things off them, and having to haul them out of our packs where they were face-down, troughing on our expedition food. Then the topic of conversation changed. 'He takes drugs,' one announced solemnly, pointing at one of their number, who looked a little sheepish but did not deny the fact. They were all ten or eleven years old. They continued at length about their drug-taking prowess, and it would be tempting to dismiss it as childish bravado, but the statistics unfortunately show that they were probably telling the truth.

The lives of Inuit peoples are harsher than I can imagine. Even during the few months of Arctic summer when the temperature rises above freezing, when the land and sea isn't bound in by ice, it's still pretty challenging, with horizontal rain and wind making a mockery of modern clothing fabrics. In days gone by, youngsters would have been expected to head out on to the pack ice in temperatures colder than your freezer at home, to cut a hole in the ice and catch fish, or stalk seals that would almost always escape. How on earth can the traditional ways of life be preserved? Thankfully, here in Pangnirtung, even though you can see the trappings of the modern world and how they impact on the local people, there is also a tremendous pride in the knowledge and practices of the past. The local visitor centre has a vast repository of information and relics from the old Inuit way of life. Well-informed, and clearly proud young guides will show you around, expounding in depth on the ways of their elders. There are still functioning Inuit hunting tents around the town, and the people still go on whale, seal and bear hunts, although nowadays with large-calibre weapons rather than harpoons.

'You're going to die out there,' one of the young boys told me in a matter-of-fact voice. He'd taken my book of climbing on Baffin Island and was scanning through the photos. 'You crazy, you going to die.' Delivered with the same certainty as if he were telling me that we would get cold.

At around midnight, our outfitter Joavee arrived to take us down to the chartered boat, which would carry us across the Cumberland Sound, aiming to ride the high tide as far as possible. It was eerie, skimming across the glassy flat water with huge hulking mountains reflected in the mirror. We were joined by Jimmy, who had worked for twenty years as a ranger in the park, and had seen the place change dramatically over time. He was a sprightly sixty-year-old, with deep etchings in his face, the mark of long years spent outdoors in Arctic conditions.

'These people will blow your mind, I tell ya,' he said, gesturing to Joavee who was driving the boat. 'You know how they used to hunt seals here?'

Tim and I shook our heads to show we did not.

'One of the kids would put on a sealskin and crawl over the ice, real slow, making little grunting noises. They'd take all day getting closer and closer to one of them small seals, like a harp seal, then when they got super close they'd grab it, stick it under their arm and walk off with it. Crazy.'

We had a giggle at that one. Victorian kids being sent up chimneys had it easy.

'What can you tell us about the whaling here?' I asked. 'Is it dying out, or still pretty big?'

'No, no, it's huge,' Jimmy responded. 'I mean, it's much more regulated, there's quotas for how many they can take, but it still brings in the whole community, you know. So bowheads, they get three a year – but that's for the whole of Nunavut.'

That didn't seem like much, Nunavut is the whole of Northern Canada and bigger than Mexico. Bowheads are pretty big though. They're named for their colossal heads, which can make up 40 per cent of their total length. They're also reputed to be the oldest mammal on Earth. A bowhead whale caught in Alaska in 2007 had a harpoon head embedded in its 60-centimetre blubber layer that dated from 1879. Others have been found with harpoon points made of jade and ivory, and scientific study of otoliths (bones in the ear) and the amino acids in eye lenses have suggested the whales may live to the ripe old age of two hundred and twenty!

'They get fifty beluga and narwhal, but to be honest they take much more than that, and there's plenty to sustain it. You get the bunny huggers complaining, but without the whale harvest, this way of life would die.'

We clustered together in the lee of the cabin on our bouncing metal boat, trying to keep the wind from cutting through to any exposed piece of flesh. Jimmy gestured up to the mountains around us.

'When I started working here in the 1980s, every one of these valleys you see around you had a hanging glacier.'

We looked at them now, every single one was empty of ice.

'They'd been like that ten thousand years, since the last ice age, and they all went in two decades. When I hear politicians and oilmen talking about how climate change ain't real, I want to bring them up here and show them. Here it's not just about numbers and statistics, you can feel it, see it with your own eyes.'

Tim and I nodded, eager to learn as much as we could.

'The last few years local people in Pang started getting stung by wasps they didn't even have names for. And they have names for everything here! They're catching gluts of fish they ain't never caught before, but running out of the fish they've lived on for a hundred generations. When I started here, the elders could tell you when the pack ice would break up to within a day. Now they're often a month out!'

We nodded. This tallied with what I'd heard on my other ex-peditions to the Arctic. All of a sudden starving polar bears were wandering through towns, desperately scavenging food from city dumps, hybridising with brown bears to form so called 'pizzly' bears.

According to the WWF, climate change is happening twice as fast in the Arctic as elsewhere on Earth. The sea ice has decreased by 15 per cent in my lifetime, and most predictions suggest I could live to see a year where there is no sea ice whatsoever over the North Pole. None.

One of the reasons things are exacerbated in the Arctic is due to 'positive feedback loops', where cause and effect starts to spiral out of control. Quite often elements of complex systems that have not been understood or accounted for cause effects to accelerate far beyond what computer modelling may have predicted. The 'albedo effect' is a case in point. It sounds obvious, but white reflects light. Shiny snow and ice reflects sunlight back out into space. As we start to lose glaciers, snowpack and pack ice, instead of shiny white there is now the absorbing blue of the sea, or the easily warmed brown of rocks and tundra. Hence the lack of snow and ice is causing an increase in temperature that itself speeds melting. Another element I learned about while making a climate-change documentary in Arctic Alaska is permafrost. Much of the far north of our planet has ancient soils that remain frozen throughout the year to a decent depth. Until recently, nobody was aware of the enormous amounts of organic deposits that had been bound into the icy ground. As the ground thaws, they release carbon gases into the atmosphere – particularly methane, which is even more powerful as a greenhouse gas than CO_2. Warmer temperatures mean more melting permafrost, leading to more carbon gases and even more warming: another disturbing positive feedback effect.

Polar bears have been the poster child of climate change, and for good reason. They rely so heavily on the pack ice to find and catch their seal prey; particularly the mothers when they have young cubs in the spring. In turn, the bears are followed by numerous hangers on, such as the beautiful ivory gull and Arctic fox, both of which rely on the scraps left by the big killer. Without the pack ice they will have to adapt to a wholly different life on land, coming into conflict with men, and their guns. Many Arctic seals, including walrus, depend entirely on the ice as a place to rest, to haul out, and to raise their young.

A global increase of 2°C could be too much. The Hollywood

movies about the planet being plunged into the freezer overnight are hopefully overstated, but the threat of the Gulf Stream being shut off, and the resultant chill across Europe, is very real indeed.

Climate and weather, though, are two very different things. While the climate here may be warming inexorably, the weather was anything but. Furious wind was channelling down the valleys and howling about our ears. Constant rain, sleet and hail was being blown horizontally into our faces, as if we were being peppered with soggy buckshot.

We were carrying our huge packs, plus our daypacks, along with a good deal of extra food and fuel for the guys who would be somewhere further up the valley. I was also making a film of the trip for my sponsors, which meant carrying a fair load of cameras, batteries, etc. I'd leave the camera on a tripod, wander off into the distance allowing it to film me, then return to retrieve it; even doing whole river crossings and then going back over to collect the camera! I would guesstimate we started off with packs in the 35–40 kilo range, which takes considerable effort to get off the ground and on to your back. Once in place, it stunts your walking, cuts into your shoulders, and needs to be constantly shifted about in order to prevent the pain beating your shoulders and traps.

Baffin Island lies within the area of 'compass unreliability', where proximity to both the magnetic North Pole and real North Pole makes carrying an old-fashioned compass pretty pointless. After throwing in the presence of copious amounts of magnetic rock, your compass needle spins around and around aimlessly. We carried GPS as a last resort, but found simple continuous map reading extremely easy, using the obvious landmarks of the towering granite leviathans around us.

As much as expeditions are a purification process, they are also a continually evolving learning curve. It doesn't matter how long you've been doing expeditions and how experienced you are, no two situations are identical in their demands, and it takes a few days before you get your head together. Here, heading up towards Asgard, I felt like a total beginner. I either had too much clothing on or not enough. For the first week, merely to pack my bag each morning took nearly an hour, and that was before trying to get it sitting balanced and comfortable on my back. Every time I needed to find anything important I had inevitably put it right at the bottom, or I'd go through a dozen different bags and compartments before finding it. Straps and clothing rub, muscles ache in new places – I was completely out of sorts.

I could sense Tim's judging eyes as I tried to figure out how to cook dinner using the absolute minimum of fuel and fuss. Then when I went to wash the dishes, I found a nice clear puddle, and thoughtlessly plunged the pan into the water, seeing a faint slick of oil skim across the surface and grains of rice sink to the bottom. This puddle would also be the precious water we'd be drinking out of. I cursed my stupidity, prayed it would dissipate before Tim saw my rookie mistake, and ladled mugs of water into the pot and took it away to scrub it out elsewhere.

In any endurance situation, you inevitably hang on to little magic feathers: a preferred pair of insoles, favourite trail mix, perhaps Vaseline around hot spots on your feet. This magic feather is something you convince yourself is *the* secret, and you come to totally psychologically rely on it. For me it was my trekking poles. I was convinced that, with this load and my dodgy ankle, they were essential, and hence that I would be lost without them. This is all well and good, but does mean that psychologically you come to rely on them, and if you lose them, then it crushes your spirit.

The peaks of the valley are all named after Norse gods and mythology. Greenlandic Vikings first came here over a thousand years ago, naming Baffin 'Helluland' (place of huge rocks), and the first climbing parties in the 1950s paid homage to them with these

Norse names. There is Mount Odin, Baldr (the son of Odin), Frigga (Odin's wife), Loki, Freya, Midgard (Middle Earth) and of course Asgard, the domain of the gods. We were dropped off at Overlord Peak, then two days into the walk in Mount Thor took over the horizon. The god of thunder is an appropriate namesake for a peak of such imposing grandeur. It's like a breaking tsunami, with the face of the wave comprising 1,800 metres of smooth granite, the biggest vertical-drop cliff face on the planet. Its presence is ominous, dominant, almost derisive. As the Arctic air is so clear, with no buildings or trees for scale, and the mountains so huge, it's a struggle to get any sense of perspective. We walked towards Thor for hours and hours and it still didn't appear to get any closer. It beggared belief that the mountain we were here to climb could dwarf even Thor. Each one possesses seemingly impervious miles of vertical rock, as if Yosemite's El Capitan had bred countless bigger offspring. But this being the Arctic, these peaks were cut through by glaciers, fed by the vast ice cap that lay to the north of us. It was the northern summer by this time, when the sun drops below the horizon for a few dusky hours around midnight, but it never gets truly pitch-dark. Much of the snow in the valleys had melted away, and thunderous waterfalls plummeted from the hanging glaciers and unseen rivers above us. This portion of Baffin Island has not changed much since the last ice age. Indeed, the Penny ice cap above us *is* the last ice age, a remnant of the ice sheet that covered the north till 18,000YA. The rock was formed about two billion years ago, but due to the fierce effects of the winter freeze, summer thaw and glacial action, it is still an environment in flux. The moraines were the most unstable and dangerous I'd ever been on, with every rock seemingly ready to tumble.

Walking through the tundra can be a treat or a horror, based entirely on the whim of the weather. For several days the wind howled down the channel of the valley at gale force, carrying horizontal rain with it. The temperature was above zero, but it felt colder. Walking out of the lee of a big boulder into the full force, it near took you off your feet. There is a saying amongst smug adventuring types that 'there is no such thing as bad weather, only bad clothing'. This is horseshit of the worst possible order. It's true that clothing can help with the cold; I've been to the Arctic in winter when the thermometer registered a temperature of minus forty and it felt even colder thanks to the considerable wind chill, but with modern goose-down and Teflon clothing you can remain comfy, even cosy. However, when the temperature is only hovering around zero but it's wet, and you're doing something active, you can't wear too many base layers else you'll overheat, and thick gloves seem like overkill. You alternately shed and add layers, and can't take a rest as the cold hammers home at you instantly. The coldest and most bedraggled I have ever been is not in the Antarctic or high Himalaya, but winter mountaineering in Scotland. There, plunging ice axes into frozen turf as there's not enough ice, with vicious winds cutting through your best Gore-Tex and wet snow or rain hammering through every gap in your clothing is a special kind of vile. As sodden gloves start to freeze to your ice axes the pain is exquisite, a burning fierce chill that turns your fingers into lumpen paws. It's no surprise that some of the finest of all mountaineers cut their teeth in the winters of the Scottish highlands. It's there they learn how to suffer. For several days, the weather here in the Baffin summer was much the same.

Arctic hare were abundant and confiding, coming within metres of us and our tents. They're one of the eleven animals worldwide that change to winter whites and back again come the summer. We saw them in their scruffy transitional stage, halfway between winter whites and summer brown. Life is impossibly tough for these bounding survivors; in the winter they dig short burrows in the snow, but for the rest of the year they make do with shallow depressions called forms in the lee of rocks, merely stamping down the springy vegetation. At our approach they'd stand upright like meer-kats to get a good look at us, before returning to their unappetising tundra tea. As nutriment is so hard to come by here, Arctic hare will cheerfully eat rotting carrion meat, and even go out on to sea ice to eat seaweed. They are adaptable strong swimmers, and need to be, for Arctic fox, wolf and wolverine tracks and scat are plenti-ful. I also saw a magnificent gyrfalcon, the largest falcon on Earth, hammering over a glacial moraine, piercing call echoing around the amphitheatre of its highland home. Here and on Greenland to the east, pure white morphs of these extraordinary raptors are found, prized beyond gold by Arabian falconers. In twelfth-century China they were used for hunting swans, plummeting into them on the ground as they do with most of their prey. In 2011 it was discovered that many gyrfalcons spend much of the winter hunting out over the pack ice, effectively becoming the world's only seabird of prey! The one we saw was undoubtedly hunting the poor Arctic hares, which would have stood little chance at the end of those thundering talons.

The most numerous mammals are rarely seen: lemmings, small round rodents that provide the bulk of food for all the Arctic carni-vores. Lemmings go through occasional surges and plunges in their populations, with knock-on effects for the predators that feed on them. In periods of extreme high populations Norway lemmings will disperse in vast numbers, which gave rise to the image of lem-mings committing suicide by throwing themselves over cliffs. In the 1958 Walt Disney film *White Wilderness*, this myth was 'captured' on camera. The film purported to show a lemming migration, with the animals then throwing themselves into the Arctic Ocean where they drowned. It was filmed at the Bow River near Calgary with cap-tive animals (not a species of lemming that actually migrate), which were pushed off the cliff into the river by a revolving platform!

To progress to our peak, we needed to cross the rivers that piss down off the glaciers. Most were a chilly knee-deep wade. Others were raging waist-high surges that threatened to carry us out to the Arctic Ocean. This is potentially fatal when you're burdened with a pack loaded with a month's food, camping gear, fuel and climbing equipment. The first day, Tim and I stopped at each crossing to remove our socks and trainers and replace them with river shoes. Eventually, though, the streams were so numerous that I gave up and tramped on through them, relying on continual motion to stop my feet from freezing. Self-supported expeditions are a purification process, a lesson in simplifying life. When you're at home doing your first pack, you think you're being conscientious casting aside iPods and underwear, decanting sunblock and bug spray into old-fashioned film canisters. After a day hefting a pack the weight of a teenager, a new kind of ruthlessness sets in. Labels are cut out of clothing, you decide to halve your daily calorie intake, take one pair of socks for a month and instead of taking your cosy down jacket you'll wrap up in your sleeping bag at the end of the day. At my second repack, I decided to lose my sleep mat. Thereafter I used a small square of foam to keep my torso off the ground, and the ropes to keep my lower half up off the rocks. At the fourth repack, I even abandoned my tent, taking a chance on the sky, barometer and weather reports. Instead of carrying suds and scourers to clean pots, we mixed glacial silt with cold water to grind off bits of porridge and pasta, cursing oily foods when the waxy fat stuck to the pots and our fingers.

Our backs ached and muscles screamed. The butt and shoulders were the worst, though after the first week there didn't appear to be any part of my body that wasn't hurting. Tim and I distracted ourselves with the thought that soon we would meet Singer and the other expedition. We tramped on to a grassy plateau, littered with boulders the size of houses, and our eyes were caught by a flash of yellow too big to be natural: one of the expedition's tents. They were expecting us sometime within a window of a few days, yet even so greeted us with slightly stunned wide eyes. Some of the crew had already been there for a month with no contact with the outside world, and it was clear that nerves and relations had been frayed within their camp.

Singer himself was found holding court at the rock garden kitchen. A huge slab of rock shaped like the spinnaker of a giant yacht provided the perfect windbreak, and created a snug little site where everyone could escape the furiously gusty rain-laden hooley. We were warmly greeted with hugs and handshakes, and one of the number, Adam, set to making us cups of fresh coffee while we shed our backpacks and made our introductions. Adam seemed to be the nicest man in the whole world, with a constant easy smile and no evidence of any ego whatsoever. He set to making us a dinner of lentils, quinoa and freeze-dried vegetables in the shadow of the massive boulder. I'd brought two sides of Canadian smoked salmon as a gift for the crew, and big chunks of delicious oily fish turned the goo into a luxurious stew. The backs of Adam's fingers were covered in grotesque black scabs, weapons-grade sunburn from carrying loads up here with no sunscreen and a fair complexion.

Lizzie looked like a traveller chick you might see in a beach bar in Goa; she had straggly curly brown hair, a deep tan and bountiful freckles, her nose was pierced with a simple stud, and she was decked out in tie-dye spandex tights. However, her hands and feet told the story of the month she'd already spent in Baffin and how hardcore she was. Tough, chapped fingers that looked as if they belonged to someone who shovelled coal for a living. The rest of the crew called her the 'Energiser bunny', and talked in awe of her energy and drive. We were to find out just how true that was.

Then there was Singer himself. He was like something out of a Gabriel García Márquez novel: long, unkempt, curly dark hair, with an intense and uncompromising gaze. He only came up to my chest, yet radiated an energy and character that took over the entire rock garden. Singer had spent the last month walking from Overlord up to Summit Lake and back again, dropping off food and fuel for their expedition. He'd walk for seven or eight hours till he got tired, then plop his bivvi bag down and sleep a few hours, before carrying on. Time of day had come to mean nothing to him, and he'd quite happily yomp through the night if he felt like it. Over the years, Singer had nailed some preposterous first ascents, including two weeks on the face of Thor, climbing the whole thing solo. Bonkers.

As we chatted away, it became clear that there had been a certain amount of tension in their little commune, and that Singer and the others were in the process of packing up to head back down to Pangnirtung. Tim and I were perplexed to hear this, as we'd assumed we'd have some company heading up into the mountains. We were also devastated we wouldn't get to spend more time with them; they seemed like the kind of people I need to have in my life! The only bonus was that they had left a cache of food, fuel and climbing equipment up at Crater Lake with one of their number called Jeff. This meant we wouldn't have to do two trips up to Crater load-carrying food and fuel, but could do it in one push. Also, Lizzie was keen to join us heading up to Asgard, so our team was now three.

Before they left to head back to the relative civilisation of Pang, there was a reminder of what is so special about people who wander the world's wild places. I'd brought a satellite phone with me from the UK, in order to post social media messages to keep my sponsors happy. My technology, though, had been refusing to work, leaving us with no connection to the outside world, and no emergency bail-out system should anything go wrong. Shortly before he threw his rucksack on to his back, Singer fished his own sat phone out, and put it into my hands. I stared at him blankly.

'I can't take this,' I offered lamely.

'What're you gonna do if you need to call for pizza?' Singer quipped.

'But this is your lifeline . . . and they're worth a fortune!'

Singer dropped his eyes and smiled. 'I reckon you're good for it. I'll be back at a real phone in a few days, no biggie.'

It's difficult to get across quite what a big deal this was. First of all, sat phones cost as much as a second-hand car, and the calls can cost $8 a minute. It's a seriously valuable bit of kit, and Singer is no trustafarian millionaire with cash to burn. If a stranger on the streets of London came up to you and asked to use your phone for a single call, you'd probably tell them to get stuffed, but here was Singer offering to *give* me his, knowing that if I ever used it, he'd personally get billed hundreds of dollars! Not to mention the fact that when you're on a self-supported expedition, every ounce you carry is thought through and fretted over. If you worked it out, taking man-hours and transport into account, every chocolate bar here in the shadow of Mount Thor was worth about fifty bucks. Yet Singer was entrusting this golden lifeline to us both, despite having met us only twenty-four hours before.

There is a special honour amongst thieves in situations like this, a kind of 'pay it forward' feeling between people who set themselves apart through challenge and remoteness; the certainty that even if you personally don't get your reward this time, what goes around will come around sometime in the future. I've seen this kind of faith and trust amongst adventurers over and over again.

No more than twenty minutes from the rock garden, we came to our biggest river crossing. Until now we'd only crossed the side streams that coursed down from the mountainsides; this time we'd have to cross over the main Weasel River that cut down the centre of the Akshayuk valley. There used to be a hanging footbridge across the river here, but it was swept away in 2008 when a moraine dam melted, allowing a summit lake to burst its banks and flood down the valley. Now all that remains is the twisted metal of the walkway, plus a few wires and struts, and the river thundering beyond.

It's a whitewater torrent, and wading simply was not going to cut it. Luckily, a few weeks beforehand when some of the river upstream was still frozen, a member of the team had strung two ropes across the void. This we ratcheted up, and rigged into a Tyrolean traverse: a line across the rapids that we could swing over, hand over hand. As he was lighter than me, Tim was the first to step up, clipping his harness on to the line with a pulley, before throwing himself backwards to gain momentum and clear the worst of the river. Though it looks dramatic, it's a skill that climbers use all the time, and is generally one of the safer parts of such expeditions. Perhaps Tim was thinking ahead to getting the packs across, or even to the folly of having gone on an expedition with someone as poorly qualified as me. Whatever, he took his eye off the ball for one crucial moment and as he leapt off backwards, his weight caused the rope to bow like a washing line loaded with a sodden duvet. Instead of sending him zipping out over the foam, it dropped him backwards into a protruding boulder at speed. The boulder had a spike at its high point like the prow of a Viking longboat, and this thumped sickeningly into Tim's lower back, stopping him dead. Although clearly hurt, he didn't want to show it, and continued to the other side, leaving Lizzie and me to ferry the packs across. We shared few words on the other side, knowing that Tim was fiercely proud and would be furious with himself for such a simple error. Avoiding his gaze, we carried the loads to the top of the steep moraine that lines the Weasel River, and then waited for Tim to come and join us. And waited and waited. After about ten minutes I decided to go back and see what was up. And saw Tim lying prostrate on the ground halfway up the slope, clearly in agony. My heart sank into my boots. This did not look good.

To make matters worse, a ferocious gale was whipping over the moraine, blowing horizontal rain and hail into our faces. Seeking shelter behind a metre-high rock, I quickly erected my tent, got the stove on for soup, and started delving in the rucksack for drugs.

As one of the world's finest ice climbers and wingsuit fliers, Tim is tough as a bucket of iron rivets. When someone like him is wailing in pain, you have to take it seriously. Luckily I carry a med kit that's designed to deal with the very worst, and within half an hour a hefty dose of morphine had him quietened and relaxed enough that I could start probing his back to assess the damage. I gently kneaded all over the small of his back, which was completely in spasm, until I came to the culprit: a fist-sized solid lump at the top of his pelvis. I didn't even need to probe it to work out that it was pretty bad. So what now? We couldn't stay here long, our site was on the top of the moraine, utterly exposed at the place where the V-shaped valley narrowed to its tightest, funnelling the winds into a non-stop fury. The wind would blow our tents in, and Tim would be stranded up here, freezing and in agony. After a miserable hour crammed into my tiny one-man tent, deafened by the flapping of the tent walls, we decided to try the unthinkable: to get him back to the relative shelter and comfort of the rock garden.

Again we had cause to rely on the kindness of near strangers. Lizzie set to carrying our packs back across the torrent, and up to the rock garden. This left me with the task of getting my climbing partner over the Tyrolean traverse and up the steep slopes to relative safety. First I gave Tim the remainder of the morphine, plus a full dose of anti-inflammatories, then I took him under my arm and started to walk him. I was instantly reminded of quite how hard it must have been for my mate Tarquin, carrying me down when I'd smashed my back and foot. And I'm a whole bunch heavier than Tim. Tim showed remarkable fortitude. It was evidently a struggle even to put one foot in front of the other, yet he battled on, clipping himself on to the line and gingerly swinging out on to the traverse line.

After another painful hour we succeeded in getting Tim back to camp, and set him up a tent with an array of all our mats, down jackets and sleeping bags to wrap him up like an overfed caterpillar.

Lizzie and I were a quiet and pensive pair as we brewed coffee in the shelter of spinnaker slab. What the hell should we do now? Tim was insistent that he would be fine here in the rock garden, with all the food he could need, a comfy mossy bed and time to recuperate. His pride would be even more affronted if I insisted on abandoning the expedition to get him out, and he was adamant that Lizzie and I should continue to Asgard together, and climb it as a duo. I knew, though, that it had been a painful metre-a-minute slog to get Tim up from the river to here, and I was certain that the following morning, when the morphine and adrenalin had worn off, Tim would be way worse than he was now. He wouldn't be making the arduous walk out to Overlord anytime soon. There were no helicopters in Pang, or even within several days' flight of where we were. Our plight looked desperate. All thought should have been for Tim, but the truth was, having got him stable there was precious little else we could do for him. Perhaps we should press on, give him a chance to recover to a stage where he could hike out under his own steam?

We decided to sleep on it, to have a good think about our options. That night, the wind battered away at my tent incessantly; the earplugs and eyeshades I'd nicked off the plane could not keep the elements at bay, and the wind seemed to be taunting me, laughing at my failure on this my most treasured of adventures. Next morning I woke at around seven, and lay in my sleeping bag not wanting to brave the chill for a few hours. Finally, I got up the guts to step out into the gale, and headed to spinnaker slab to make Tim a cuppa. It took me about fifteen minutes to figure out how to work

Lizzie's stove with frozen fingers, and then, having brewed up a precious cuppa, I stumbled across to Tim's tent, and more than half the hot tea blew out of the cup and all down my front. It seemed like the height of misery, and for the first time having a good excuse to get the hell out of there seemed like a blessing. When I zipped down Tim's tent, though, I found Lizzie and Tim inside in intense conversation. They had clearly been chatting for a good while, and had run through a whole range of options. Lizzie was still keen to climb, Tim was loath to let his mistake impact my grand adventure. To her credit, Lizzie was still open to the idea of carrying on with me, even after Tim was no longer part of the plan. That was a pretty bold move. She knew Tim by reputation to be one of the finest climbers in the world, but she didn't know me at all, had no idea of my climbing abilities, and was taking a massive gamble. What she was seeing and hearing of my qualities cannot exactly have been doing much to convince her I was solid. We sat and had a frank conversation about the realities of what we would be taking on.

'If we do this,' she said, 'I don't mind leading the hard stuff, but this is a big deal – I'm risking my life just going up on that mountain. I'm not here to guide you up the thing. If you think it's beyond you, we should forget it.' She wasn't exaggerating. And this was very obviously my cue to bow out, but I didn't take it. It meant too much to me. If Lizzie was willing to take a chance, then I was sure as hell going to give it a go. We found an uneasy equilibrium, determining to climb, but with me very aware of what I was asking of her, and what was at risk. She did at least give a nod to my mountaineering background: 'I'll need you to talk me through the glaciers and ice and that – that's not my thing.'

So it was decided: we would continue up the valley to meet Jeff at Crater Lake, deserting my friend. It felt like the greatest of betrayals, but I knew I would have wanted the same in Tim's place.

Actually it made a pleasant change that it wasn't me that had done something dumb!

Setting Tim up with piles of easily accessible food, a pee bottle, and plenty of warm stuff, Lizzie and I set off the following afternoon, hoping the thunderous wind and rain would ease somewhat. It didn't. It was almost as if the gods were coming out to curse me for my betrayal. The battle up the valley was all into the fierce headwind, leaning forward with faces parallel to the ground in an effort to ease our progress into the wind tunnel. The sleety rain made a mockery of our waterproofs, and icy river crossings left us drenched to the waist. I set myself a rule of an hour's hard walking followed by a three-minute break for a mouthful of chocolate and to massage my aching buttocks. Lizzie instantly made good on her reputation, always seeming to be a kilometre ahead of me. If I stopped for my three minutes, she'd disappear completely, so after a while the hourly break went out the window.

Our final challenge came towards the end of the trek. It was eleven at night, pretty dark, and by now very cold. Before we could make camp, we needed to do one last big river crossing before making our way up to Summit Lake. When we reached it, my heart sank. The flow was sixty metres wide, in three main channels. The water was café-au-lait brown, churning with glacial silts. The glacier that gave birth to it was probably half a kilometre away, so it was as cold as freshwater could get. It looked as if it was probably waist-deep through much of it, and without a lot of care it could be quite serious. When you stopped and listened for a while, over the roar of the water itself you could hear the faint clock-clocking of big rocks being rolled down the flow. It looked like death on a stick. I stripped down to my pants, split my pack into two, and started across with the smaller pack. It was worse than it looked. The icy water thundered around my thighs, tickling my testicles, which instantly retracted up into my belly.

I picked my way across, my feet and legs already losing all sensation. One of the rules with river crossings is not to attach your pack to yourself, so you can ditch it if you fall in. The other is not to jump between boulders, as a single misplaced foot can have horrendous consequences. I'd been merrily ignoring these rules ever since leaving Overlord, but here I picked my way with incredible caution, knowing that any wrong move could result in a very ignominious end. No more than thirty metres downstream the river plunged over a small but tumultuous falls. Get swept into that and you would die, no questions asked. The park official's last words to us before we left Pang were ringing in my ears: 'From here on in, you're on your own.'

The last channel was the most dramatic and deepest. Halfway over, I stumbled, face-planted, and one of my poles disappeared. I scrabbled around, getting back to my feet, completely drenched. The pole was gone. Almost on my knees, I made the far bank, puffing and panting, and frozen solid. The wind and rain stopped me resting for even a minute. I had to go back, get the rest of my pack, and repeat the whole nasty procedure, this time with only one pole.

We made summit camp long after midnight, shivering, bitterly cold and utterly exhausted. Well, I was. Lizzie seemed to have a fair bit of fuel left in the tank, and immediately set to making tea and food. Jeff was asleep in his tent, so we decided to leave introductions till the following morning.

I woke sore and tired, to hot sunshine beating down through the yellow wall of my tent. The wind had eased, and I poked my head out to gaze upon a view of staggering beauty. The sky was blue, teased with fluffy clouds gently scudding along in a ludicrously light breeze. Peaks of a celestial grandeur appeared to me for the first time, thrones of giant deities that must surely sit on either side of the valley holding court over the trivial matters of man. My first thought was to make my allotted time window to call down to Tim and find out how he was doing. I'd left the other dodgy sat phone with him, and miraculously it chose this one window to work, and we managed a couple of three-minute conversations, during which he imparted the remarkable news that he was to be rescued! He'd got in touch with the park's office in Pang, and found out that in three days a chartered helicopter was to arrive in Auyuquittuq bearing rich photographers who wanted to take snaps of Mount Thor before continuing up to the north where there was a small settlement. They had a space in the chopper, and were prepared to take Tim out with them.

It was with a happy heart that I headed over to join Lizzie, who was brewing up porridge with dried blueberries and peanut butter. She was sitting beside the stove in her bright purple lycra tights with a white-bearded wiry man, wearing a black and gold Cornish rugby beanie, and an ancient climbing jacket that was older than me. Jeff had been resting high up at Summit Lake with the idea of hiking solo round the Turner Glacier. A dyed-in-the-wool mountain man, he was still smashing big mountain routes that would have broken men in their twenties . . . and he was a few months shy of his seventieth birthday! Even more extraordinary, Jeff had decided he wanted to join us in climbing Asgard.

His decision was without doubt influenced by word on the sat phone that we had an extended high-pressure system that would last for a week or more. With the clouds burning away and wind calming to near nothing, Baffin began to transform into a world of magic and legend. Blue skies framed the monoliths and watery sunshine polished the cliff faces. Suddenly every single peak beckoned to us, as if screaming, 'Climb me!' Dwarf fireweed blooms turned the slopes into a barrage of purple, dotted with white mountain avens like bunches of hardy daisies. All around us, life was frantically trying to make the most of these short summer weeks.

All over the tundra, wild cotton sprouted perfect white pompoms. The Inuktitut word for it is 'what looks like snow geese' and they value it above all other natural materials, using it to make wicks, and mixing it with charcoal to heal the wound after an umbilical cord is cut. Yellow mountain saxifrage flowers bloomed alongside boulders that had cascaded down from the peaks hundreds of years ago. A covering of lichen lent them incredible texture, bright like orange peel, black and crispy as paper ash, greens, whites, yellows. It turned every aged boulder into a work of modern art. A miniature forest of mosses and grasses sprouted, and we found mountain sorrel with green leaves that turn red over time and have a bitter but not unpleasant taste. Nothing grows more than ankle height; there are no trees, no shrubs – nothing can withstand the ten months of snow and eternal punishing winds.

For those precious days of sunshine, this valley is one of the natural wonders of the world. Every time I looked up from placing one foot in front of the other, I was greeted by a view that almost stopped my heart. At times we just stopped and stared at a mountain for hours as it changed with the light, and as high clouds seethed, grew and dissolved like smoke about the spiky summits.

The sole negative was that, once the temperature began to rise and the wind eased, the mosquitos took their chance to feed. When we awoke, they'd be waiting in squadrons on the mesh door of the tent, drawn in by the scent of CO_2 from the occupant breathing within. These were big, black mossies, strong fliers and even stronger biters. We rarely stood still, walking around windmilling our arms, plastering ourselves with as much bug spray as we could bear. It was no use, though, they seemed to actively enjoy the flavour of the repellent. Worryingly, populations of mossies are evolving with a gene that is resistant to DEET, the active chemical in conventional insect repellents. It's unlikely to be happening on Baffin, where repellent-coated humans form such a small part of the diet. The mossies we encountered were just titanium-encrusted fighter pilots, capable of biting clean through clothing.

With a few days for rest and consolidating our equipment, it was a further four days before we reached our final high base camp. It was a tricky day's trek, stumbling over fresh moraines with infinite care. I was starting to think I had the whole thing dialled, when I stumbled underneath a rock the size of my backpack and dropped it on to my foot. Somehow managing to internalise the cry of shock and pain, I rolled it aside carefully, fully expecting to find my foot pancaked like a cartoon character squished under an anvil. Mercifully, I'd only suffered bruising and a nasty cut, but I kept it to myself. Last thing I wanted was for Lizzie and Jeff to see me as a dangerous weak link.

Finally we crested a ridge and got our first view of Asgard, the realm of the gods. There is no debating the extraordinary beauty of the place. For students of symmetry, it is aesthetic perfection: two identical cylindrical fortresses two kilometres high. The mountaineer can appreciate its magnificence, but that contemplation is always tempered with fear. With the knowledge of all that could go wrong on its faces, failure is the absolute least of your worries.

The route we had chosen to take was first climbed by Doug Scott in 1972. For any climbers out there, he took forty pitches of mostly E-grade climbing to reach the summit, with two crux pitches at around E4 or E5. We had longer ropes, and superb conditions, but I for one had nothing like his level of skill. It would be one of the hardest climbs of my life.

Despite being tired from the laden lunge up the mountains to the base of Asgard, we decided to climb the following day, taking advantage of the wondrous weather window. I busied myself filming timelapses of the mountains changing under the evening light, while sorting out my kit for the following day. To take four power bars for the day, or five? To bring a Gore-Tex, or my small down jacket? Lizzie had decided not to take a water bottle, and go with Tim's method of relying on a free straw she'd pinched from a McDonald's at the airport on the way out. I had a litre of water, but would hope to find a source to refill it on the route. All the while, the huge buttresses of our peak glowered down on us, contemptuously judging me for my temerity in thinking I could even imagine attempting to climb there.

We rose at four. Asgard loomed above us, 1,200 metres of steep, overhanging or vertical granite – that's three times higher than the Empire State Building, or ten Shards. In order to get on to the route, we had to tiptoe down the glacier that rolled alongside it, keeping clear of yawning crevasses. As the sun crept over the ridgelines, blessing us with life-giving warmth, we reached the base of the buttress and began kitting up, standing in a patch of soggy gravel.

In my conversations with Tim before the climb, he'd assured me that he would take on the harder sections. I for my part was desperate to do at least some share of the leading, if for no other reason than to exorcise my demons. How to proceed with Lizzie and Jeff? It was instantly clear that both were better climbers than me. Lizzie is a self-confessed 'dirt-bag' climber, who lives in her van and travels the world climbing, taking short-term jobs to fund her habit. She was technically the strongest climber, and would probably lead the hardest pitches. Jeff had years of experience and was frighteningly comfortable on lower-grade rock, and was totally oblivious to height and exposure. He would take off the rope and solo on ground that Lizzie and I both needed to be roped up for. It was possible that for me to take on the lead would only slow us down, and certainly offer little to our performance as a group. All the same, it was important to me. On the third pitch, I stepped up to take the lead, but Jeff had already started the process. All the way up the fourth, I was steeling myself to take over, no matter what the rock was like.

At the belay, I took all the cams, nuts and quickdraws from Lizzie, and set off. To begin with, the crackline was extremely easy. I strode up it without bothering to place any gear, figuring that fast movement was more important than protection. Then it steepened, and the mega fissure I'd been following dwindled to a meagre finger crack. Proper climbing, right at the limit of my ability. Judgement hour. Would I crumble again? I forced myself not to think, not to contemplate the beating of blood in my ears. Instead, I thought back to the skills I'd studied for crack climbing back in the Peak District. My fingertips were taped up, my hands protected with rubber mitts. I jammed them into the crack, then cammed them sideways, forming a crude lock to pull on. The ancient granite may as well have been made of sandpaper it was so textured. My finger-tips would pay for it later, but for now they stuck, and I continued upwards. Two-thirds of the way through my first seventy-metre pitch, the test. The crack ran out, meaning I had nowhere to place any protection, but the climbing stepped sideways, on to blank slab. The obvious spot to stop was a ledge perhaps another ten metres on. I would have to push through. I breathed deeply, forcing myself to concentrate. 'This is not hard,' I told myself. 'Don't look down, focus on the moves, push through it.' A finger twist, a smearing toe hold, step away from the security of the cammed hand and put my faith in the grip of my climbing shoe rubber. Weight shift, knees splayed to keep hips close to the rock, loll over like I'm swaying to a slow dance tune. Reach up slowly, don't overbalance, pray there's something for my fingers, and step . . .

Before I knew it, I was at the belay. Before I set about fixing a number of cams and nuts in order to bring Jeff and Lizzie up safely, I breathed out, and silently high-fived myself. They had no idea quite what a big deal this was for me, and I wasn't about to let them see. Instead I kept my conquered demons inside, and passed on the gear for the next pitch. Which was a bona fide nightmare. A corner with a fingercrack at its corner, vertical for its entirety, and stern even for Lizzie who led it. But then I started climbing and realised that the crack was too narrow for my fat fingers! With the others high above me, I sneakily slipped a cam into the crack, and pulled on that instead. All's fair in the high mountains after all.

We were less than a third of the way up and really starting to enjoy ourselves, when we had a moment of horror that brought us straight back to reality; the climber's worst nightmare. Suddenly from far above, there was a distant but growing roar. The closest I can come to it is the sound of the storm troopers' X fighters in the original *Star Wars* films, or perhaps the whine of a distant dragon. I knew I'd heard the noise before, but it took a beat before my memory clicked. 'ROCK!' We pulled ourselves in tight to the face, me hugging Lizzie in close, trying to cover her with as much of my back as possible, while boulders thundered down on us. The biggest must have been football-sized, and hit about fifty metres above us, smashing and exploding. The aftermath felt like that scene from the film *Gravity*, when space flotsam fires past the astronauts piercing everything. I have been caught in bullet crossfire twice in my life: once in a riot in East Timor, the second time while riding atop a train in Cambodia which was strafed with fire by the Khmer Rouge. The pieces fizzed past our ears with exactly the same sound as those flying bullets. A grapefruit-size chunk from that height would have smashed through our helmets. I took an acorn-sized piece to my thigh, which merely gave me a dead leg that later blossomed into an ugly black bruise. As pebbles bounced harmlessly over us, pinging on our helmets, we dared look around us and make sure no one had been injured. Our hearts were thumping, and the colour had drained even from Lizzie's freckled face.

It was a sickening moment of vulnerability, and that was when my nerves began to fray. This wasn't helped when we hit easier ground and Jeff removed the rope in order to move more quickly.

The climbing wasn't especially hard, but the consequences of any mistakes are so unthinkable that you over-concentrate. One particularly strenuous corner pitch was followed closely by another where I had to step out on to a completely blank face, the drop yawning miles below me. I wouldn't say I am particularly scared of heights – you couldn't very well do this if you were – but my stomach lurched into my boots. 'Don't fall now, Backshall, don't fall now'.

Because I didn't know my climbing partners that well, and was so aware of my inferiority to them, I was desperate not to make mistakes. I watched every footfall like a hawk, tracking the movement of my ropes above and below me in the desperate desire not to unroot loose rock and cause another *Gravity* moment. At one point, Jeff and I were climbing simultaneously. For perhaps a minute, he was directly below me. Feeling the pressure of his presence breathing down my neck, I rushed my decision-making and reached out for a solid-looking flake with my left hand. It turned out to be more fragile than it appeared, and fractured off. I swung out, barndooring away from the face, but managed not to fall. The sliver of rock, though, dropped straight down on to Jeff and whacked into the back of his hand. He swore violently and shook his hand in fury. 'That fucking hurt,' he screamed at the rock in front of him, but it was clearly directed at me and my inadequacy. An apology would have been futile. I focused on the rock and climbed on.

Trying to keep the weight down, we'd carried straws with us, counting on being able to suck seeping water from the rocks as it trickled down. Unfortunately the dry spell had shut off the flow. All our water had run out by noon. By midnight, we were still some way from the summit, pushing on, throats parched, limbs leaden, tendons cramping. At one point I was standing at the belay for what seemed like hours while Jeff battled with the lead on one of the hardest pitches. Water was dripping off the rock in front of me, one tedious drop at a time. Keeping tight hold of the rope in my belay plate, I leaned in to the rock and, pressing as close as I dared, allowed the droplets to fall on to my parched tongue. I had to take care not to lean in too far, as the rock was by this time icy cold and I was afraid my tongue might freeze to the face! Ten or so drops did nothing more than heighten my thirst, making it infinitely worse.

Though the Arctic summer never gets truly dark, the sun does set. Once it has gone behind the horizon, the sky turns a deep inky blue, the temperature drops by around ten degrees, and everything takes on a far more serious air. We pulled on our down jackets, but it was nowhere near enough to stem the penetrating chill as it tried to inject its icy kiss through to our very bones.

As so often with mountaineering, the sting was in the tail. No more than a hundred metres from the summit, we were hit by the hardest climbing on the whole route. Only the best climbers could lead these chimneys and cracks, especially up here on the top of the world, and having already been going for twenty hours. Jeff screamed and yelled his way up the route as if the hounds of Hades were snapping at his heels.

I pulled myself on to the summit at exactly 1 a.m. It was the darkest and coldest hour. The mountains and valleys were purple and black as deep bruises, the starless sky somewhere between dusk and twilight, yet the snow and ice appeared to be lit from within, glowing ghostly radioactive white. We knew we couldn't stay here long. We had a terrifying, dangerous and unprotectable descent ahead of us, and daren't let our guards down. However, for a few minutes the stress was forgotten. We found a big snowmelt puddle to slake our furious thirsts, and took a few photos, though they could never capture the wonder of that panorama. To the horizon in every direction was nothing but wilderness. Unclimbed Arctic summits, little-known or seldom-visited valleys. Out to the coast, the kingdom of the Inuit, beluga, narwhal and ice bear. We knew that there was nobody in this whole vast wild world but us.

The world looks different from a height, and here, on this privileged throne, life itself was thrown into perspective. The things I wanted and wished for back home seemed empty and vain. The words of Mallory popped into my head: 'What we get from this adventure is just sheer joy . . . That is what life means and what life is for.' For those perfect moments, I would not have wished to be anywhere else on Earth.

But never has the climber's maxim about the summit being only halfway there been more true. It began much as we expected, finding a reasonable lower-off point to abseil down towards the saddle between the two towers of Asgard. I think it was only two big rappels to get us down, and though we were dead tired, and concentrating on taking care not to bounce too hard on the ropes and dislodge loose rock, it was no more than you'd expect from an adventure in the big hills. From the saddle, we faced about 600 metres more descent to get back to our base camp. It was well off vertical, and a chossy mess of loose gravel and slabs of rock that would shift and slide to the slightest touch. Normally this slope would have been bound in with snow and ice, making for an easy roped descent. But our unseasonal warm weather had seared away any hint of snow. It was out of the question to descend on the rope. The movement of the cord across the boulders would have unseated them and started lethal rockfalls. Jeff led the way down, unroped. We followed with painstaking care, sometimes sliding down on our backsides, but never able to allow that slide to last more than a metre or so for fear of gathering speed and plummeting into the void.

In adventure, people often talk about different classifications of fun. Type one fun is in the moment: fear-free, pure pleasure. An example would be driving to the base of a sunny crag and rock climbing under blue skies, with a nice picnic and a cold beer at the end of the day. Type two fun is generally only enjoyable in retrospect. It can involve moments of peril, but seems way better when you're telling the story back in the pub afterwards. Many of my days climbing are like this – most fun when they're safely done! The descent of Asgard was type three. Type three fun consists of altogether darker experiences that cannot be recalled without a shudder of horror. Constant mind-altering terror, the drip drip of hydrochloric acid to the nerve endings that irrevocably changes your life. It was seven hours of pure hell, every single second tense with the knowledge that a misplaced toe could cause a landslide that would kill the two people I was climbing with. I know that Lizzie and Jeff didn't struggle like I did on the climb itself. Lizzie was much more adept and Jeff much more experienced than me, and they both enjoyed almost all of the ascent. But no human being could have got through that descent without feeling they'd stressed away several years of their life.

When we finally made it to solid ground, twenty-seven hours after we'd set off, I was about as relieved as I can ever remember feeling. Not even taking time to eat, I crawled into my sleeping bag and instantly collapsed into a dead, unconscious sleep, despite it being the fiercest, hottest part of the day.

Four or five days later, and we were already borne back to the rock garden, trekking under our heaviest loads so far, loathe to leave anything behind to sully this wild paradise. It was remarkable how much the tundra had transformed since we'd first trekked these trails only a few weeks before. It seemed that summer had come to the tundra overnight: a blaze of purple and yellow from the fireweed and saxifrage, fields of wild cotton shaking about merrily, and puffball mushrooms like little deflated footballs. With the thin, nutrient-poor soil, the temperatures and winds, little can survive outside of these few bright months, but now, given the chance, life was leaping forward with glee. The wildflowers were in a hurry to bloom and pollinate, many merely by the wind, others using the few bugs which were now making their appearance felt. We stripped down as much as we dared, but couldn't go too far because the mossies were able to plunge their mouthparts through thin clothing. Every time you stopped to draw breath, you could see them probing with their stabbing mouthparts like a prospector jabbing for oil. Eventually, pay dirt! Usually at the shoulders or backside, where fabrics are drawn tight to skin.

We saw big wolf spiders scuttling along with puckered white egg sacs clasped beneath them in their jaws, and as I descended a moraine I came upon clumps of discarded snowy owl feathers. I studied them intently, but they were all well-used feathers, scattered in ones and twos with perfect quills, suggesting they have been moulted out rather than snipped off by predators (birds of prey leave neatly clipped ends, mammals such as foxes tear feathers out in clumps and leave smears of spittle behind).

I did find one kill site, an explosion of white feathers, probably from a gull. Looking around I discovered the blocky droppings of a wolverine, and the five-toed and clawed teddy bear footprints characteristic of the species. I also came across numerous wolf scats with tapered ends, alongside huge spread-out footprints. The wolf was moving easily but with determination, progressing in a straight line. It's often difficult to sense how many wolves are in a group purely from their tracks, as they practice something called 'register', walking in the footprints of the animal in front. But having followed this male for two days, I saw no sign of another. He was alone, probably using the valley as a corridor to move between territories. At every stop I craned my neck, desperately hoping for a glimpse of a white Arctic wolf, but it never showed its face.

Two species of butterflies fluttered weakly, blown from one bloom to another like a hanky shaken loose from a pocket on a gusty day. On a sunny 1 August we saw our first bumblebee. And then within hours they were commonplace. They were furrier than the bumbles we get here in the UK, and for good reason. While most insects are cold-blooded, *Bombus polaris* will bask and vibrate its wings in the mornings, gaining a body temperature not too far away from that of a mammal. The big hairy abdomen stores all that heat, allowing the bee to stay active in all but the most unpleasant of conditions. And it needs to make the most of its time. There may be no more than five or six weeks of activity, during which time the queen must lay a clutch of eggs that would hatch out into female workers, going off to collect pollen and nectar. The next brood would be reproductive, made up of queens and drones. These would then mate, and the fertilised queens would seek out a burrow – perhaps an abandoned lemming tunnel – which they would occupy for the winter, freezing throughout their tissues. When the thaw finally came, the whole process would be repeated.

Far more intriguing, though, is the case of the second Arctic bee species, *Bombus hyperboreus*. Lone, mated queens emerge from their burrows when the warm weather comes, much like their smaller cousin. That is where the similarity ends. For this is a cuckoo bee, and never builds a colony of her own. Instead she invades the colony of the smaller bee, kills the queen, and uses a heady cocktail of chemical pheromones to usurp her workers, turning them into slaves that will feed the cuckoo's own offspring. In a bitter world, where survival hangs on a slender thread, this cruel enslavement is a terrible twist.

This bizarre and macabre interplay between parasite and host is far more important and omnipresent most people realise. On our Bhutan expedition, I watched in wonder as a big praying mantis laid her ootheca or egg case. She spun her abdomen around, spraying out a kind of foam, almost like an ice-cream man making a Mr Whippy. She then laid her eggs inside the protective foam, which started to harden as soon as she had finished. And before she could wander more than a few centimetres away, two tiny wasps had landed on the egg case. As I looked on, they produced giant needle-like stingers from their behinds, longer than their entire bodies – and plunged them into the still soft foam. These were their ovipositors or egg-laying tubes, and with them they were laying their own eggs into the ootheca. These eggs would hatch out before the mantis nymphs, and eat them alive.

In Latin America we've done a lot of work with the world's biggest wasp, the tarantula hawk. These wasps have a body as long as my thumb, with the wingspan of many hummingbirds. They battle with huge tarantulas, catch them, paralyse them with their sting, and then drag them to their burrow, where they lay a single egg on them. This hatches out into a fat maggot that eats the spider from the inside. And not only that; it eats around the internal organs, so the spider doesn't die, and the meat stays fresh. And it manages that, despite having a brain that's about a quarter of the size of a full stop.

We don't know how this works. Evolution, it seems, is smarter than we are. In his entire career working with the natural world, and coming up with a theory that was the single greatest threat to organised religion, Darwin wrote almost nothing in his life that called his god and creationism into question. Until he thought about these parasitic wasps (the *ichneumonidae*) and their victims. He wrote: 'I cannot persuade myself that a beneficent & omnipotent God would have designedly created the *Ichneumonidae* with the express intention of their feeding within the living bodies of caterpillars.' And perhaps the most distressing fact for any religious naturalist is the omnipresence of parasitism; there are around 80,000 different species of these parasitic wasps, munching out the insides of many other animals.

For every beautiful miracle you find in the natural world there are dozens of sinister parasites eating their prey's insides out, using it as a living larder, causing it unimaginable agony. Modern biological theory suggests that natural selection has been driven by parasites since the very dawn of time. Ideas such as the Red Queen hypothesis (named after the Lewis Caroll's character of the same name) suggest that in the biological arms race of life, we are running to stand still in our desperate struggle to stay ahead of parasites. At the same time as hosts develop mechanisms to beat the parasites, the parasites are developing ever-more sophisticated means of subverting these protective facets. So much of what we consider essential in the forms of modern animals could have originally developed for this very purpose, from the development of the cell wall, to the emergence of an immune system and antibodies, to the very skin we live in. There is even strong evidence that sexual reproduction came about because it allowed for mutation, a way for organisms to recombine their genes and reorganise their genomes. Thus some offspring would develop variations that enabled them to deal better with the ever-present parasites.

We like to think that we, as an intelligent all-conquering mammal, are the pre-ordained purpose of life and that there has been an inevitable evolution towards complexity, with us as the final glorious result. But that couldn't be less true. Evolution doesn't have a purpose, there is no grand plan, and complexity only emerges accidentally as a way to solve various biological challenges, most of which involve things that burrow into our flesh and eat us from the inside. We are nothing more than a warm, dark, damp place for parasites to nurse their babies.

I guess you could see this theory as being incredibly grim and negative, but I find it liberating. It's evolutionary theory meeting existentialism head on. If there is no purpose to life other than to deny tapeworms a good feed, if we are not inherently special, and life has no grand plan or meaning, then we have to find a meaning for ourselves, and in doing so, in looking at the world through the eyes of a child, and wanting to understand it all, we can encounter a planet of infinite unimaginable natural wonders – no matter how grim they are.

The world and the mountains too are ambivalent to us, grinding on in geological time. It is part of human nature to believe in fate, to believe that some things are 'meant to be', or predetermined. To my mind this is purely human vanity. It is wanting to believe that we are intrinsically important, that in some small way the universe has a plan for us. We like to build a picture of the world where we matter. But we don't. The world is as ambivalent to us as the mountains are. The planet is as unconcerned with our time here as the mountains are with those that climb them. So we must find a purpose for life ourselves. Whether that is to be an athlete, an aesthete, a parent, a tyrant, or a teacher. Each of these things have merit. It is up to us to decide, to find our own meaning of life.

My meaning of life? Well, it's surprisingly simple. The mountains have taught me that our time here is fleeting. The merest blink of an eye. When I stood on top of Mount Upuigma, I was the first to summit a mountain whose rocks were 1.8 billion years old, and formed before there was life on our planet. What is my four score years and ten in its shadow? I don't want to waste a second of my precious time here on Earth. I want to achieve as much as is possible, to make a life that is bigger than my years, I want to achieve as much ecstasy, and bring as much to as many other people as possible. In the words of the great poet (Mel Gibson's Braveheart!) 'Every man dies, not every man truly lives.'

As we made our way back down the mountain, we returned to the caches we had left behind, beginning the process of setting ourselves back into the real world. To begin with, on being reunited with my tent and sleeping mat, it was a boon: I got my first decent night's sleep. But as we continued down, reloading with all the things we'd discarded, it felt as if I was burdened with ridiculous luxuries. Did I really bring a coffee maker and grounds all the way up here? And then the joy of that first cup, everyone sitting around the camp stove, eyes wolfish, saliva practically dripping from lips as the coffee brewed, wanting to be the first so desperately, but also wanting to show the selflessness of being last. No Italian barista could ever brew anything that could taste as divine and decadent as that coffee would. Many people in the modern world never experience true hunger, a meal earned through physical suffering, or eaten in clean air with the world's most intoxicating landscapes. They have never known the sheer joy of eating a fish you've speared yourself on a beach barbecue, and never eaten a squashed sandwich on the summit of a hard-won peak. I am convinced that no one, whether gourmets or kings, has experienced flavours like I savoured here.

That's the real joy of expeditions. It's the Buddhist divestment of attachments. It's certainly true that in these situations you are better the less you can make do with. It's so easy to put all your faith in one particular object, and come to rely on it, as I did my walking poles. But this is about discovering simplicity. Pretty soon you come to the realisation that everything in modern life is a sham. It is of no ultimate consequence what cereal we choose, who follows us on Facebook, what house we live in, how much our accountant can trim from our taxes. Up on high, life is crystal clear. The only things of consequence are friendship and kinship, finding the perfect spot for the daily poo, savouring a cup of coffee or soup. My pal Carol's flapjacks tasted finer at midnight on Asgard rock than anything Heston Blumenthal could create.

My joy was tainted by melancholy, as I realised that within a week or so I would be back in the modern world and frantically checking out who'd replied to my last Tweet. This clarity would be gone. I would back to being manipulated by advertisers and media, conned into believing a whole bunch of insignificant things were important. But at this moment I knew what I was all about, I saw the core of me. Standing on top of a mighty peak and looking out to the horizon, heart full of joy. Not done for anyone else or for thought of any gain whatsoever. Just for the now.

On the way down the mountain, running loads to where we would finally be picked up, we passed Mount Thor. It is such a dominant peak, so incredibly imposing. To a mountaineer its very existence is an invitation. I stared at it for many hours. The southern ridge didn't look so bad. My two climbing partners were not surprisingly totally over climbing, and didn't offer to join me, so the next morning I rose early and set off for the mighty Thor. It looked as though I'd have to traverse a vile moraine to bypass the glacier and get on to its slopes, so it was a pleasant surprise to discover the moraine was actually pretty ancient, consolidated with moss and lichen, nothing like as challenging as those leading up Asgard. I decided to keep going. A thousand metres higher up, and I'd reached the buttress that marks the southern end of the Thor massif. From the ground it had looked like near vertical ground, far too challenging to be taking on solo. However, as I got higher, it became clear that you could clamber around the back of it. Might as well carry on I thought. On reaching the ridgeline, I tiptoed to the edge, greeted by the dizzying yawn of infinite drop; the highest vertical cliff on the planet. Overcome with a desperate urge to hurl myself off, to soar through the valley below on phoenix wings, I sat on the edge with my feet swinging over space as the sun broke through the clouds to bathe me in faded golden light. One by one the faces of the peaks on the other side of the valley began to explode into life, reflecting amber mirrors given texture and depth by the new light. I checked my watch: 1,200 metres above sea level. Thor is 1,800, leaving 600 more metres of ascent, plus getting back down to camp. I looked up towards the upper slopes, shrouded in ever-evolving clouds.

I could make out several precipitous pitches of climbing, not beyond my abilities, but with stomach-gurgling exposure. With a climbing partner it'd be a grand adventure. On my own, without any equipment, it would be a fright-fest, and I'd had my share of that over the last few days.

There was no questioning, none of the usual guilt, no beating myself up over my failure. I'd come here with no agenda and no expectation. For now, it was enough to sit there on Thor's grand shoulder like some tiny pixie advisor to the great god, looking down at the world, utterly content.

AFTERWORD

I sit writing this now at the conclusion of another epic expedition to the mountains, one which yet again left me humbled. I'd gone back to the tepuis of Venezuela with John and Ivan to attempt another first ascent of a stunning mountain called Amauri. This time the perfect orange rock of Upuigma was replaced with nasty, greasy black choss, which fell apart to the touch. It was horrible. We had six days sleeping on piles of jagged rocks, climbing on stinking fly-blown ropes that had inadvertently been dragged through the slick of human waste underneath 'jobby tree' where we all took our morning ablutions. We were scorched in unexpected sun, then frozen to hypothermia in tropical storms, and the Gran Sabana of Venezuela had taken on a totally different character in my imagination.

We had chatted some days before with one of the local Pemon, who had told us that the tepuis harbour evil spirits, and that they do not want to be climbed. Both Ivan and John took huge falls, rockfall could easily have killed any one of us, and the mountain certainly appeared to have a malevolent spirit that would simply not be appeased until we decided to give up and turn down (at which point it instantly stopped raining and the sun came out!). This time, though, there was a certainty about the retreat that left me more comfortably philosophical than usual. I will never look back and say 'what if?' about Amauri as I do with all my other dismal disasters. There was no choice or option to our turning back, and hence no sense of failure. If the mountain beat the finest tepuis climber in the world, then there was nothing I could do or offer to change things. I quickly formed the opinion that in this case our inability to reach the summit was itself a triumph. It proved that the mountains could still be bigger than us, that even with the best possible people on our team, even with every bit of modern technology, there were still mountains that refuse to be tamed, that may possibly never be conquered, and surely that is one of the most important and exciting things about adventure. Would it even be adventure, if you *knew* that you would succeed?

And that's not the only addition to my thinking on climbing and adventure in general. It seems so much has changed in so little time. On Amauri tepuis, hanging in my harness at a fragile belay for six hours with the void beneath me, while John battled on above and plummetting rocks fizzed past my ears, for the first time I found myself thinking, 'I don't want to die here, I have so much to live for.' Strange that it should have taken so long for such a simple and obvious sentiment to come to me. It's mostly down to Helen, to falling in love for the first time, and starting to think of a future with family and children. Maybe I'm finally starting to grow up.

One thing that strikes me is that, in amongst all of these words, there is scant encouragement to others to follow in my footsteps and take to the hills, and that is unforgivable. Particularly as so much of the latter part of my life has been devoted to trying to convince people – especially kids – to get outside and discover adventure in all its many forms. Perhaps reading of shit-soaked ropes and fizzing rockfall, many readers will be thinking, 'I wouldn't do that for all the tea in Tibet.' That would be a tragedy, for there is no doubt in my mind that we all have so much wonder to discover in the world's wild and high places. The mountains have a power unlike any other environment, and you don't have to risk your life to experience their majesty. There is solace for the bereaved or clinically depressed in a wild sunrise, even the elderly or infirm can find their way up peaks on funiculars and cable cars; the least adventurous person on Earth can get a kick of achievement from strolling up a humble fell, and winter sports make the wonders of high places attainable for many who daren't venture far from modernity. Go to the hills, it will make your life better, it will make you a better person, it will make you happy, I guarantee it! But a word of caution. All who venture into the mountains, no matter at what level, have a responsibility to be prepared, to either acquire the correct help, or to gain the experience necessary to take care of themselves. I can joke now about my early mountain experiences, but the fact is that my laissez-faire attitude could have killed someone. There is no excuse nowadays for not getting the right advice, training and equipment, a simple internet search will show you how. Mountain Rescue costs money, can involve environmental degradation (trees chain-sawed to make emergency helipads, fuel dumped onto wild lands to lighten the load, gear and garbage left behind) and these inutterably heroic individuals lose members every year during rescue attempts. Don't let it be you that has to call for the cavalry, unless it simply cannot be avoided.

In the wider world of the mountains, the biggest development since I finished writing was the devastating earthquake in Nepal in early 2015, and the effects that had on another Himalayan mountaineering season. Somehow amongst so much human tragedy it seems ludicrous trying to justify expeditions, rationalising our own First World desire for pleasure, challenge and danger in the big hills. Surely they are just the ultimate pointless luxury, a shameful waste of money that could be put to more noble causes? Eventually, though, as the rubble clears, and the Nepalese start to rebuild their lives, the Sherpas will need mountaineers' tourist dollars more than ever. No one in Nepal would thank me for saying, 'they've suffered so much, we shouldn't go there just to climb mountains'. Again, the hills often pose more questions than answers.

And then, while I was putting the finishing touches to this book, David got in touch with me with the devastating news that Sammi had been killed. By this point Sammi was 36, and one of the finest extreme altitude mountaineers in the world, having climbed ten 8000m peaks, eight without supplementary oxygen. The previous year we had chatted about attempting K2 together, and he had gone on to summit in some style. However, on the descent of Annapurna, it seems that at around 7100m both Sammi and Pemba, the Sherpa he was climbing with, took a fall, with the cost of both their lives. The news stung me harder than I expected. I hadn't seen Sammi in person for several years, but we chatted regularly on email, and I cheered his every achievement, sometimes living vicariously through him, as he hit the high hills while I had to work. He seemed invincible. And I wasn't alone in thinking this, another climber commented; 'there are some people who seem to live charmed lives, and you think they will survive no matter what. Sammi was one of these for me.'

But the mountains care nothing for human fortitude. The world's strongest man or finest mountaineer would still be specks of dust to a serac collapse or big avalanche. Annapurna is now the most dangerous mountain on Earth. On K2 one person dies for every four people that summit. On Annapurna it is about one to two. Thirty-five per cent death rate odds. Summit or die, Russian roulette where not one but two of the chambers are filled with bullets. There is no other area of human life where such odds would be acceptable. Sammi will always be in my mind when I'm in the big hills. His huge bison laugh, ruddy cheeks and icy eyes. If the hills can take the finest of us, they will not hesitate to take a hacker like me. Blue skies Sammi, you will be much missed.

GLOSSARY

Abseil/rappel – descending on fixed ropes.

Aid-climbing – climbing where instead of pulling on the rock you pull directly on to the gear, a method that can enable you to get up pitches that would be impossible free.

Alpine style – going fast and light, leaving super early in the morning, trying to conquer a route in one main attack.

AMS – Acute Mountain Sickness.

Arete – a ridge-like feature on steep rock.

Belay – holding the rope of another climber, paying it out or taking it in as they proceed, providing their safety should they fall. When used as a noun it denotes the place you stop in order to belay.

Belay stance – the position a belayer takes up on the rock, snow or ice, in order to belay their partner safely and effectively.

Bergschrund – the huge crevasse at the head of the glacier.

Big wall – climbing a big wall (!) but by a method that involves painstaking hauling up of gear, usually done over many days sleeping out on ledges.

GLOSSARY

Bolt – permanent protection placed into the rock, allowing for much safer 'sport' climbing.

Cam/friend – expanding metal camming device that is placed in cracks and locked in place. Most of the time.

Carabiner – the vaguely 'O'-shaped chunks of metal that are the mainstay of a 'rack' and are used to run rope through.

Cornice – the breaking wave effect of snow at the top of a ridgeline, blown in one particular direction. This often forms a dangerous undercut formation.

Couloir – a steep gully often filled with snow or ice.

Crag – a cliff face used for climbing.

Crampons – metal pins that can clip onto the underside of stiff mountaineering boots in order to facilitate safe passage on ice and snow.

Crevasse – gaping chasms in glaciers, which form one of the greatest dangers of mountaineering.

Crux – the most difficult move or pitch of a climb.

Deep-water solo – climbing on your own without ropes, but with deep water below you to splash into if you fall.

Dihedral – a corner of rock, much like an arete.

Dry tooling – climbing on rock using ice axes and crampons.

Exposure – empty air to the side or below a climber, and also the sense of fear and unease one gets in the same situation.

First ascent – the first person or team to climb a particular mountain or route.

Free climbing – different to solo or free solo, freeclimbers ascend using traditional protection, and without using 'aid'.

Gear – pieces of equipment that are placed into rock in trad climbing in order to catch you should you fall.

Grade – the often esoteric set of numbers or letters applied to a rock climb or mountain that attempts to portray how hard or easy it will be to climb.

HACE – High-altitude Cerebral Edema, the most serious altitude-related illness, without immediate descent often results in brain damage or death.

HAPE – High-altitude Pulmonary Edema, the build-up of fluid in the lungs at altitude, usually treated with Diamox and Dexamethasone.

Hyperthermia – when a human body's core temperature rises above normal levels.

Hypothermia – when a human body's core temperature drops below normal levels.

Hypoxia – lack of oxygen.

Jumar – a metal gripping device that allows you to climb vertical rope.

Lead – the person who climbs first, placing 'gear' as they go to protect themselves.

Moraine – places where rocks have been dumped by a glacier's flow. They can be at the end (terminal), sides (lateral), or right in the middle (medial) of the glacier.

Moulin – giant drain holes that allow surface meltwater to flow down into the guts of a glacier.

Moving together/simul climbing – when on ground that is well within the ability of a climbing team, to move as one across the ground, without stopping to belay.

Nuts – chunks of soft metal that can be pressed into a crack to take on a similar function to cams.

Pitch – climbs are broken down into sections, which need to be smaller than one entire rope length. The lead climbs this pitch, the second follows, then they move on to the next.

Rack – the full set of equipment needed to make a traditional climb.

Scree – small, loose broken-up rocks. Can also be described as 'choss'.

GLOSSARY

Second – the person who climbs second, taking the gear out that the lead has placed. They are supported by the rope above and in little danger of a fall.

Serac – when a glacier goes over steep ground it may form huge blocks of ice. These seracs can collapse and lead to disaster.

Solo/free solo – ascending with no rope or gear whatsoever. The most pure, and most lethal form of the climbing arts.

Traditional climbing/Trad – using gear such as cams, nuts and slings to climb natural rock.

Traverse – to climb sideways, horizontally across a rockface.

Whipper – to 'take a whipper' is to take a big fall, but be caught by the rope.

Zipper – when all of your gear peels out of a crack, extending your 'whipper'.

BIBLOGRAPHY

Anker, Conrad, *The Lost Explorer: Finding Mallory on Mt Everest* (Constable, 2013)

Boardman, Peter, *Sacred Summits: A Climber's Year* (Vertebrate Digital, 2003)

Bonatti, Walter, *Mountains of the Mind: A History of a Fascination* (Granta, 2008)

Bonington, Chris, *Annapurna South Face: The Classic Account of Survival* (Book Faith, 2008)

Breashears, David, *Last Climb: The Legendary Everest Expeditions of George Mallory* (MapQuest.com, 1999)

Cave, Andy, *Thin White Line* (Arrow, 2009)

Cherry-Garrard, Apsley, *The Worst Journey in the World* (Vintage, 2010)

Coffey, Maria, *Where the Mountain Casts Its Shadow* (Hutchinson, 2003)

Coffey, Maria, *Fragile Edge: A Personal Portrait of Loss on Everest* (Mountaineers Books, 2012)

Curran, Jim, *K2: Triumph and Tragedy* (Hodder & Stoughton, 2013)

BIBLIOGRAPHY

Davis, Wade, *Into the Silence: The Great War, Mallory and the Conquest of Everest* (Vintage, 2012)

Dawe, Heather, *Adventures in Mind* (Veterbrate, 2013)

Deimberger, Kurt and Mantovani, Robert, *K2: A Challenge to the Sky, 1954-2004* (Smithmark, 1995)

Gadd, Will, *Ice and Mixed Climbing Modern Technique* (Mountaineers Books, 2003)

Harrer, Heinrich, *Seven Years in Tibet* (Harper Perennial, 1991)

Harrer, Heinrich, *The White Spider* (Harper Perennial, 2005)

Helprin, Mark, *A Soldier of the Great War* (Harcourt, 1991)

Herzog, Maurice, *Eiger Dreams: Ventures Among Men and Mountains* (Pan, 2011)

Houston, Charles S., *K2: The Savage Mountain* (Lyons Press, 2009)

Krakeur, John, *Into the Wild* (Pan, 2007)

Krakeur, Jon, *Into Thin Air* (Pan, 2011)

Lee, Alastair, *Baffin Island* (Frances Lincoln, 2012)

Matthiessen, Peter, *The Snow Leopard* (Vintage, 1988)

Messner, Reinhold, *Everest: Expedition to the Ultimate* (Vertical Digital, 2014)

Messner, Reinhold, *All Fourteen 8000ers* (Crowwood, 1988)

Norgay, Jamling Tenzing, *Touching My Father's Soul: A Sherpa's Journey to the Top of Everest* (Ebury 2002)

Partridge, Keith, *The Adventure Game* (Sandstone, 2015)

Rebuffat, Gaston, *The Mont Blanc Massif* (Baton Wicks, 2005)

Reeves, Mark, *Hanging by a Thread* (Constable, 2009)

Schmid, Stephen E., ed., *Climbing: Philosophy for Everyone* (Wiley-Blackwell, 2010)

Simpson, Joe, *The Game of Ghosts* (Vintage, 1994)

Simpson, Joe, *Touching the Void* (Vintage, 1998)

Simpson, Joe, *Beckoning Silence* (Vintage, 2003)

Torbert, Andy, *Extreme Adventures* (Bantam, 2015)

BIBLIOGRAPHY

Tyson, Andy, and Clelland, Andy, *The Illustrated Guide to Glacier Travel and Crevasse Rescue* (Falcon Guides, 2009)

Venables, Stephen, *Everest: Summit of Achievement* (Bloomsbury, 2013)

Willis, Clint, *High: Stories of Survival from Everest and K2* (Thunder's Mouth Press, 1998)

INDEX

INDEX

INDEX

INDEX

ice-climb 74–7
  camp 76
ganja 71–2
Garhwal Himalaya, the 54
glaciers 23–8
golden langur monkeys 255
Gomer (Sinai expedition
  member) 35
Gran Sabana National Park 199–200,
  200, 203, 207
greenhouse gases 299
Greenland 304
Greenwood, Steve
  Borneo expedition 130–1, 133–4,
    145, 151
  appearance 131
  Upuigma expedition 202, 203,
    209
  arrival at Upuigma summit 230–1
  Upuigma summit
    exploration 233–4
Griffith, Jonathan 191–2
griffon vultures 76–7, 263
Grindelwald 22–3, 31
Guiana Shield expedition 200–4. *see
  also* Upuigma
Guyana 200, 201
gyrfalcon 304

HABE (High Altitude Bottom
  Evils) 115, 178–9
HACE (High Altitude Cerebral
  Edema) 115, 178
hammerhead flatworm 145
handicap principle, the 38–40
Handslip, Sanna 258, 263, 268–70
hanging glaciers 24–5
HAPE (High Altitude Pulmonary
  Edema) 115, 170, 178

Harding, Ian 242–3
Hardiwar 54
Harrison's Rocks, Tunbridge
  Wells 18–22
Hawley, Elizabeth 192
Hideyuki (Japanese student) 11–12
high altitude acclimatisation 111–13,
  165–7, 171–4
high Himalayan trek
  departure 62–3
  Gangotri 63–6
  food 65–6, 87
  scenery 66, 77
  encounter with Moni Baba
    66–9
  high-altitude migraine 69–70
  arrival at Gangotri glacier 72–4
  on the Gangotri glacier 74–7
  sunburn 77
  night 78
  tents 78–9
  endurance exercise 79–84
  Anthony's rebellion 82
  snow skills training 85–6
  team bonds 86–7
  wildlife 86–8
  weather 88–9
  attempt on the summit 88–94
  sense of accomplishment 94–6
  end of 96
high-altitude bulimia 170, 174
high-altitude migraine 69–70
high-altitude mountaineering 154–5,
  155, 189. *see also* Cho Oyu;
    high Himalayan trek
high-place phenomena 124–5
Hillary, Edmund 156
Himalayan blue sheep 88
Himalayan chough 86

INDEX

INDEX